D1753406

AMBRA |V

Matthias Boeckl (Hg/Ed)

DER CAMPUS DER WIRTSCHAFTSUNIVERSITÄT WIEN
VIENNA UNIVERSITY OF ECONOMICS AND BUSINESS CAMPUS

Stadt · Architektur · Nutzer
City · Architecture · User

AMBRA |V

INHALT
CONTENTS

VORWORT Christoph Badelt, Rektor	**6**	**PREFACE** Christoph Badelt, Rector
GESCHICHTE		**HISTORY**
FÜLLE UND HÜLLE Zur Institutions- und Baugeschichte der Wirtschaftsuniversität Wien 1873–1982 Markus Kristan	**8**	**NEVER ENOUGH AND NOTHING TO SPARE** On the Institutional and Architectural History of Vienna University of Economics and Business 1873–1982 Markus Kristan
ZWEI WETTBEWERBE FÜR EINEN CAMPUS Franziska Leeb	**14**	**TWO COMPETITIONS FOR ONE CAMPUS** Franziska Leeb
STARKE IDENTITÄTEN POLARISIEREN Dietmar Eberle im Gespräch mit Edith Schlocker	**22**	**STRONG IDENTITIES POLARIZE** Dietmar Eberle in conversation with Edith Schlocker
EINE LEBENDIGE STADT Wolf D. Prix im Gespräch mit Matthias Boeckl	**25**	**A LIVELY CITY** Wolf D. Prix in conversation with Matthias Boeckl
MASTERPLAN		**MASTER PLAN**
INTEGRAL UND DIFFUSIONSOFFEN Der Masterplan von BUSarchitektur Isabella Marboe	**28**	**INTEGRAL AND PERMEABLE** The Master Plan by BUSarchitektur Isabella Marboe
RAUM UND KOMMUNIKATION Reflexionen zur Campus-Philosophie Gerlinde Mautner	**38**	**SPACE AND COMMUNICATION** Reflections on the Campus Philosophy Gerlinde Mautner
BAUTEN · NUTZER · THEMEN		**BUILDINGS · USER · THEMES**
EIN NEUES LEBENSGEFÜHL Das Library and Learning Center von Zaha Hadid Architects Matthias Boeckl	**42**	**A NEW QUALITY OF LIFE** The Library and Learning Center by Zaha Hadid Architects Matthias Boeckl
WAS IST EIN LEARNING CENTER? **WIE FUNKTIONIERT ES?** Statements Cordula Rau	**56**	**WHAT IS A LEARNING CENTER?** **HOW DOES IT FUNCTION?** Statements Cordula Rau

INHALT / CONTENTS

GEBAUTE LERNLANDSCHAFT — **62** A BUILT EDUCATIONAL LANDSCAPE
Das Teaching Center von BUSarchitektur / The Teaching Center by BUSarchitektur
Isabella Marboe / Isabella Marboe

INTEGRATION ARCHITEKTONISCHER UND STRUKTURELLER KOMPLEXITÄT — **74** THE INTEGRATION OF ARCHITECTURAL AND STRUCTURAL COMPLEXITY
Konstruktions-Highlights am WU Campus / Construction Highlights on the WU Campus
Andrei Gheorghe / Andrei Gheorghe

SCHICHTEN UND FÜLLUNGEN — **82** LAYERS AND FILLING
Das Departmentgebäude und Student Center von Atelier Hitoshi Abe / The Departments and Student Center by Atelier Hitoshi Abe
Matthias Boeckl / Matthias Boeckl

STUDIEREN AM WU CAMPUS — **92** STUDENTS ON THE WU CAMPUS
Statements / Statements
Robert Temel / Robert Temel

HEITERKEIT ALS PROGRAMM — **98** JOLLY GOOD FUN
Das Department- und Administrationsgebäude von CRAB studio / The Department and Administration Building by CRAB studio
Cordula Rau / Cordula Rau

DER GRÜNE CAMPUS — **110** THE GREEN CAMPUS
Energie-Design-Konzepte / Energy Design Concepts
Malgorzata Sommer-Nawara, Bernhard Sommer / Malgorzata Sommer-Nawara, Bernhard Sommer

EIN SPIEL MIT PARALLELOGRAMMEN — **118** AN INTERPLAY OF PARALLELOGRAMS
Departmentgebäude von Estudio Carme Pinós / Department Building by Estudio Carme Pinós
Ulrich Tragatschnig / Ulrich Tragatschnig

DER NEUE CAMPUS AUS SICHT DER LEHRENDEN — **128** THE NEW CAMPUS FROM THE VIEWPOINT OF THE TEACHERS
Statements / Statements
Ulrich Tragatschnig / Ulrich Tragatschnig

NICHT-KARTESIANISCHE GEOMETRIEN — **134** NON-CARTESIAN GEOMETRIES
Eduardo Arroyo über die Executive Academy im Gespräch mit Gudrun Hausegger / Eduardo Arroyo on the Executive Academy in conversation with Gudrun Hausegger

SCHNITTSTELLEN – ARBEITS-BEZIEHUNGEN ZUR GEBAUTEN CAMPUS-UMWELT — **146** INTERFACES – WORK RELATIONSHIPS IN THE ARCHITECTURE OF THE CAMPUS
Statements / Statements
Daniel Grünkranz / Daniel Grünkranz

SICH NICHT FÜRCHTEN — **152** TO NOT BE AFRAID
Über die große Aufgabe, eine Universität auf die grüne Wiese zu bauen / About the challenge of constructing a university from scratch
Maximilian Pammer, Christoph Sommer / Maximilian Pammer, Christoph Sommer

ZAHLEN · DATEN · FAKTEN — **156** FACTS AND FIGURES

KURZBIOGRAFIEN — **157** SHORT BIOGRAPHIES

VORWORT

GEBAUTE IDEALE
EIN UNIVERSITÄTSCAMPUS DES 21. JAHRHUNDERTS

CHRISTOPH BADELT

Der Abschluss des ersten Studienjahres am neuen Campus der Wirtschaftsuniversität Wien ist ein guter Zeitpunkt für den Rückblick auf eines der ambitioniertesten Bauprojekte der Zweiten Republik, für eine erste Bilanz und für einen Ausblick.

Die Reaktionen der Öffentlichkeit auf den Neubau, viele Medienberichte und die Erfahrungen der Universitätsangehörigen zeigen uns, dass hier eine sinnvolle und nachhaltig wirksame Investition gelungen ist. Ein öffentliches Universitätsgebäude von heute dient nicht nur Bildungszwecken im engeren Sinne, sondern ist auch Ausdruck einer Vision sowie Träger gesellschaftlicher Verantwortung. Mit der Wahl des Bautyps Campus und seiner zentralen Lage inmitten einer europäischen Metropole ist eine klare Positionierung der Universität als lebendiger Bestandteil von Stadt und Gesellschaft verbunden. Der Wunsch nach Offenheit und Interaktion war Leitlinie dieser Entscheidung.

Unsere Universität steht für eine Vielfalt an Sichtweisen auf Wirtschaft und Gesellschaft, für Weltoffenheit in Bezug auf den akademisch-intellektuellen Austausch und in Bezug zum realen Wirtschaftsleben, für Verantwortung gegenüber Wirtschaft, Gesellschaft und Politik, einen nachhaltigen Beitrag zu einem besseren, anderen Wirtschaftsleben zu leisten und für Innovation und ein neues Denken, das die Phänomene der Wirtschaft im 21. Jahrhundert mit neuen Methoden erfasst und zeitgemäße theoretische Erklärungen wie praktische Handlungsanleitungen generiert.

Der Campus drückt diese Inhalte aus und liefert darüber hinaus auch Mehrwert für Stadt und Gesellschaft. Mit seiner offenen Anlage lädt er zur Nutzung durch alle Stadtbewohner und Besucher ein, seine vielfältigen Einrichtungen tragen zur positiven Transformation des Stadtquartiers bei. Man kann das Bauprojekt auch mit „harten Zahlen" umschreiben: Hier wurden rund 100.000 m² Nutzfläche geschaffen, knapp 4.000 Räume, davon 90 Hörsäle und Seminarräume mit einer Gesamtkapazität von 5.000 Nutzern und rund 3.000 Arbeitsplätze für Studierende. Es wurden aber auch 1.000 Fahrradabstellplätze gebaut und 230 Bäume gepflanzt.

Wir haben versucht, all jenes räumlich umzusetzen, was uns an einer Universität, wie wir sie verstehen, besonders wichtig ist. Forschung und Lehre stehen im Zentrum des universitären Lebens und alles andere wird darum herum gedacht und gebaut: Die attraktivsten Räume dieses Campus werden von den Studierenden für Arbeitsplätze in der Bibliothek genutzt. Der Campus steht auch für Internationalität und Weltoffenheit – er wurde von mehreren internationalen und hoch angesehenen Architektinnen und Architekten gebaut. Es wäre falsch gewesen, ihn nur von einem Architekten oder einer Architektin bauen zu lassen, denn unsere Universität steht für eine Vielfalt von Fächern, Perspektiven und Forschungsmethoden. Der Campus ist auch ein wichtiger Wirtschaftsfaktor, die Universität ist stolz auf ihre gute Kooperation mit der österreichischen Wirtschaft, die sich etwa in langfristigen Sponsoringbeziehungen ausdrückt.

Viele Aspekte unseres Verständnisses von Universität sind ganz unmittelbar in bauliche Strukturen übersetzt. Zum Beispiel gibt der Campus Raum für gesellschaftliches, kulturelles und politisches Leben, er ist daher ohne Zaun errichtet: Die Universität ist offen für das gesellschaftliche und kulturelle Leben dieser Stadt. Der Campus ist auch nach den Prinzipien eines „Green Buildings" gebaut, wir beziehen 70 % der Energie für Heizung und Kühlung aus Geothermie und bei den einzelnen Bauten wurde besonders auf Energieeffizienz geachtet. So steht der Bau auch für eines der wichtigsten Prinzipien, die unsere aktuelle gesellschaftspolitische Diskussion prägen: Das Prinzip der Nachhaltigkeit. Die Wirtschaftsuniversität will und muss im Sinne der Nachhaltigkeit wirken.

Das vorliegende Buch ist der Architektur und dem Leben am Campus gewidmet. Es ist eine erste Standortbestimmung zur Frage, ob die oben beschriebenen Ideale erreicht werden konnten. Renommierte Autorinnen und Autoren verschiedener kulturwissenschaftlicher und technischer Fachrichtungen beschreiben die Geschichte des Projekts, die einzelnen Bauten und technische Spezialaspekte. Es kommen aber auch jene zu Wort, für die der Campus gebaut wurde: Studierende und Lehrende, Mitarbeiter aus den verschiedensten Bereichen des komplexen Uni-Lebens. Großzügige Illustrationen und Grafiken tragen zum hohen dokumentarischen Wert dieser repräsentativen Publikation bei. Sie beweist vor allem eines: Dass mit diesem international höchst beachteten Projekt eine funktionierende Basis für eine dynamische Entfaltung der Institution gelegt und die Voraussetzung geschaffen wurde, weiterhin substantielle Beiträge zur wirtschaftlichen und gesellschaftlichen Entwicklung zu liefern.

PREFACE

BUILT IDEALS
A UNIVERSITY CAMPUS FOR THE 21ST CENTURY

CHRISTOPH BADELT

The end of the first academic year on the new campus of Vienna University of Economics and Business is a good point in time to look back at one of the most ambitious construction projects of the Second Republic in Austria for an interim review and a prospect.

The public reactions to the new campus, the many media reports, and the experiences of the university staff and students reveal the success of the sensible and sustainable investment that has been made here. A contemporary public university building not only serves educational purposes in the narrower sense; it is also the expression of a vision and bears social responsibility. The choice for the campus typology and the central location at the heart of a European metropolis clearly positions the university as a lively component of the city and society. The desire for openness and interaction was a guiding principle behind this decision.

Our university stands for a plurality of perspectives on economy and society, for a cosmopolitan approach to academic-intellectual exchange and to real economic life, for responsibility toward economy, society, and politics, for a sustainable contribution to a new, better economic reality, for innovation and a new paradigm that tackles the economic phenomena of the twenty-first century with new methods and thereby generates up-to-date theoretical explanations and best practices.

The campus gives shape to these contents; moreover, it also affords an added value for the city and society. The publicly accessible complex is an open invitation to be used by all inhabitants of the city and its visitors; its diverse facilities make a contribution to the positive transformation of the district. One can also describe the project with "hard facts and figures": Approximately 100,000 square meters of usable area have been created, almost 4,000 rooms, of them 90 lecture halls and seminar rooms with a total capacity of 5,000 users and 3,000 workplaces for students. Additionally, 1,000 bicycle parking places have been provided and 230 trees planted.

We have attempted to spatially implement everything that is of vital importance for a university in our definition. Research and teaching are at the heart of university life, and everything else is conceived and built around it: The most attractive spaces on this campus are used by students as workplaces in the library. The campus also stands for internationality and cosmopolitanism – it was built by a number of international and highly acclaimed architects. It would have been wrong to have only one architect design it all as our university represents a diversity of subjects, perspectives, and research methods. The campus is also an important economic factor; the university is proud of its valuable cooperation with the Austrian economic sector, which manifests, for example, in long-term sponsoring relationships.

Many aspects of our understanding of a university have been directly translated into built structures. For example, the campus provides space for social, cultural, and political life – that's why there is not a fence around it. The university is open for the social and cultural life of this city. The campus has also been built according to the principles of "Green Buildings": We obtain 70 % of our energy for heating and cooling from geothermy, and energy efficiency was a particular focus in the design of the individual buildings. Hence, the WU Campus also exemplifies one of the most important principles that currently inform sociopolitical discussions: the principle of sustainability. The University of Economics and Business strives to and must act in the spirit of sustainability.

The book before you is dedicated to the architecture and the life on campus. It is a first inventory on the question whether the above-described ideals could be attained. Renowned authors from various cultural-scientific and technical disciplines describe the history of the project, the individual buildings, and the technical earmarks. But also the people for whom the campus was built have their say: the students and teachers, the staff from diverse realms in the complex university life. Exceptional illustrations and graphics contribute to the high documentary value of this representative publication. But, above all, it evidences one thing: This internationally highly-esteemed project provides a functioning basis for the dynamic evolution of our institution, and the prerequisites are in place to continue making substantial contributions to economic and social progress.

Weltausstellung Wien, 1873: Eine Metropole entsteht
Vienna International Exhibition, 1873: A rising metropolis

FÜLLE UND HÜLLE
ZUR INSTITUTIONS- UND BAUGESCHICHTE DER WIRTSCHAFTSUNIVERSITÄT WIEN 1873–1982

MARKUS KRISTAN

Am 4. Oktober 2013 wurde der neue WU Campus eröffnet. Mit diesem neuen Standort auf dem ehemaligen Gelände der Wiener Weltausstellung von 1873 kehrte die Wirtschaftsuniversität Wien (WU) an den Ort zurück, an dem exakt 140 Jahre zuvor ihre Geschichte mit dem anlässlich der Ausstellung zur Betreuung ausländischer Delegationen und zur Aufnahme von Handelskontakten gegründeten „Cercle Oriental" begonnen hatte.

NEVER ENOUGH AND NOTHING TO SPARE
ON THE INSTITUTIONAL AND ARCHITECTURAL HISTORY OF VIENNA UNIVERSITY OF ECONOMICS AND BUSINESS 1873–1982

On October 4, 2013 the new WU Campus officially opened. With this new location on the former terrain of the Vienna International Exhibition of 1873, Vienna University of Economics and Business (WU) returns to the site where precisely 140 years ago its history began with the "Cercle Oriental", an organization founded on the occasion of the exhibition to support foreign delegations and welcome trade partners.

Da nach dem Ende der Weltausstellung viele der orientalischen Ausstellungsobjekte in Wien verblieben waren, wurde zu deren Aufbewahrung 1874 das „Orientalische Museum"[1] gegründet. 1886 folgte nach dem Vorbild des „Musée commercial" in Brüssel eine Umbenennung in „Handelsmuseum", das 1896 von der Börse in das ehemalige Palais Festetics in Wien-Alsergrund, Berggasse 16 übersiedelte.

Zur Verbesserung der österreichischen Handelsbilanz wurde auf Betreiben des Museums am 18. August 1896 dem Handelsminister ein Memorandum überreicht, in dem die Gründung einer „Export-Akademie des k. k. österreichischen Handels-Museums" vorgeschlagen wurde.[2] Für die neu gegründete Institution wurde am 22. Mai 1898 ein provisorisches Organisationsstatut erlassen.[3] Die langatmige Bezeichnung wurde später auf „k. k. Exportakademie" vereinfacht. Für die feierliche Eröffnung war der 1. Oktober 1898 vorgesehen. Infolge der Ermordung von Kaiserin Elisabeth in Genf am 10. September 1898 nahm man jedoch von einer formellen Eröffnungszeremonie Abstand und nahm formlos am 1. Oktober 1898 den Lehrbetrieb im Palais Festetics auf.

Internationale Vorgängerinstitutionen für die Exportakademie waren beispielsweise die „Handelsacademie" in Hamburg, gegründet 1767, die „Hautes études commerciales de Paris" (HEC Paris), gegründet 1881, und die „London School of Economics and Political Science", gegründet 1895.

As many of the Oriental exhibition objects remained in Vienna after the end of the exhibition, the "Oriental Museum"[1] was founded in 1874 to ensure their safe-keeping. In 1886, following the example of the "Musée commercial" in Brussels, it was renamed as the "Trade Museum" and moved from the stock exchange to the former Palais Festetics in the 9th district Vienna-Alsergrund on Berggasse 16.

As a measure to improve the Austrian trade balance, the museum presented the trade minister a memorandum on August 18, 1896, proposing the foundation of an "Export Academy of the Imperial Austrian Trade Museum".[2] A provisional organizational statute was issued on May 22, 1898 for the newly founded institution.[3] The long-winded name would later be simplified as the "Imperial Export Academy". The opening festivities were planned for October 1, 1898. But owing to the murder of Empress Elisabeth in Geneva on September 10, 1898, they refrained from a formal opening ceremony, and teaching customarily commenced in Palais Festetics on October 1, 1898.

International predecessor institutions for the Export Academy were, for example, the "Trade Academy" in Hamburg, founded in 1767, the "Hautes études commerciales de Paris" (HEC Paris), founded in 1881, and the "London School of Economics and Political Science", founded in 1895.

**Romano & Schwendenwein:
Palais Festetics, Wien / Vienna 1858**

Weltausstellung, Wien 1873: Japanische Galerie
Vienna International Exhibition, 1873: Japanese Gallery

Alfred Keller: k.k. Exportakademie (ab / from 1919: Hochschule für Welthandel, ab / from 1975: Wirtschaftsuniversität), Währingerpark, Wien / Vienna, 1915–1917

GESCHICHTE / HISTORY

Carl Appel: Hochschule für Welthandel, Zubau / Addition, Philippovichgasse, Wien / Vienna, 1954–1956

Kurt Eckel: Hochschule für Welthandel, Zubau / Addition, Gymnasiumstraße, Wien / Vienna 1969–1974

Carl Appel: Hochschule für Welthandel, Hörsaal / Lecture Hall, 1954–1956

Alfred Keller: k.k. Exportakademie, Währingerpark, Eingangshalle / Entrance Hall, Wien / Vienna, 1915–1917

Die ständig anwachsende Zahl von Hörern brachte das Bedürfnis mit sich, die Akademie aus ihrem bisherigen Verband mit dem k.k. österreichischen Handelsmuseum zu lösen und in eine selbständige Einheit umzugestalten. Zu diesem Zweck wurde der Verein „Exportakademie" gegründet, der am 1. August 1915 die Akademie vom Verein k.k. österreichisches Handelsmuseum übernahm. Die wichtigste Aufgabe des neu gegründeten Vereines war es, den bereits 1914 begonnenen Neubau der Exportakademie trotz der Kriegsereignisse voranzutreiben. Kriegsbedingt musste der Architekt Alfred Keller[4] räumliche und ausstattungsmäßige Abstriche von seinem ursprünglichen Planungskonzept machen. Das noch nicht zur Gänze fertiggestellte Gebäude wurde 1916 bezogen, die offizielle Eröffnung folgte am 20. März 1917.[5]

Der Neubau wurde auf einer Parzelle des aufgelassenen Währinger Friedhofes, einem großen Grünareal in Wien-Döbling, an der Ecke Gymnasiumstraße/Philippovichgasse in einem Mischstil aus Klassizismus, Neobarock und Heimatschutz errichtet.[6] An seiner künstlerischen Ausschmückung waren die Bildhauer Karl Stemolak, Michael Powolny, Franz Barwig, Theodor Stundl und Wilhelm Heyda sowie die Maler Adolf Groß, Oskar Laske, Josef Beyer und Alfred Keller (zugleich auch Architekt des Hauses selbst) beteiligt.[7]

The steadily growing number of students entailed the need to dissolve the academy's previous association with the Imperial Trade Museum and to restructure it into an independent entity. To this end, the "Export Academy" association was founded, which took over the academy from the Imperial Austrian Trade Museum association on August 1, 1915. The most important task of the newly formed association was to spur the construction of the Export Academy's new building, which had already began in 1914, despite the parallel events of World War I. Due to the war, architect Alfred Keller[4] had to make spatial and furnishing cuts in his original planning concept. The academy moved into the not entirely finished building in 1916, and the official opening followed on March 20, 1917.[5]

The new building was constructed on a plot in the vacated Währing cemetery, an expansive green zone in Vienna-Döbling, on the corner of Gymnasiumstraße and Philippovichgasse in a mix of Classicism, Neo-Baroque, and Heimatschutz styles.[6] Responsible for its artistic decoration were the sculptors Karl Stemolak, Michael Powolny, Franz Barwig, Theodor Stundl, and Wilhelm Heyda as well as the painters Adolf Groß, Oskar Laske, Josef Beyer, and Alfred Keller himself.[7]

GESCHICHTE / HISTORY

Kurt Hlaweniczka: Wirtschaftsuniversität Wien, 1978–1982
Vienna University of Economics and Business, 1978–1982
Leherb: Europa, Fayence in der Eingangshalle
Europe, Faience in the entrance hall

Die Umwandlung der „Exportakademie" in die „Hochschule für Welthandel" erfolgte durch den Beschluss der Nationalversammlung der im Jahr zuvor gegründeten Ersten Republik am 21. Oktober 1919. Den AbsolventInnen wurde von da ab der akademische Grad eines „Diplomkaufmannes" verliehen. Das Promotionsrecht, die AbsolventInnen zu „Doktoren der Handelswissenschaften" zu ernennen, erhielt die Hochschule im Jahr 1930.

Von 1954 bis 1956 wurde entlang der Philippovichgasse nach Plänen von Carl Appel[8] ein Zubau errichtet. 1969 bis 1974 folgte ein längs der Gymnasiumstraße gelegener weiterer Zubau nach Plänen von Kurt Eckel[9].

Ein neuerlicher, nunmehr dritter Namenswechsel der Institution erfolgte im Zuge der Universitätsneuorganisation 1975, als die „Hochschule für Welthandel" in „Wirtschaftsuniversität Wien" umbenannt wurde.

Trotz der beiden Zubauten blieb die Raumnot der WU bestehen. Nach dem Scheitern einiger Vorprojekte (Überbauung des Jüdischen Friedhofes, Erweiterung entlang der Gymnasiumstraße, Grundstück in der Türkenschanzstraße, Verlagerung nach Niederösterreich) entstand die Projektidee eines Universitätszentrums in der Althanstraße mit Überbauung der Gleisanlagen (nach amerikanischen Vorbildern) der Franz-Josefs-Bahn als erstes Großprojekt dieses Typs in Österreich. Zeitgleich suchten auch andere unter drückender Raumnot leidende Institute der Universität, der Creditanstalt und der Post Bauland für neue Räumlichkeiten. Dadurch entstand nach und nach das Projekt Universitätszentrum Althanstraße (UZA). Zur Finanzierung des Großbaus wurde der Bau von privater Seite vorfinanziert, um dann 15 Jahre hindurch von der Republik Österreich geleast zu werden. Das Wiener Architekturbüro von Kurt Hlaweniczka[10] wurde als Generalplaner beauftragt.[11]

Der von den Planern unternommene Versuch, das UZA in seinen ungewöhnlich großen Ausmaßen durch kleinräumliche Gliederungen in die Umgebung einzufügen, ist kaum gelungen.

The Export Academy would then transform into the "University of World Trade" on October 21, 1919 following a decision by the national assembly of the First Republic, which was founded in the year before. From then on graduates were awarded the academic degree "University Trained Merchants". In 1930 the university received the right to award doctorates and title graduates "Doctors of Commercial Science".

Between 1954 and 1956 an extension was built along Philippovichgasse in accordance with the design plans of Carl Appel.[8] Between 1969 and 1974 another extension was added along Gymnasiumstraße following the design by Kurt Eckel.[9]

The institution would undergo a further, now third name change with the University Reorganization Act of 1975, when the University of World Trade was renamed "Vienna University of Economics".

Despite the two extensions, the WU's growing demand for space remained a problem. After the failure of a number of predecessor projects (building over the Jewish cemetery, further extension along Gymnasiumstraße, properties on Türkenschanzstraße, and relocation in Lower Austria), a project idea emerged for a university center on Althanstraße by building above the railway tracks (like American precedents) of the Franz Joseph line – the first large-scale project of this kind in Austria. Simultaneously, there were other institutes of the University, the Creditanstalt bank, and the Austrian Post service with desperate shortages of space, which were also in search of sites for new buildings. This gradually led to the project University Center Althanstraße (UZA). To finance this major project the construction was prefinanced by the private sector and then leased by the Republic of Austria for 15 years. The Viennese architectural firm of Kurt Hlaweniczka[10] was commissioned as the general planner.[11]

The intention of the designers to integrate the extraordinary scale of the UZA into the surroundings through small-scale components cannot exactly be called a success. "The new

"Insgesamt erweckt der Neubaukomplex den Eindruck einer klirrenden Landschaft aus Glasflügeln, zwischen denen man sich fürs erste nur schwer orientieren kann."[12]

Ähnlich wie schon der Vorgängerbau in Wien-Döbling erhielt auch der Neubau eine reiche künstlerische Ausstattung.[13] Auf Wunsch des Architekten wurden mehrere Künstler mit der Ausschmückung des Gebäudes beauftragt: Hier wirkten die Maler Franz Grabmayr, Peter Klitsch und Maitre Leherb (Helmut Leherbauer) sowie die Bildhauer Horst Aschermann, Oskar E. Höfinger und Josef Schagerl.

Die Bauarbeiten am WU-Gebäude begannen 1978. Im Jahre 1982 wurde die neue WU bezogen.[14] Die Raumnot war prolongiert – das Haus war für 9.000 Studierende geplant worden, aber die Universität verzeichnete nun bereits 9.863 Inskribierte. Am Gebäudekomplex des UZA wurde noch bis 1995 weitergebaut.[15] Die WU linderte ihre bereits notorische Raumnot durch Anmietungen rundum, begann sich aber bereits mit dem neuen Universitätsgesetz 2002 auch als Institution neu zu erfinden – ein Prozess, der letztlich in die Planung des WU Campus mündete.

complex evokes an overall impression of a bone-chilling landscape of glass wings between which one has great difficulty finding orientation."[12]

Similar to its predecessor in Vienna-Döbling, the new building also received a wealth of artistic furnishings.[13] At the request of the architect, different artists were commissioned with the decoration of the building: The painters Franz Grabmayr, Peter Klitsch, and Maitre Leherb (Helmut Leherbauer) and the sculptors Horst Aschermann, Oskar E. Höfinger, and Josef Schagerl were chosen for this task.

Construction work on the WU buildings commenced in 1978. In 1982 the new WU was inhabited.[14] But the lack of space was only prolonged: The house was designed for 9,000 students, but by that point the university already had 9,863 students enrolled. Work continued on the UZA complex till 1995.[15] The WU mitigated its already notorious lacking space through renting spaces in the area. But with the new Austrian Universities Act 2002, it already began to reinvent itself as an institution – a process that ultimately led to the plan for the WU Campus.

---

1 Eine Zusammenfassung der Geschichte des Orientalischen Museums findet sich in: http://www.wieninger.com/assets/Uploads/orient-mus-paris-wieninger.pdf (Johannes Wieninger, Das orientalische Museum in Wien, 1874–1906), Zugriff am 29. Jänner 2014.
2 Anton Schmid, Geschichte der k. k. Exportakademie, in: k. k. Exportakademie (Hrsg.), Die k. k. Exportakademie in Wien. Zur Erinnerung an die Eröffnung des neuen Akademiegebäudes im Herbst 1916, Wien 1916, S. 13.
3 Ludwig Strauss, Die Reform des Deutschen Handelsrechtes und ihre Bedeutung für Österreich, Wien 1899, S.149.
4 Alfred Keller (1875–1945) war ein in Graz geborener österreichischer Architekt, Maler und Grafiker. Seine Bautätigkeit erstreckt sich von 1908 bis zu seinem Tod. Stilistisch folgten seine frühen Bauten noch dem Späthistorismus, später dem Heimatschutz-Stil und schließlich einer gemäßigten Moderne. Hauptwerke Kellers, der auch Mitglied des Hagenbundes und Professor an der Technischen Universität Wien gewesen war, sind das Polizeigebäude auf der Rossauer Lände in Wien (1902–04), das Gerichtsgebäude in der Riemergasse in Wien (1906–08), eine Reihe von Hotels und Villen in Graz und Kroatien sowie Arbeitersiedlungen in der Steiermark.
5 K.k. Exportakademie. Bericht über die feierliche Eröffnung des neuen Akademiegebäudes am 20. März 1917, Wien 1917.
6 Friedrich Achleitner, Österreichische Architektur im 20. Jahrhundert. Ein Führer in vier Bänden. Band III/3. Wien: 19.–23. Bezirk, St. Pölten/Salzburg 2010, S. 21. Die heutige Adresse des Gebäudes ist Franz-Klein-Gasse 1. Franz Klein (1854–1926) war ein österreichischer Jurist, Hochschullehrer und Politiker.
7 Alfred Keller, Das neue Akademiegebäude, in: Die k. k. Exportakademie in Wien. Zur Erinnerung an die Eröffnung des neuen Akademiegebäudes im Herbst 1916, Wien 1916, S. 35–48 (Ansichten und Grundrisse); Alfred Keller, Das neue Gebäude der k. k. Exportakademie in Wien, in: Der Architekt. Monatshefte für Bau- und Raumkunst, 21. Jg., Wien 1916/1918, S. 129–137; Ferdinand Fellner Ritter von Feldegg, Alfred Keller, in: Österreichische Bauzeitung (Wiener Bauindustrie-Zeitung), 35. Jg., Heft 11, Wien 1918, S. 81–83, T. 65–67.
8 Carl Appel (1911–1997) war ein österreichischer Architekt. Appel prägte von der Wiederaufbauzeit nach dem Zweiten Weltkrieg bis in die 1970er Jahre das Baugeschehen in Österreich maßgeblich mit.
9 Kurt Eckel (*1921) ist ein österreichischer Architekt. Er studierte an der Technischen Universität Wien. 1955 gründete er sein eigenes Architekturbüro in Wien. Ein weiteres markantes Werk Eckels in Wien ist der Funkturm im Arsenal, der zeitgleich mit dem Zubau der Hochschule für Welthandel errichtet wurde.
10 Kurt Hlaweniczka (*1930) ist ein österreichischer Architekt, der in den 1970er, 1980er und 1990er Jahren oftmals in Arbeitsgemeinschaft mit anderen Architekten in Wien und Niederösterreich eine Reihe von großen Wohn- und Verwaltungsbauten schuf (Wohnpark Alt-Erlaa mit Harry Glück; Technisches Zentrum der Creditanstalt mit Karl Schwanzer, Harry Glück, Franz Requat und Thomas Reinthaller; Pensionsversicherungsanstalt der Angestellten gemeinsam mit Hannes Lintl; Rehabilitationszentrum der Allgemeinen Unfallversicherungsanstalt in Klosterneuburg gemeinsam mit Hannes Lintl).
11 Vgl.: Manfred Wurzer, Universitätszentrum Althanstraße. Versuch einer Projektdokumentation, Diplom-Hausarbeit am Institut für Organisation und Materialwirtschaft an der Wirtschaftsuniversität Wien, Wien 1984; Überbauung des Wiener Franz-Josefs-Bahnhofs, in: Österreichische Ingenieur- und Architekten-Zeitschrift (ÖIAZ), 140. Jg., Heft 4, Wien, April 1995.
12 Harald Sterk, Bauen in Wien. Das letzte Jahrzehnt 1976 bis 1986, Wien 1986, S. 125.
13 Universitätszentrum Althanstraße: artifizielle Ausgestaltung, Wien 1983.
14 In das alte Gebäude der WU zogen mehrere Universitätsinstitute ein.
15 Walter Jaksch, Edith Fischer, Franz Kroller, Österreichischer Bibliotheksbau. Architektur und Funktion, Bd. 2: 1945–1985, Wien – Graz Köln 1992, S. 106–115; Elmar Schübel, Der Universitätsbau in der Zweiten Republik. Ein Beitrag zur Entwicklung der universitären Landschaft in Österreich, Horn 2005, S. 235–245.

1 A summary of the history of the Oriental Museum can be found in: Johannes Wieninger, Das orientalische Museum in Wien, 1874–1906, http://www.wieninger.com/assets/Uploads/orient-mus-paris-wieninger.pdf, accessed January 29, 2014.
2 Anton Schmid, "Geschichte der k. k. Exportakademie," in Die k. k. Exportakademie in Wien. Zur Erinnerung an die Eröffnung des neuen Akademiegebäudes im Herbst 1916, ed. k. k. Exportakademie (Vienna: Verlag Der K. K. Exportakademie, 1916), 13.
3 Ludwig Strauss, Die Reform des Deutschen Handelsrechtes und ihre Bedeutung für Österreich (Vienna: Manz, 1899), 149.
4 Alfred Keller (1875–1945) was a Graz-born Austrian architect, painter, and graphic designer. He was active as an architect from 1908 until his death. In stylistic terms, his early buildings still followed late Historicism, later works the Heimatschutz style and subsequently a tempered modernism. A member of the Hagenbund and professor at Vienna University of Technology, Keller's principal works included the police building on Rossauer Lände in Vienna (1902–04), the court house on Riemergasse in Vienna (1906–08), a number of hotels and villas in Graz and Croatia, and workers' settlements in Styria.
5 Imperial Export Academy report about the festive opening of the new Academy building on March 20, 1917. (Vienna: 1917).
6 Friedrich Achleitner (ed.), Österreichische Architektur im 20. Jahrhundert. Ein Führer in vier Bänden. Wien: 19.–23. Bezirk, vol. III/3 (St. Pölten/Salzburg: Residenz Verlag, 2010), 21. Today the address of the building is Franz-Klein-Gasse 1. Franz Klein (1854–1926) was an Austrian lawyer, university teacher, and politician.
7 Alfred Keller, "Das neue Akademiegebäude," in Die k. k. Exportakademie in Wien. Zur Erinnerung an die Eröffnung des neuen Akademiegebäudes im Herbst 1916 (Vienna: 1916), 35–48. (views and floor plans); Alfred Keller, "Das neue Gebäude der k. k. Exportakademie in Wien," Der Architekt. Monatshefte für Bau- und Raumkunst, 21 (Vienna: 1916/1918): 129–137; Ferdinand Fellner Ritter von Feldegg, "Alfred Keller," Österreichische Bauzeitung (Wiener Bauindustrie-Zeitung), 35/11 (Vienna: 1918): 81–83, T. 65–67.
8 Carl Appel (1911–1997) was an Austrian architect. He played a decisive role in Austrian architecture from the post-Second World War reconstruction period until well into the 1970s.
9 Kurt Eckel (*1921) is an Austrian architect. He studied at Vienna University of Technology. In 1955 he founded his own architecture office in Vienna. Another distinctive work by Eckel is the radio tower on the Arsenal terrain, which was built at the same time as the extension of the University of World Trade.
10 Kurt Hlaweniczka (*1930) is an Austrian architect who built a series of residential and administrative buildings in Vienna and Lower Austria in the 1970s, 80s, and 90s, often in working groups with other architects (Alt Erlaa residential park with Harry Glück; Creditanstalt technical center with Karl Schwanzer, Harry Glück, Franz Requat, and Thomas Reinthaller; Pensionsversicherungsanstalt der Angestellten with Hannes Lintl; Rehabilitationszentrum der Allgemeinen Unfallversicherungsanstalt in Klosterneuburg with Hannes Lintl).
11 Cf. Manfred Wurzer, Universitätszentrum Althanstraße. Versuch einer Projektdokumentation, Diplom-Hausarbeit am Institut für Organisation und Materialwirtschaft an der Wirtschaftsuniversität Wien (Vienna: 1984); "Überbauung des Wiener Franz-Josefs-Bahnhofs," Österreichische Ingenieur- und Architekten-Zeitschrift (ÖIAZ), 140/4 (Vienna, April 1995).
12 Translated for this publication from: Harald Sterk, Bauen in Wien. Das letzte Jahrzehnt 1976 bis 1986 (Vienna: Harold, 1986), 125.
13 University Center Althanstraße: artificial decoration, Vienna, 1983.
14 A number of university institutes also moved into the old WU building.
15 Walter Jaksch, Edith Fischer, and Franz Kroller (eds.), Österreichischer Bibliotheksbau. Architektur und Funktion, 1945–1985, Wien–Graz, vol. 2 (Cologne: 1992), 106–115; Elmar Schübel, Der Universitätsbau in der Zweiten Republik. Ein Beitrag zur Entwicklung der universitären Landschaft in Österreich (Horn: Berger, 2005), 235–245.

2
WETTBEWERBE FÜR EINEN CAMPUS
TWO COMPETITIONS FOR ONE CAMPUS

FRANZISKA LEEB

Auslober eines Architekturwettbewerbs seien gut beraten gut zu wissen, was sie wollen oder – sich des Nichtwissens bewusst – mit großer Offenheit auf ein überraschendes Ergebnis einzulassen, lautet eine oft vertretene Meinung. Überraschungen gab es in der Wettbewerbsgeschichte des WU Campus einige, zumindest aus der Sicht von außen. Analysiert man die Geschichte der Projektentwicklung und nimmt Ausschreibungen und Juryprotokolle unter die Lupe, stellt sich heraus, dass vieles, was so unerwartet schien, durchaus in der Struktur der auf viele Eventualitäten bedachten Auslobung bereits kalkuliert war.

Optionen offen gehalten

Im Dezember 2007 wurde der EU-weite, offene Realisierungswettbewerb für die Generalplanung des Universitätskomplexes ausgelobt, der in „architektonischer, ökonomischer und ökologischer Hinsicht den Vorreiteranspruch der WU verkörpern" möge. Der Auslober erklärte, mit dem Gewinner Verhandlungen entwe-

It's a widely-held opinion that organizers of an architectural competition should be well advised to know what they want or – knowing that they don't know – to have an open mind for surprising results. And there were several surprises in the competition history of the WU Campus, at least seen from the outside. If you analyze the project development process and have a closer look at the tenders and protocols, you will discover that much of what seemed unexpected was in fact already anticipated in the structure of a call for tenders open to many eventualities.

Options Left Open

In December 2007 there was an EU-wide open architectural competition for the general planning of the university complex, which should "embody the WU's pioneering claims in architectural, economic, and ecological terms". The organizer stated that there would be negotiations with the winner either about the overall planning of the site and the Library and Learning

Wettbewerb für die Generalplanung 2007–08:
Siegerprojekt von BUSarchitektur
Competition for the general planning 2007–08:
winning project by BUSarchitektur

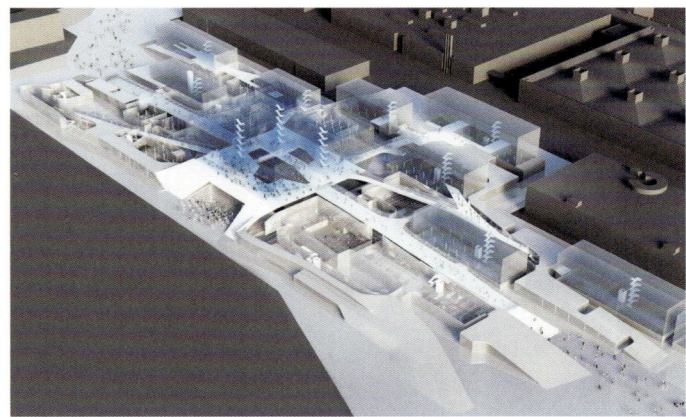

**Wettbewerb für die Generalplanung 2007–08:
Projekt von Berger + Parkkinen**
Competition for the general planning 2007–08:
project by Berger + Parkkinen

**Wettbewerb für die Generalplanung 2007–08:
Projekt von Flatz / Zeytinoglu**
Competition for the general planning 2007–08:
project by Flatz / Zeytinoglu

der über die übergeordnete Planung des Projektstandortes sowie des Library and Learning Center und/oder weitere Teile bis zum Gesamtprojekt zu führen. Es wurde damit also nicht explizit in Aussicht gestellt, dass der oder die Siegerin damit rechnen kann, mit dem Gesamtprojekt beauftragt zu werden. Eine Teilbarkeit des Areals in mehrere Baufelder war somit bereits eine mögliche Variante. Hochkarätig besetzt war die Jury, mit Wolf D. Prix als Vorsitzendem, unterstützt unter anderen von den Architekten Dietmar Eberle, Brian Cody, Bettina Götz und Ernst Hubeli. Ob es an der großen Aufgabenstellung lag oder einer zu wenig offensiven Werbung um internationale Teilnehmer, darüber kann man im Nachhinein nur mutmaßen: Jedenfalls hatte die Jury am 2. April 2008 nur 24 Einreichungen vorliegen, im Wesentlichen von durchaus nicht unbekannten Büros aus Österreich, fünf Bewerbern aus Deutschland und einem Atelier aus Portugal.

Drei Einreichungen blieben nach zwei Bewertungsdurchgängen der Jury im Rennen: Berger + Parkkinen Architekten (Projekt 8), die Arbeitsgemeinschaft Flatz_architects + Architekturbüro Zeytinoglu mit Idealice Landschaftsarchitektur (Projekt 17) sowie BUSarchitektur & Partner (Projekt 23). Zu viele, anonym nicht zu klärende Fragen blieben offen, sodass sich das Preisgericht entschloss, mit diesen Bewerberinnen am darauffolgenden Tag einen sogenannten Dialog[1] zwecks Klärung zu führen. Am Ende war klar, dass Projekt 8 (einstimmig), Projekt 17 (10:2) und Projekt 23 (7:5) überarbeitet werden sollen, wobei neben der Verbesserung projektspezifischer Detailprobleme das Augenmerk besonders auf die Freiräume gelegt werden sollte.

In der entscheidenden Sitzung am 9. Mai 2008 traute schließlich das Beurteilungsgremium dem Projekt von BUSarchitektur das größte Potenzial zu, ein gelungener Campus zu werden. Während der Masterplan gefiel, hält das Protokoll aber auch fest, dass „wie bei allen anderen Projekten auch … die architektonische Umsetzung des Library and Learning Centers nicht überzeugen" konnte. Am Vorschlag von Berger + Parkkinen würdigte man „die Qualität der im Masterplan teilweise umgesetzten Campus-Atmosphäre", den in Ost-West-Richtung durch die Anlage führenden „Broadway" – eine witterungsgeschützte Hauptstraße – und auch die Nord-Süd-Verbindungen zwischen Messe und Prater sah man dezidiert positiv. Nicht punkten konnte das sehr über-

Center and/or additional buildings when not the entire project. Hence, the prospect that the winner can expect to be commissioned with the complete project was not raised explicitly. The division of the site into numerous building plots was thus already a potential variant. There was a top-notch jury with Wolf D. Prix as the chair and other members including architects Dietmar Eberle, Brian Cody, Bettina Götz, and Ernst Hubeli. Whether it was due to the scale of the formulated task or because the call for international participants was not advertised well enough, we can only speculate after the fact: In any case, on April 2, 2008 the jury only had 24 submissions on the table, most of them from reputed offices in Austria, five applicants from Germany, and one studio in Portugal.

After two evaluation rounds there were three submissions still in the race: Berger + Parkkinen Architekten (Project 8), the working group Flatz_architects + Architekturbüro Zeytinoglu with Idealice Landschaftsarchitektur (Project 17), and BUSarchitektur & Partner (Project 23). Too many questions remained open that couldn't be clarified on the anonymous basis of the authors. This led to the jury's decision to hold a so-called dialogue[1] for clarification on the following day. In the end it was clear that Project 8 (unanimous), Project 17 (10:2), and Project 23 (7:5) needed to be reworked. In addition to improvements in project-specific details, special attention should be devoted to the issue of the open spaces.

In the decisive jury meeting on May 9, 2008 the assessment board entrusted the project by BUSarchitektur with having the most potential to become a successful campus. They were pleased with the master plan, however the protocol also stated: "as is the case with all of the other projects […] the architectural design for the Library and Learning Center is not convincing." The proposal by Berger + Parkkinen was recognized for "the quality with which the campus atmosphere was partially implemented in the master plan"; the east-west "Broadway" traversing the complex – a weather-protected main street – and also the north-south connection between the Messe Wien exhibition grounds and the Prater were decidedly positive aspects. On the other hand, the very coherently organized project couldn't score points with the open spaces and the repetitive

sichtlich organisierte Projekt hingegen mit den Außenräumen und der sich wiederholenden ruhigen Form der Baublöcke, die nicht den Geschmack der Jury getroffen haben. Beim Projekt von Flatz/Zeytinoglu fand die Idee des polyatmosphärischen Städtebaus Anerkennung, bei der dörfliche und städtische Stimmungen einander überlagern und eine hohe Qualität des öffentlichen Raums entsteht. Ebenso gefiel das Library and Learning Center als klare Markierung in der Mitte, man fand allerdings Defizite funktionaler Natur und stellte eine „starke Hierarchisierung der verschiedenen Geschosse in qualitativer Hinsicht" fest.

Final wurde beschlossen, mit den Autoren des Gewinnerprojektes „Verhandlungen über einen Generalplanervertrag für den Neubau der Wirtschaftsuniversität Wien auf Grundlage seines überarbeiteten Masterplans" zu führen. Die öffentlichen Wege und übergeordneten Verkehrs- und Erschließungsflächen, deren notwendige Infrastruktur und die Landschaftsarchitektur sollten Gegenstand dieses Generalplanervertrages sein und der Gewinner, also das Team BUSarchitektur um Laura Spinadel, verpflichtet werden, „das Architektenteam auf Grundlage von weiteren Wettbewerben bzw. einem Wettbewerb mit mehreren Losen zu erweitern."

133 Bewerber für vier Baufelder

Jury und Auslober machten also keinen Hehl daraus, dass der erhoffte große Wurf nicht dabei war.[2] Zu pragmatisch und zu wenig visionär für die Maßstäbe des Bewertungsgremiums waren offensichtlich die Zugänge der einzelnen Einreicher angelegt.

In den folgenden Monaten entwickelte daher die Projektgesellschaft als Bauherr mit der Generalplanerin, der im Zuge der Verhandlungen auch die Realisierung des Hörsaalzentrums zugesprochen wurde, den Masterplan weiter und beschloss, einen weiteren Wettbewerb mit Präqualifikation in mehreren Losen auf Basis des Siegerprojektes auszuloben. Im Juli 2008 war es soweit. Insgesamt 133 Architekturbüros aus aller Welt – die Liste liest sich wie ein Katalog der nationalen und internationalen Architekturszene – bewarben sich für den zweistufigen, nicht offenen Realisierungswettbewerb für die einzelnen Gebäude.

Neben dem bereits an BUSarchitektur vergebenen Bauplatz für das Hörsaalzentrum (Bauplatz Ost 1 – O1) standen vier weitere Baufelder zur Disposition: Südlich davon der Bauplatz O2, auf dem es externe Dienstleister (ED) unterzubringen galt, in zentraler Lage jener für das Library and Learning Center (kurz LLC), im Westen das Baufeld W1 für ein Departmentgebäude und die Executive Academy sowie das Baufeld W2 für den Verwaltungstrakt. Jedes bewerbende Büro hatte neben Referenzen auch Präferenzen für das gewünschte Bearbeitungsgebiet abzugeben. Nach erfolgtem Ranking der Besten wurden jeweils sechs den Baufeldern zugeordnet. Darunter fand sich nur ein Büro aus dem Kreis der Preisträger des erstens Wettbewerbs und zwar jenes von Wilhelm Holzbauer.

calm form of the buildings, which didn't meet the taste of the jury. The project by Flatz/Zeytinoglu was celebrated for the idea of poly-atmospheric urban planning, where rural and urban ambiences intermingle and result in high-quality public spaces. Also the Library and Learning Center as a distinguishing mark in the middle had definite appeal, however the jury found that the functional nature of the design had deficits with a "strong hierarchy of the different storeys in qualitative terms".

Ultimately the jury decided to hold negotiations with the authors of the winning project "about a general planner contract for the new Vienna University of Economics and Business complex on the basis of its reworked master plan". The public paths and the superordinate traffic and access zones, their required infrastructure, and the landscape architecture should be the subject of this general planner contract, and the winners – Laura Spinadel and her team at BUSarchitektur – were obliged to commit themselves to "expanding the team of architects on the basis of further competitions or a competition with several stages".

133 Submissions for Four Building Plots

The jury and client made it no secret that the competition had not produced the desired solution in "one stroke".[2] The approaches of the individual applicants were obviously too pragmatic and not visionary enough for the standards of the assessment board.

Hence, the project company "Wirtschaftsuniversität Wien Neu GmbH" as client continued with the elaboration of the master plan in the following months together with the general planner – who was also awarded with the design of the Teaching Center in the course of the negotiations – and, on the basis of the winning project, another competition was tendered with prequalification for a number of building plots. In July 2008 the time had come. A total of 133 architectural offices from around the world – the list reads like a "who's who" of the national and international architecture scene – made submissions for the two-stage, non-open architectural competition for the individual buildings.

Besides the plot already assigned to BUSarchitektur for the Teaching Center (Building Plot East 1 – O1), four other sites were in question: Building Plot O2 to the south, which was designated for external service providers (ED); at the center one for the Library and Learning Center (LLC for short); Building Plot W1 to the west for a department building and the Executive Academy; and Building Plot W2 for the administrative tract. In addition to references, each office that applied had to submit preferences for the desired work area. Following a ranking of the best, six proposals were assigned to each respective building plot. Among them was only one office from the winners of the first competition, namely Wilhelm Holzbauer.

>

Realisierungswettbewerb für die Einzelgebäude, 2008: Der Campus mit den Siegerprojekten von Zaha Hadid Architects, BUSarchitektur, Atelier Hitoshi Abe, CRAB studio, NO.MAD, Estudio Carme Pinós
Competition for the individual buildings, 2008: Winning projects by Zaha Hadid Architects, BUSarchitektur, Atelier Hitoshi Abe, CRAB studio, NO.MAD, Estudio Carme Pinós

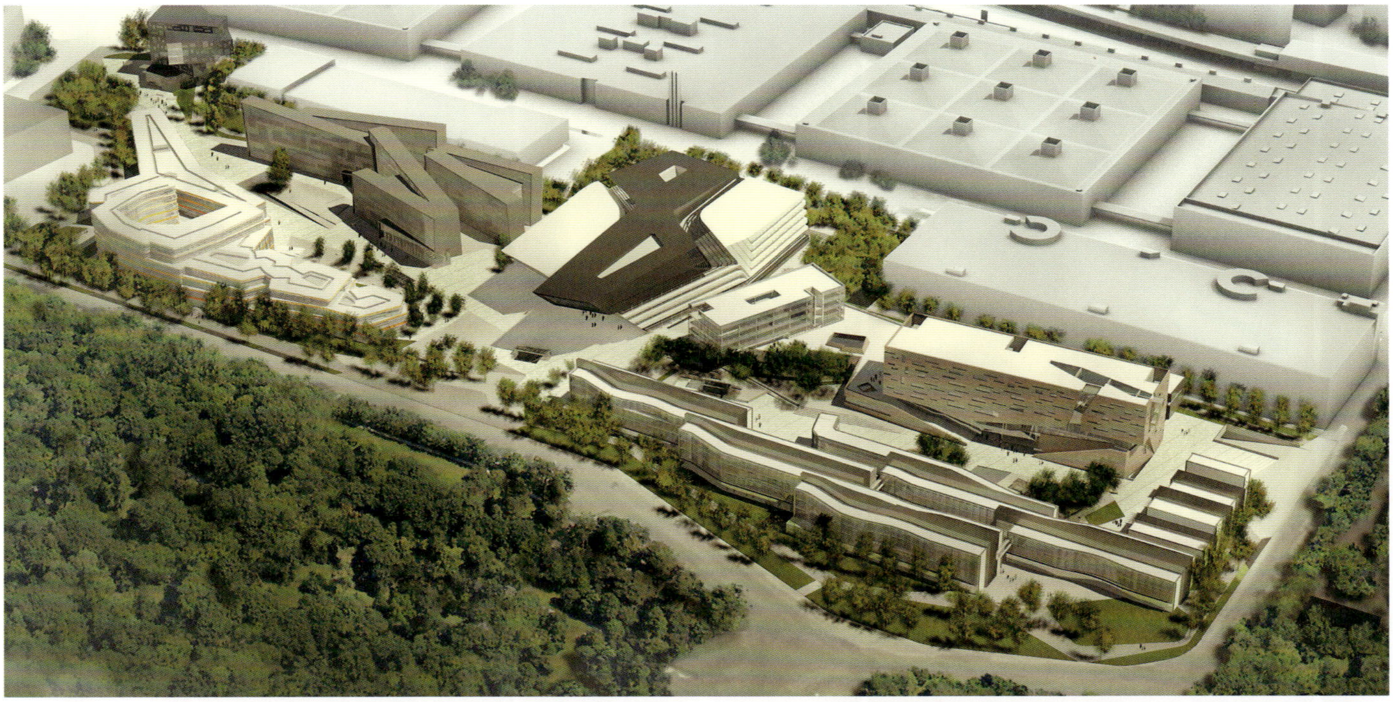

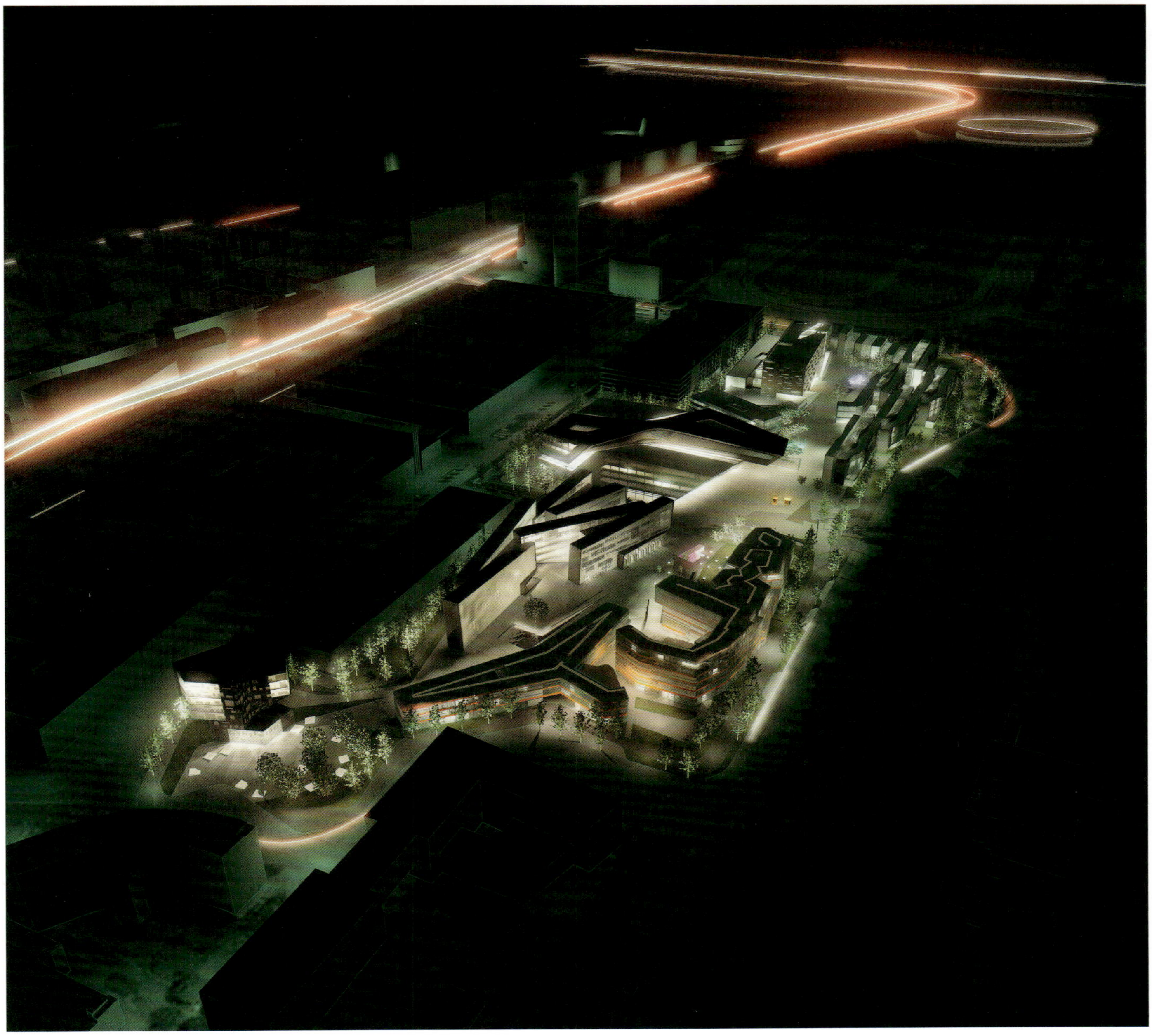

WETTBEWERBE / COMPETITIONS

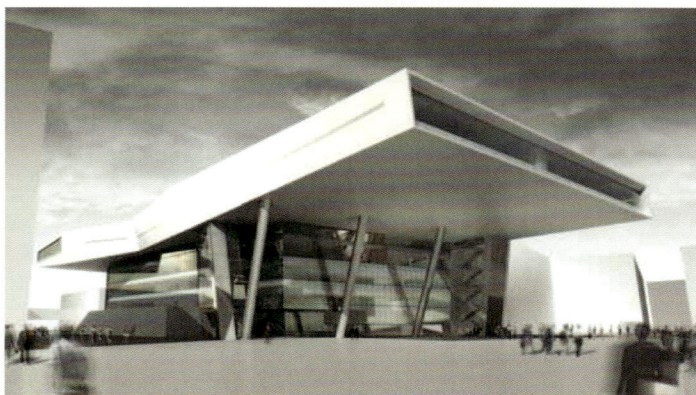

Realisierungswettbewerb für die Einzelgebäude, 2008: Projekte für das Library and Learning Center von Zaha Hadid Architects (oben), Hans Hollein (links), Morphosis Architects (rechts)
Competition for the individual buildings, 2008: Projects for the Library and Learning Center by Zaha Hadid Architects (top), Hans Hollein (left), Morphosis Architects (right)

Die finale Entscheidung

Am 8. Oktober 2008 lagen der Jury die skizzenhaften Darstellungen der Projektanten vor, aus denen drei für die 2. Stufe ausgewählt wurden. Als weiteres Prozedere beschloss die Jury, drei bereits in die Vorprüfung involvierte Experten (die Architekten Andreas Burghardt und Paul Katzberger sowie Bauingenieur Wolfgang Vasko), die dem Preisgericht gegenüber zur Verschwiegenheit verpflichtet sind, zu beauftragen, ein Kolloquium mit jedem für die zweite Runde qualifizierten Wettbewerbsteilnehmer durchzuführen, um eine Reihe von Punkten, bei denen die Jury im Zuge der ersten Stufe Erläuterungsbedarf sah, zu besprechen. Ebenso entschied man sich, dass die Teilnehmer im Zuge der Preisgerichtssitzung am 25. und 26. November für Erläuterungen zur Verfügung stehen sollten, die Anonymität also aufgehoben werden solle.

Library and Learning Center

Beim „Herzstück" LLC beeindruckte das Gremium die „dynamische und faszinierende Formensprache" des Beitrages von Zaha Hadid, der als das mit Abstand am weitesten entwickelte Projekt klassifiziert und daher mit dem ersten Preis bedacht wurde. Morphosis Architects wurde die überzeugendste Lösung des Themas „Bibliothek" attestiert, zu kurz gekommen sei aller-

The Final Decision

By October 8, 2008 the jury had received the designers' draft representations, from which three were selected for the second round. As an additional procedure, the jury decided to commission three experts – who were already involved in the prequalification stage (the architects Andreas Burghardt and Paul Katzberger and engineer Wolfgang Vasko) and sworn to secrecy in face of the jury – to conduct a colloquium with each of the competition participants who qualified for the second round and discuss a number of points from the first stage where the jury needed further explanation. Likewise, they decided that the participants should be present for questions at the jury meeting on November 25 and 26, hence annulling the anonymity.

Library and Learning Center

For the LLC centerpiece of the campus, the jury was won over by the "dynamic and fascinating formal language" of the contribution by Zaha Hadid, which was seen as being the most elaborated project by far and thus awarded first prize. Morphosis Architects delivered the most convincing solution on the topic "Library", however too little account was paid, above all, to the functional aspects of the "Learning Center" – thus second place. Hans Hollein's proposal came in third: The functionality

dings vor allem in funktioneller Hinsicht der Aspekt des „Learning Centers", daher nur Zweiter. Hans Holleins Beitrag wurde drittgereiht. Obwohl Funktionalität und leichte Orientierbarkeit zwar gewürdigt wurden, übte man Kritik an der zu geringen Flexibilität sowie an „der Formensprache der einzelnen Bauteile".

Baufeld 02

Am Baufeld 02 bildete das Atelier Hitoshi Abe mit einem zum Prater durchlässigen Projekt die Anforderungen des Masterplans perfekt ab. Leichtigkeit, Einfachheit und filigrane Anmutung bestachen obendrein – also Platz eins. Bevk Perović Arhitekti schufen mit einer Plattform und Rampen eine Verbindung zwischen Campus und Prater. Im Sockel mit den öffentlichen Bereichen sah das Preisgericht eine störende wie auch unwirtschaftliche Barriere. Insgesamt konnte man dennoch eine gewisse Offenheit und Leichtigkeit erkennen: Platz zwei. Als „städtebaulich interessant" wurde der Beitrag von Josep Llinás Carmona bewertet. Die regelmäßige Kammstruktur empfand man als harmonisch, unbefriedigend allerdings die zu erwartenden Belichtungsprobleme: Platz drei.

and easy orientation were positively noted; however it was criticized for its low level of flexibility and the "formal language of the individual building components".

Building Plot 02

Atelier Hitoshi Abe's solution for Building Plot 02 with its permeations to the Prater perfectly implemented the requirements in the master plan. Above all, its lightness, simplicity, and filigree character captivated the jury – first place. Bevk Perović Arhitekti created a connection between the campus and Prater with a platform and ramps. However, the public areas in the plinth represented a disruptive and uneconomic barrier in the jury's opinion. Nevertheless, the overall project did possess a certain openness and lightness – second place. The proposal by Josep Llinás Carmona was graded "interesting in urban planning regards". The recurrent comb structure was harmonic, but the lighting problems that could be expected were unsatisfactory – third place.

Realisierungswettbewerb für die Einzelgebäude, Baufeld 02: Siegerprojekt von Hitoshi Abe
Competition for the individual buildings, Plot 02: Winning project by Hitoshi Abe

WETTBEWERBE / COMPETITIONS

Baufeld W1

Vielfältige Durchgänge und Blickverbindungen im Projekt von Carme Pinós wurden als angemessener Ausdruck des Masterplans im Baufeld W1 betrachtet. Nicht nur in der Horizontalen den Fluss durch das Gelände gewährleistend, sondern auch auf Belebung in der Vertikalen bedacht wurde der ökonomisch und ökologisch als zweckmäßig gewürdigte Entwurf mit dem ersten Preis auf diesem Baulos bedacht. Das Departmentgebäude von NO.MAD arquitectos konnte die Jury vor allem wegen einer zu großen Freifläche, die dem Platz vor der Bibliothek unerwünschte Konkurrenz gemacht hätte, nicht vollends überzeugen. Die Executive Academy hingegen wurde als „städtebauliches Highlight am Zugang zum Campus" gesehen und daher ein zweiter Preis vergeben. An dritter Stelle landete das Projekt von Holzbauer und Partner, dem Funktionalität zugestanden wurde, dessen „sehr konservative Architektursprache" allerdings als ebenso wenig passend erachtet wurde wie die städtebaulich kaum wirksame Executive Academy.

Mit dieser Entscheidung wurde zugleich die Empfehlung an den Bauherrn verbunden, mit der Erstplatzierten das Verhandlungsverfahren über die Planung des Departmentgebäudes auf diesem Baufeld zu führen und über die Planung der Executive Academy mit dem Zweitplatzierten zu verhandeln, wofür der verhandelte Bauplatz in Folge auf zwei Architekten aufgeteilt wurde.

Building Plot W1

The various passageways and intersecting vistas in the project by Carme Pinós for Building Plot W1 were deemed an appropriate translation of the master plan. It granted the desired horizontal flow through the site while offering a lively vertical solution as well. The economic and ecological design was best-suited for this plot and awarded first prize. The department building by NO.MAD arquitectos was not entirely convincing for the jury, primarily due to the large public zone in the plan, which would create an undesirable rivalry with the plaza in front of the Learning Center. In contrast, the Executive Academy was seen as an "architectural highlight at the entrance to the campus" and thus awarded second prize. Praised for its functionality, the project by Holzbauer and Partner landed in third place. However, its "very conservative architectural language" was not fitting nor was the ineffective design for the Executive Academy.

Along with these decisions came the recommendation to the client to enter into negotiations with the first place winner about the design of the Department Building on this building plot and with the second place winner for the design of the Executive Academy, which led to the division of the site into two individual plots.

Realisierungswettbewerb für die Einzelgebäude, geteiltes Baufeld W1: Projekte von Estudio Carme Pinós (oben), NO.MAD (unten)
Competition for the individual buildings, split Plot W1: Projects by Estudio Carme Pinós (top), NO.MAD (bottom)

Realisierungswettbewerb für die Einzelgebäude, Baufeld W2: Projekte von CRAB studio (links), Guillermo Vázquez Consuegra (rechts)
Competition for the individual buildings, Plot W2: Projects by CRAB studio (left), Guillermo Vázquez Consuegra (right)

Baufeld W2

Beim Verwaltungsgebäude von CRAB studio/Peter Cook erhoffte sich die Jury von versetzten Geschossen, Nischen und Höfen eine Vielfalt, die eine „typisch studentische Atmosphäre" erzeugt und sprach ihm den ersten Preis zu. Am Projekt von Guillermo Vázquez Consuegra Arquitecto machte man interessante Akzente aus. Zu massiv erschien aber der nördliche Riegel und zu starr der Südtrakt Richtung Prater: Platz zwei. Auf dem dritten Rang landete das Projekt von Eric Owen Moss, das nach Ansicht der Jury neben zu vielen Büros ohne direkten Blick ins Freie auch einen gravierenden städtebaulichen Makel aufwies: die dominante Turmlösung hätte das LLC in den Hintergrund gedrängt.

Lohnende Taktik

Wohl nie zuvor hat ein österreichisches Bauvorhaben ein dermaßen dichtes Feld von Stars der globalen Architekturszene zur Teilnahme animieren können. War der Wurstelprater nebenan um 1900 eine internationale Sensation, so ist es heute der Campus der Wirtschaftsuniversität. Allein dafür hat sich die ausgeklügelte Wettbewerbstaktik im Vorfeld gelohnt.

Building Plot W2

With the offset floors, niches, and courtyards in the Department and Administration Building by CRAB studio/Peter Cook, the jury anticipated a diversity that would create a "typical student atmosphere" and presented him first prize. The proposal by Guillermo Vázquez Consuegra Arquitecto offered interesting accents. But the block to the north seemed too massive and the southern tract facing the Prater too rigid: second place. Third place was given to the project by Eric Owen Moss: In the eyes of the jury there were too many offices without a direct view outdoors, but moreover it represented a serious flaw for the urban plan: The dominant tower would have pushed the Learning Center into the background.

A Worthwhile Tactic

Likely never before has an Austrian building project animated the participation of such a dense cast of stars from the global architecture scene. The international sensation that the Wurstelprater amusement park was in 1900 has been passed on to the WU Campus today. And that alone is enough evidence that the sophisticated competition tactic was worthwhile.

---

[1] **Bundesvergabegesetz 2006, § 155 Abs 6:** „..... Die Bewerber können bei Bedarf aufgefordert werden, zur Klärung bestimmter Aspekte der vorgelegten Wettbewerbsarbeiten Antworten auf Fragen zu erteilen, die das Preisgericht in der Niederschrift festgehalten hat. Über den darüber stattfindenden Dialog zwischen den Preisrichtern und den Bewerbern ist ein umfassendes Protokoll zu erstellen, das der Niederschrift anzuschließen ist. ..."
[2] **siehe dazu auch:** „Starke Identitäten polarisieren – Dietmar Eberle im Gespräch mit Edith Schlocker" in diesem Band.

[1] **Austrian Federal Contracts Act 2006 § 155 para. 6:** "When necessary, applicants can be asked to answer questions for the clarification of certain aspects of the submitted competition work, which the jury has recorded in the minutes. A detailed protocol is to be made of the dialogue between the jury members and the applicants and supplemented to the minutes."
[2] **See** "Strong Identities Polarize – Dietmar Eberle in conversation with Edith Schlocker" in this publication.

STARKE IDENTITÄTEN POLARISIEREN

DIETMAR EBERLE IM GESPRÄCH MIT EDITH SCHLOCKER

Edith Schlocker: Es ist in Österreich ungewöhnlich, dass eine ganze Universität komplett neu gebaut wird. Und zwar als Campus, wie man ihn von angelsächsischen Ländern kennt. War das Ihre Idee, waren Sie doch seit Beginn der Diskussionen über einen Neubau als Berater und dann als Juror mit dabei?
Dietmar Eberle: Die Bundesimmobiliengesellschaft (BIG) hat mich als Berater engagiert. Sie wie die Verantwortlichen der Universität davon zu überzeugen, dass international alle wirklich guten Hochschulen als Campus organisiert sind, war allerdings Knochenarbeit. Gibt es meiner Meinung nach doch auf der ganzen Welt keine Institution in der Größe der Wiener WU, die ihr komplexes Programm in einem einzigen Gebäude unterbringt. Die Idee, wieder eine riesige Maschine zu bauen, aus den Köpfen der Bauherren zu vertreiben, war allerdings nicht leicht.

Was ist an mehreren Gebäuden prinzipiell besser als an einem einzigen?
Dass sie überschaubar sind, Identität entwickeln, nicht zuletzt, weil die Maßstäblichkeit stimmt. Gebaut im Idealfall von den besten Architekten der Welt. Nachdem man nach der österreichischen Vergabeordnung diese aber nicht freihändig aussuchen kann, wurde ein Wettbewerb ausgelobt.

Einer von zwei, war der erste doch vor allem dem Masterplan gewidmet. Warum zwei Stufen?
Weil in der ersten Ausschreibung immer noch die ursprüngliche Idee des großen Wurfs in der Form eines einzigen Gebäudes nachgewirkt hat. Das Ergebnis des Wettbewerbs war dementsprechend niederschmetternd. Aber es ist der BIG genauso wie der Universität hoch anzurechnen, sich von dieser Idee zu verabschieden. Und sich zu überlegen, wie es nun weitergehen soll. Der den Wettbewerb juristisch begleitende Kurt Dullinger hat die rechtlichen Grundlagen für den zweiten Wettbewerb dann ganz nach unseren Wünschen formuliert. Ohne ihn gäbe es die WU in ihrer heutigen Form sicher nicht.

Indem beim zweiten Wettbewerb die funktional nun bereits definierten einzelnen Gebäude ausgeschrieben wurden.
Exakt. Die Ausschreibung war weltweit offen und wir Juroren haben außerdem Architekten, die wir besonders schätzen, eingeladen mitzutun. Anders geht es nicht. Hätten sich sonst doch so manche der Kollegen, die nun gebaut haben, sicher nicht an dem Wettbewerb beteiligt.

Den Masterplan dazu hat der Gewinner des ersten Wettbewerbs, BUSarchitektur aus Wien, entwickelt. Verbunden mit der Zusage, eines der sechs Gebäude zu bauen.
Das war der Kompromiss. Sie haben außerdem die gesamten Außenanlagen gestaltet.

War die Entscheidungsfindung in diesem zweiten Wettbewerb schwierig? Ist neben Ihnen doch u. a. Wolf Prix in der Jury gesessen, ein Kollege, dessen Architekturverständnis so grundsätzlich anders ist als das Ihre.
Überhaupt nicht. Prix und ich können uns über Qualität wunderbar einigen. Auch wenn wir prinzipiell ganz andere Wertvorstellungen haben. Die Ergebnisse der Jurysitzungen waren auf alle Fälle einstimmig.

An dem Wettbewerb haben sich 133 Büros aus aller Welt beteiligt. Ausgesucht wurden sechs Projekte mit völlig unterschiedlichen Architektursprachen. Bewusst?
Das war Teil des Programms. Auch, dass ein sehr starker Außenraum die Kraft haben sollte, diese heterogenen Teile zu verknüpfen. Diesem müssen wir noch etwas Zeit geben, sich zu entwickeln. Ob er dann diese Aufgabe übernehmen kann oder nicht, wird sich zeigen.

War ein Aspekt der Auswahl der sechs Projekte auch das Kriterium, wie die Gebäude miteinander korrespondieren?
Dieser Diskussion haben wir Juroren uns ziemlich konsequent enthalten. Weil auf einem guten Campus gerade diese Unterschiedlichkeit den Reiz ausmacht.

Inzwischen ist die WU besiedelt mit rund 24.000 Studierenden und etwa 1.500 Menschen, die hier arbeiten. Funktioniert es?
Ich bekomme jedenfalls keine gegenteiligen Rückmeldungen. Alle scheinen sehr stolz auf den neuen Campus zu sein, der offensichtlich schon in dieser kurzen Zeit eine starke Identität entwickelt hat. Aber eines ist klar: Starke Identitäten polarisieren.

Teil des Konzepts war es auch, die Universität zu öffnen, durchlässig zu machen. Auch räumlich. Ist das gelungen?
Ich hätte mir eine viel stärkere Durchmischung von universitären mit öffentlichen Funktionen, viel mehr „normales" Leben am Campus gewünscht. Deshalb waren uns auch die im Masterplan fixierten Übergänge und Anbindungen an die Welt außerhalb so wichtig.

INTERVIEW

Das alte WU-Gebäude hat keine 30 Jahre gehalten. Wird dem neuen Campus dieses Schicksal erspart bleiben?
Ein solches ereilt nur gesichtslose Gebäude, weil sie niemand mag. Und die neue WU hat eine Architektur, die sich wohltuend von jener anderer österreichischer Universitäten unterscheidet.

Was bei öffentlichen Bauten die Überschreitung der ursprünglich veranschlagten Kosten vergessen lassen würde?
Das mit den Kostenüberschreitungen bei öffentlichen Großprojekten ist eine ganz schwierige Problematik. Weil die Strategie international immer die gleiche ist. Und die anfangs behaupteten niedrigen Kosten sich praktisch nie einhalten lassen. Worüber sich allerdings nur mehr Außenseiter wundern. Aber es geht nicht anders, um ambitionierte Projekte zu ermöglichen.

Sie stehen für nachhaltiges Bauen, für ein Rücksichtnehmen auf den Ort, die Situation, den Inhalt. Gilt das auch für die sechs neuen WU-Gebäude?
Das große Thema der Nachhaltigkeit ist in Zukunft die Langlebigkeit eines Gebäudes. Und diese hängt mehr mit seiner Identität als mit den Betriebskosten zusammen. Auch die Relation zum Ort war im Fall der WU obsolet, nicht zuletzt, weil dieser so nichtssagend ist. Sich auf Gebäude der Umgebung zu beziehen hätte keinen Sinn gemacht. Noch dazu, da die neuen so stark sind.

Tut es einem engagierten Architekten, wie Sie es sind, eigentlich leid, als Juror an so einem reizvollen Projekt nicht teilnehmen zu können?
Die Aufgabe hätte mich sicher gereizt. Ob ich mitgemacht hätte, weiß ich allerdings nicht. Hab ich mich doch seit rund 20 Jahren in Österreich an keinem öffentlichen Wettbewerb mehr beteiligt. Nicht zuletzt wegen der Art, wie diese ausgeschrieben werden.

STRONG IDENTITIES POLARIZE

DIETMAR EBERLE IN CONVERSATION WITH EDITH SCHLOCKER

Edith Schlocker: In Austria it is quite uncommon to have an entire university completely rebuilt – and namely as a campus as we know it from Anglo-Saxon countries. Was that your idea, given you were involved from the very beginning as an advisor and then as a juror?
Dietmar Eberle: I was engaged as an advisor by the Bundesimmobiliengesellschaft (BIG – Austrian Federal Real Estate Company). However, convincing them and the responsible people at the university that all really good universities are organized as a campus was really quite back-breaking work. To my knowledge there are no institutions in the world the size of Vienna University of Economics and Business (WU), which accommodate their complex programmatic requirements in one single building. Getting the idea of once again building a gigantic machine out the minds of the clients was certainly no easy task.

What is the main advantage of several buildings as opposed to just one?
They are manageable, they develop identity, not least because the scale is right. And in the ideal case, they're built by the best architects in the world. But the Austrian Federal Contracts Act stipulates that one cannot freely choose the architects, so a competition was tendered.

One of two as the first one was mainly dedicated to the master plan. Why these two steps?
Because the original idea of one stroke in the form a single building still resonated in the first tender. The result of the competition was correspondingly crushing. But due credit should be given to the BIG and the University for parting with this idea and thinking about how it should go forward. The legal advisor of the competition Kurt Dullinger then formulated the legal basis for the second competition totally in line with our wishes. Without him there definitely wouldn't be the WU in its present form.

Since the individual buildings were already tendered with their respective functions in the second competition?
Precisely. The tender was international, and we jurors also invited architects we greatly respected to participate. It doesn't work otherwise. Then some of the colleagues who have now built on the campus certainly wouldn't have participated in the competition.

The master plan was developed by the winner of the first competition, BUSarchitektur from Vienna. In combination with the confirmation to design one of the six buildings.
That was the compromise. They also designed the complete outdoor facilities.

INTERVIEW

> Alle scheinen sehr stolz auf den neuen Campus zu sein, der offensichtlich schon in dieser kurzen Zeit eine starke Identität entwickelt hat. Aber eines ist klar: Starke Identitäten polarisieren.

———

> Everyone seems to be very proud of the new campus, which has obviously developed a strong identity in a very short period of time. But one thing is clear: Strong identities polarize.

Was coming to the decision in the second phase difficult? Wolf Prix, among others, was also in the jury with you, a colleague whose understanding of architecture is fundamentally different than yours.
Absolutely not. Prix and I were in complete agreement about the quality. Even though we do have very different values and priorities. The results of the jury sessions were in any case unanimous.

133 offices from around the world took part in the competition. Six projects with entirely different architectural languages were chosen. A conscious decision?
That was a part of the program. And also that a strong outdoor area should have the power to connect these heterogeneous elements. This still needs some time to develop. Whether it can accomplish this task or not remains to be seen.

Was the criterion of how the buildings correspond with one another also an aspect in the selection of the six projects?
We jury members refrained quite consequently from this discussion. Because it is exactly this diversity that is particularly appealing on a good campus.

In the meanwhile the WU is populated by approximately 24,000 students and 1,500 staff. Does it work?
I haven't received any responses indicating the contrary. Everyone seems to be very proud of the new campus, which has obviously developed a strong identity in a very short period of time. But one thing is clear: Strong identities polarize.

A part of the concept was also to open up the university, to make it transparent. Also spatially. Was this successful?
I wanted a far stronger mix of university and public functions, far more "normal" life on the campus. That's why the transitions and connections to the outside world defined in the master plan were so important to us.

The old WU building didn't even last 30 years. Will the new campus be spared such a fate?
Such a fate only befalls faceless buildings because nobody likes them. And the new WU has an architecture that is refreshingly different from that of other Austrian universities.

Which also makes exceeding the initial budget of public buildings easier to forget?
Overrun costs in large-scale public projects are a very difficult problem. Because the strategy is always the same around the world. And the initially claimed low costs can never be maintained in practice. But only outsiders are surprised by this. There is no other way to facilitate ambitious projects.

You are an advocate of sustainable building, for taking the place, the situation, and the content into consideration. Can this also be said about the WU buildings?
The big topic of sustainability has to do with the durability of a building in the future. And this depends more on its identity than on the operating costs. Also the relationship with the place was obsolete in the case of the WU, not least because it is so trivial. Making references to the surrounding buildings would have made little sense. Even more so as the new buildings have such strong character.

Wasn't it a shame for an engaged architect like yourself to be a jury member and thus not able to participate in such a prestigious project?
The opportunity definitely would have been thrilling. But I don't know if I would have participated. I haven't been involved in a public competition in Austria since about 20 years. If nothing else because of the way in which they are tendered.

EINE LEBENDIGE STADT

WOLF D. PRIX IM GESPRÄCH MIT MATTHIAS BOECKL

Matthias Boeckl: Sind anonyme Architekturwettbewerbe das geeignete Instrument, um das beste Bauprojekt zu finden?
Wolf D. Prix: Bei Wettbewerben, die angeblich anonym sind, zerbricht sich manchmal die Jury den Kopf, ob ein Projekt vom Architekten X oder Y stammt. Da sage ich dann immer: Hallo, es ist doch egal, von wem das ist – ist es ein gutes Projekt oder ein schlechtes? In weiterer Folge ist es aber dann schon sehr wichtig, dass man weiß, wer das Gebäude zu verantworten hat und ob er das auch planen kann. Deshalb bin ich ja gegen die anonymen Wettbewerbe und es ist mir auch gelungen, bei der Wirtschaftsuniversität Wien dieses Anonymitätsgesetz zu durchbrechen.

Für den WU Campus in Wien gab es einen ersten, EU-weiten Wettbewerb 2008. Warum war danach noch ein zweiter nötig?
Als ich angerufen wurde, ob ich den Vorsitz für den WU Campus übernehmen würde, war die Ausschreibung für den ersten Wettbewerb schon draußen. Ich habe dann natürlich sofort heftig polemisiert, weil ich eben befürchtete, dass nichts daraus werden kann, wenn man alles auf einen Schlag macht und noch dazu anonym. Anscheinend war auch die Ausschreibung nicht sehr verlockend, da sich nur wenige Architekten beteiligt hatten. Und auch das Ergebnis war nicht prächtig, muss ich sagen. Im Laufe der Diskussionen hat sich dann herauskristallisiert – und daran waren Auftraggeber und Nutzer sehr interessiert –, dass man den Wettbewerb erweitert und eine zweite Stufe veranstaltet, um das eigentlich gewünschte Campus-Konzept zu vertiefen, das im ersten Projekt nicht richtig ausformuliert war. Denn es hat geheißen: Eine Universität, sozusagen. Und jeder der einreichenden Architekten glaubte daher, er könne alles machen. Das war eine Verführung, das gebe ich zu. Ein Campus-Konzept im weitesten Sinne konnte man aus den Beiträgen nicht ablesen. Nur beim Projekt von BUSarchitektur konnte man mehrere Baufelder erkennen.

War es für Dich von Anfang an klar, dass das Programm nur mit einem Campus-Typ gelöst werden kann? Was sprach grundsätzlich gegen eine kompakte Lösung?
Erstens die Situation am Bauplatz im Prater. Zweitens Rektor Badelt von der Wirtschaftsuniversität. Und drittens die Vorstellung einer räumlich aufgelösten Universität, die Atmosphäre für kreatives Denken schafft. Das Interessante an einem Campus ist natürlich die Vielfältigkeit. Wir haben uns vorgestellt, dass eine Vielfalt von Konfigurationen auf Baufeldern lebendige Räume schafft, in denen man sich gerne bewegt. In der Vorbereitung für die zweite Stufe gab es dann auch den Wunsch der Nutzer, dass das Projekt eine internationale Ausstrahlung haben soll. Da lag der Schluss nahe, internationale Architekten einzuladen. Daraus wurde dann ein mehrstufiger Wettbewerb mit Präqualifikation. Die Baufelder wurden zwar zugelost, aber die Planer waren nicht anonym. Denn ich habe darauf bestanden, dass die Architekten die Gelegenheit haben sollten, ihr Projekt zu erklären. Je komplexer die Gedanken hinter einem Gebäude sind, desto weniger können das unerfahrene Juroren lesen. Und ich bin nicht dazu da, das alles zu übersetzen. Das war das Argument, warum man sich entschieden hat, die Architekten im letzten Durchgang ihre Projekte erklären zu lassen. Und das hat sich bewährt.

Das hat ja auch den Vorteil, dass der Bauherr weiß, mit wem er es überhaupt zu tun hat.
Ja. Ich muss auch sagen, dass der Nutzer beim WU-Wettbewerb sich wirklich engagiert hat. Ich habe noch nie bei einem Wettbewerb erlebt, dass der Nutzer derart am Vorgang, an den Projekten und an den Architekten interessiert war. Außerdem entspricht das Ergebnis tatsächlich dessen Vorstellung. Ich wünschte, dass Wohnbezirke genau so lebendig wären wie dieser Uni-Campus. Wenn man etwa in der Nähe der neuen WU die Lasallestraße überquert und in jenes Gebiet kommt, das ich Klein-Bukarest nenne, erlebt man ein Quartier, das von der Zwergpudel-Stadtplanung auf Ostblock-rektangulär reduziert wurde. Das ist eine absolute Stadt-Fehlplanung. Ich kann mir vorstellen, dass man auf dem WU Campus lieber wohnen würde als in diesem Stadtentwicklungsgebiet am ehemaligen Nordbahnhofareal. Stadträumlich finde ich den WU Campus sehr interessant. Denn die Architekten haben gut auf die Baufelder dieses Campus mit ihren jeweiligen Formen reagiert. Es ist eine sehr lebendige Umgebung geworden, die Cafés sind voll.

Du hast in einem Interview die einzelnen Bauten als „sehr gut" und „fast sehr gut" beurteilt.
Ich bin kein Architekturkritiker. Aber ich bin überrascht, dass alle Bauten fast so realisiert wurden, wie sie im Wettbewerb präsentiert worden waren. Zumindest vom Stadt- und Campus-Konzept her. Innen soll es ja einige Änderungen

gegeben haben, aber das ist immer so. Über Details müssen wir nicht reden. Peter Cooks Gebäude etwa ist zwar durchlässig, aber seine Performance ist nicht überzeugend. Die Durchlässigkeit der Gebäude war eine wichtige Nutzer-Forderung, es sollte keinerlei Blockaden geben. Das Campus-Konzept ist ja, dass man überall queren kann, ohne von Bauten daran gehindert zu werden.

Wie kamen die Einladungen zur zweiten Wettbewerbsstufe zustande?
Weil der Auftraggeber im internationalen Architekturbetrieb nicht sehr versiert war, habe ich ihm einige Adressen gegeben. Ich als Juryvorsitzender habe aber natürlich niemanden aktiv angesprochen und auf Nachfrage nur versichert, dass es sich um einen sehr interessanten Wettbewerb handle.

Wie sieht es mit dem Nutzungsmix aus? Sind monofunktionale Teilquartiere sinnvoll für die Stadt?
Die Alternative wäre die Verteilung der einzelnen Uni-Institute über die Stadt. Aber Wohnfunktionen innerhalb des Campus-Areals wären durchaus wünschenswert – einen schönen Gruß an die Wiener Stadtplanung! Es ist zwar klar, dass ein derartiges Projekt nur in einer konzentrierten Intensität realisiert werden kann, aber die Stadtplanung hätte dafür sorgen können, dass anliegende Straßenzüge wie etwa die Ausstellungsstraße keine Barrieren bilden und der Impact auf das dahinterliegende Stuwer-Viertel etwas intensiver wäre. Der WU Campus selbst ist aber ein faszinierendes Beispiel dafür, wie durch fließende Räume Buchten und Nischen entstehen können, in denen sich Treffpunkte und Cafés ansiedeln und schon nach kürzester Nutzungsdauer belebte Plätze entstehen. Das Gegenbild ist der orthogonale Blockraster wie am ehemaligen Nordbahnhof – da gibt es keine Chance für derartige Entwicklungen. Aber zurück zum WU-Wettbewerb: Der war wirklich eine Ausnahme vom Gewohnten. Die Voraussetzungen waren gut, der Ablauf war gut organisiert, die Jurysitzungen wurden von den Beamten nicht bürokratisch dominiert. Sondern auch sie waren offen und man konnte ihnen erklären, dass nicht jedes Projekt genau so gebaut wird, wie es im Wettbewerb gezeigt wird, denn ein Wettbewerbsprojekt ist kein Einreichplan. Das ist eine wichtige Botschaft, jeder Vorsitzende bei jedem Wettbewerb müsste das eingangs dezidiert feststellen. Besonders ausländische Architekten können ja nicht die lokale Bauordnung im Detail kennen. Hier kam jedenfalls ein gutes Ergebnis zustande. ▬

A LIVELY CITY

WOLF D. PRIX IN CONVERSATION WITH MATTHIAS BOECKL

Matthias Boeckl: Are anonymous architectural competitions the right instrument for finding the best building project?
Wolf D. Prix: In competitions that are apparently anonymous the jury sometimes wonders whether a project was by architect X or Y. I always say: Hello, it doesn't matter who did it – is it a good project or a bad one? In the process, however, it is definitely very important to know who is going to take responsibility for a building and if he or she is also able to go through with the planning. For this reason I am against anonymous competitions, and I also succeeded in breaking with this rule in the case of the Vienna University of Economics and Business.

In 2008 was the first EU-wide competition for the WU campus in Vienna. Why was a second one necessary afterwards?
When I was called about whether I would take on the chair for the WU Campus, the tender for the first competition was already on the go. Naturally, I complained heavily as I was worried that nothing would come out of doing everything in one stroke and moreover anonymously. Also the tender did not seem very seductive given how few architects participated. And the results weren't great either, I have to say. Then, in the course of the discussions, it came to the point – very much to the interest of the client and users – that the competition was to be extended by launching a second stage where the actually desired campus concept, which had not been properly articulated in the first project phase, could be better emphasized. Because previously the word was: one university, so to say. Thus each of the participating architects believed he or she could do everything. This was naturally a temptation, I have to admit. The contributions did not suggest a campus idea in the broadest sense. Only in the project by BUSarchitektur could one identify several building plots.

Was it clear to you from the very beginning that the program could only be resolved with a campus typology? What fundamentally opposed a compact solution?
To begin with, the situation of the building site in the Prater. Second, Rector Badelt from the WU. And thirdly, the notion of a spatially dispersed university, which generates an ambience for creative thinking. The interesting aspect of a campus is, of course, its diversity. We imagined that a variety of configurations on different building plots could yield lively spaces where it is a pleasure to move around. In the preparations for the second stage the users also expressed the wish that the project should have international appeal. Thus it seemed

INTERVIEW

> Wir haben uns vorgestellt, dass eine Vielfalt von Konfigurationen auf Baufeldern lebendige Räume schafft, in denen man sich gerne bewegt.

> We imagined that a variety of configurations on different building plots could yield lively spaces where it is a pleasure to move around.

only logical to invite international architects. This led to a multi-stage competition with pre-qualification. The building plots were allotted to the planners, but they were not anonymous. I insisted that the architects should have the opportunity to explain their projects. The more complex the thoughts behind a building are the less they are readable for inexperienced jurors. And I'm not there to translate everything. This argument resulted in the decision to have the architects explain their projects in the last round. And this proved to be successful.

This also has the advantage that the client knows with whom they are dealing.
Yes. I also have to say that the client and users were really engaged in the WU competition. I have never experienced a competition in which these parties were so interested in the procedure, in the projects and architects. Moreover, the result actually conforms to their visions. I wish residential districts were as lively as this university campus. For example, if you cross Lasallestraße not far from the new WU you arrive in this area that I call "Little Bucharest". You will find a quarter that has been reduced to an Eastern Bloc rectangle by a narrow-minded city planning. This is absolute urban misplanning. I imagine that people would rather live on the WU campus than in this new urban development on the grounds of the former Vienna North Station. From an urbanistic perspective I find the campus very interesting because the architects have reacted well to the building plots and their respective shapes. The result is a bustling area; the cafés are full.

In an interview you rated the individual buildings as "very good" and "almost very good".
I am not an architecture critic. But what surprises me is that all buildings were realized almost in the way they were presented in the competition. At least in terms of the urban and campus concepts. Supposedly there were some changes to the interiors, but this is always the case. We needn't talk about details. Peter Cook's project, for example, might be permeable, but its performance is not convincing. The permeability of the buildings was an important requirement from the users; there shouldn't be any barriers whatsoever. At the core of the master plan is the possibility to transverse the campus at any point without being inhibited by the buildings.

How did the invitations come about for the second competition stage?
As the client was not really well versed in the international architecture world I provided them with some contacts. But as the chair of the jury I naturally didn't actively approach anyone and, upon request, just made clear that it was a very interesting competition.

How does it look with mixed usage? Do mono-functional quarters make sense for the city?
The alternative would have been to distribute the individual university departments across the city. Indeed, residential functions within the campus terrain would have been desirable – with warm greetings to Viennese city planning! Although it is clear that such a project can only be realized in a concentrated density, the city planning authorities could have taken measures to prevent adjoining streets such as Ausstellungsstraße from forming a barrier and to intensify the impact on the Stuwer neighborhood behind the campus. However, the WU Campus in itself represents a fascinating example of how fluid spaces can create coves and niches where meeting places and cafés can settle and lively squares emerge even in a very short period of usage. The antithesis is the orthogonal grid of blocks like the one on the former North Station where there is no chance for such developments.

But back to the WU competition: It was really an exception to the norm. The preconditions were good, the procedure was well organized, and the jury meetings were not bureaucratically dominated by the public servants. They were also open, and you could explain to them that not every project is going to be built exactly in the way it was presented during the competition since a competition project is not a building permit plan. This is an important message: Every chair of a competition should decisively state that at the very beginning. Especially foreign architects cannot know the local building code down to the last detail. In the end, we achieved a very positive result.

MASTERPLAN

INTEGRAL UND DIFFUSIONSOFFEN
DER MASTERPLAN VON BUSARCHITEKTUR

ISABELLA MARBOE

Für BUSarchitektur ist der Freiraum zwischen gebauten Volumina entscheidend, um Urbanität zu generieren. Unter dieser Prämisse entwickelte das Büro auch den Masterplan des WU Campus. Dank definierter Parameter wie Wegen, Plätzen, Blickbeziehungen und Durchgängen gelang es, die sechs Architekturhandschriften am Campus zum zusammenhängenden Ganzen zu formen und in die umgebende Stadtlandschaft des Praters zu integrieren.

INTEGRAL AND PERMEABLE
THE MASTER PLAN BY BUSARCHITEKTUR

For BUSarchitektur the open space between built volumes plays an integral role in generating urbanity. This premise was also central in the development of their master plan for the WU Campus. Thanks to predefined parameters such as paths, squares, sight lines, and passageways it was possible to unite the six architectural signatures on campus into a coherent whole and integrate it into the surrounding urban landscape of Prater.

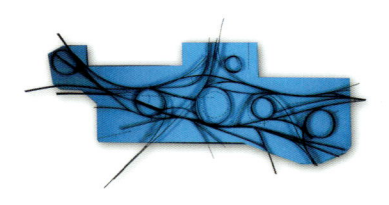

Ein Bauplatz als urbanes Magnetfeld voller Kraftlinien, die Menschen in Interaktion auf Kreuzungen, Wegen, Plätzen und Zwischenräumen erzeugen
A building site seen as urban magnetic field full of force lines, which the interaction of people induces on crossings, paths, squares, and passageways

Ein Campus als Ort der Begegnung: Studierende genießen die ersten warmen Sonnenstrahlen am grünen Dach der Mensa des Teaching Centers
A campus as meeting place: Students enjoy the first warm rays of sunlight on the green roof of the Teaching Center's Mensa cafeteria

MASTERPLAN

Ein neuer Stadtteil entsteht

Der Masterplan zum Campus der WU Wien ist so ungewöhnlich wie seine Geschichte. Sie begann am 10. Jänner 2008: Damals besichtigten alle Architekten, die sich zur Teilnahme am Wettbewerb für die Generalplanung des Neubaus der Wirtschaftsuniversität Wien angemeldet hatten, das Grundstück. Seine Nordostflanke ist rund 560 Meter lang. Sie liegt im Windschatten des Messegeländes am Rand des grünen Praters, der im Südwesten am Grundstück entlang mäandert. Wesentliche Bezugspunkte sind der runde Bogen des Hotels Messe Wien von Hermann Czech am schmalen, westlichen Ende der Parzelle, die Messe im Nordosten, die grellen Attraktionen des Prater-Vergnügungsparks und der Knick der Trabrennstraße. Im Osten grenzen die Trabrennbahn Krieau und das „Viertel Zwei" an den Bauplatz. Letzteres steht für die erfolgreiche Ansiedlung eines modernen, hochwertigen Businessquartiers in einer Gegend, die seit Generationen von Glücksspiel, Rotlicht und Kleinkriminalität geprägt ist. Andererseits ist der grüne Prater neben Wienerwald und Donauinsel eines der wichtigsten innerstädtischen Erholungsgebiete. Bereits 1766 öffnete Kaiser Joseph II. das einstige Jagdrevier der Habsburger für die Allgemeinheit. Bis heute ist es bei allen Wienern populär. Gegenüber auf der Ausstellungsstraße dominieren klassische Blockrandbebauung und Alleen, wie sie für Wien typisch sind. Seit einiger Zeit wurden hier Maßnahmen zur Aufwertung gesetzt, wie die Verlängerung der U2, der Bau des Stadion Centers und neuer Wohnanlagen. Die Strategie geht auf, der zweite Bezirk boomt.

Die Parameter, die den hybriden Charakter des Standorts zwischen Blockraster, Messe, Hotels, Stadion, „Viertel Zwei", weitläufigem Grün, Vergnügungspark, Touristenattraktion und Alltag bestimmen, sind so unterschiedlich und komplex wie das Anforderungsprofil der WU an ihren Neubau. Man rechnet mit 24.000 Studierenden und etwa 1.500 MitarbeiterInnen. Gemeinsam mit der BIG gründete die WU die Projektgesellschaft Wirtschaftsuniversität Wien Neu GmbH, die als Bauherr fungierte. Sie wünschte sich ein Library and Learning Center als Leuchtturmprojekt mit Hauptbibliothek, Gastronomie, Servicestellen für Studierende und Infrastruktur von rund 35.000 Quadratmeter Nutzfläche, sowie Departments für unterschiedliche Studienrichtungen mit Bibliotheken und Cafés, ein Hörsaalzent-

A New City District

The master plan for the campus of the Vienna University of Economics and Business (WU) is as unusual as its genesis. It all started on January 10, 2008: On this day, all architects who had registered for participation in the competition for the general planning of the new WU visited the site. Its northeastern flank measures about 560 meters. It is situated on the periphery of the Messe Wien fairgrounds and at the edge of the green Prater park, which meanders along the site to the southwest. Important reference points are the round curve of Hermann Czech's Hotel Messe Wien at the narrow western end of the premises, the trade fair complex to the northeast, the dazzling attractions in the Wurstelprater amusement park, and the kink in the Trabrennstraße. The Krieau horse trotting course and the "Viertel Zwei" neighborhood form the eastern perimeter of the building site. The latter stands for the successful development of a modern, high-quality business quarter in an area that was characterized by gambling, prostitution, and petty crime for many generations. Besides the Vienna Woods and the Danube Island, the Prater is one of the most important innercity recreational zones. Emperor Joseph II had already opened the former Habsburg hunting grounds to the general public in 1766. To this day it is widely frequented by all Viennese. The opposite side along Ausstellungsstraße is dominated by classic periphery block development and leafy avenues typical in Vienna. For some time now urban renewal measures have been underway, such as the extension of the U2 subway line and the construction of the Stadion Center and new residential complexes. The strategy works – the second district is booming.

The parameters that inform the hybrid character of this location – between block development, fairgrounds, hotels, stadium, "Viertel Zwei", green areas, amusement park, tourist attraction, and everyday city life – are as differentiated and complex as the requirements the WU stipulated for its new university. It should accommodate 24,000 students and around 1,500 staff. Together with the Bundesimmobiliengesellschaft (BIG – Austrian Federal Real Estate Company) the WU founded the project company Wirtschaftsuniversität Wien Neu GmbH to act as the client. It asked for a Library and Learning Center as a landmark project to house the main library, gastronomy and service

Masterplan des WU Campus von BUSarchitektur: Freiraum als Generator von Urbanität
Master plan of the WU Campus by BUSarchitektur: open space as generator of urbanity

rum, ein Verwaltungsgebäude und eine Executive Academy (EA) für Postgraduates. All diese Bauten sollten in einer campusartigen Struktur organisiert und so flexibel sein, dass man sie an wechselnde Bedingungen für Forschung, Lehre und Verwaltung anpassen konnte. Externe Dienstleister wie die Österreichische Hochschülerschaft, ein Fitnesscenter, Kindergarten, Supermarkt, Garagen mit 411 Stellplätzen und Parkmöglichkeiten für Fahrräder rundeten das Programm ab. Insgesamt sind es etwas mehr als 100.000 Quadratmeter Nutzfläche.

Ein Campus für 24 Stunden

Laura P. Spinadel und ihr Team um ihre Partner Jean-Pierre Bolívar und Bernd Pflüger von BUSarchitektur entwickelten für die Wiener WU ihre eigene Vision eines lebendigen, offenen Universitätscampus: Für sie ist die Aneignung von Wissen ein komplexer Vorgang an der Schnittstelle von Individuum und Gesellschaft. Außerdem war ihnen wichtig, ein 24 Stunden lang öffentlich zugängliches, durchwegbares Areal zu schaffen, von dem die ganze Stadt profitiert. Sie wollten in erster Linie ein vielschichtiges Raumkontinuum im Grünen erzeugen, das Einzelnen und Gruppen möglichst viele Optionen zur Aneignung bietet. Das Grundstück ist über 90.000 Quadratmeter groß. Der Campus sollte die Qualitäten eines gewachsenen Quartiers aufweisen. Diese definieren sich vor allem durch eine Vielfalt an Freiräumen, die darüber bestimmen, wie gebaute Volumina und ihr Umfeld erfahren, wahrgenommen und zueinander in Beziehung gesetzt werden. BUSarchitektur ging von Umriss und Größe des Grundstücks aus und überlagerte es mit bewährten städtischen Role-Models von vergleichbarem Maßstab, wie dem Petersplatz in Rom, dem Schloss Schönbrunn, dem Museumsquartier und der Strecke zwischen Stephansdom und Donaukanal. Aus der Analyse dieser Referenzbeispiele mit ihren Durchwegungen, Proportionen, Platzfolgen und deren Verhältnis von Freiraum zu Bebauung wurde das Wettbewerbsprojekt entwickelt. Dabei behielt man stets die Beziehung zum städtischen Kontext im Auge: Wesentliche Planungskriterien waren urbane Kraftfelder, Durchgänge, Wegverbindungen und Blickbezüge. Sie ließen aus dem Zusammentreffen unterschiedlicher Gebäude identitätsstiftende Orte am Campus werden. Die Vorstellung des Verhaltens von Studierenden, Lehrenden und Anrainern, sowie der Wunsch, ihre Bedürfnisse zu antizipieren, bildeten den Ausgangspunkt der Planung. Sie führten zur Idee eines „Walk Along Park", der als leicht geknickte Diagonale das gesamte Areal durchzieht, von querenden Wegen gekreuzt wird und sich zu unterschiedlichen Freiräumen öffnet. Sie werden zur Bühne für die Architektur, die sich wie eine gebaute Topografie mit Durchgängen, Terrassen, Rampen, einfassend-begrenzenden Wandscheiben, eingeschnittenen Fensteröffnungen, Plattformen und auskragenden Bauteilen in die urbane Landschaft des WU Campus einfügt. Im Prinzip streben alle Baukörper wie magnetische Kraftfelder dem Library and Learning Center in der Mitte zu, vor dem sich eine zentrale Piazza ausbreitet. Der Campus ist als Abfolge von Wegen und Plätzen für verschiedene Grade an Öffentlichkeit und Aktivität gedacht, von denen die gebauten Volumina gleichermaßen umflossen werden. Sie bilden Sequenzen aus, stellen Bezüge her, schaffen Panoramen und Horizonte und stiften so auch Identität. Diesen Ansatz verfolgten BUSarchitektur konsequent vom städtebaulichen Maßstab bis zur Organisation der Studienzonen. Damit dieses Konzept funktioniert, war es wesentlich, den Campus als Fußgängerzone zu definieren: Auf dem ganzen Areal dürfen weder Autos noch Fahrräder in der Innenzone fahren.

units for students, approximately 35,000 square meters of infrastructure, department buildings for different academic programs with libraries and cafés, an Auditorium Center, an administration building, and an Executive Academy for postgraduates. All of these buildings should be organized in a campus-like structure and offer sufficient flexibility to adapt to the changing needs of research, teaching, and administration. External service providers such as the Austrian Students Union, a fitness center, kindergarten, supermarket, garages with 411 spaces, and parking facilities for bicycles rounded out the program. In total it has an effective area of more than 100,000 square meters.

A 24-Hour Campus

Laura P. Spinadel and the team around her partners Jean-Pierre Bolívar and Bernd Pflüger at BUSarchitektur developed their own vision of a lively, open university campus for the Viennese WU: For them, the acquisition of knowledge represents a complex process that takes place at the interface between the individual and society. Furthermore, it was important to create a public area that can be accessed and traversed around the clock and is thereby beneficial to the whole city. Above all, they strove for a multilayered spatial continuum in the green, which could be appropriated by both individuals and groups alike and in as many ways as possible. The site measures more than 90,000 square meters. The campus should have the qualities of a grown quarter. These largely manifest in an array of open spaces that determine how the built volumes and their surroundings are perceived and put into a relationship with one another. BUSarchitektur took the outline and size of the site as departure points and superimposed them with time-proven urban role models of comparable scale, such as St. Peter's Square in Rome, the Schönbrunn Palace, the MuseumsQuartier, and the stretch between St. Stephens's Cathedral and the Danube Canal in the center of Vienna. The competition project was developed through the analysis of these reference examples with their thoroughfares, proportions, and sequence of spaces, as well as the ratio of open space and built fabric. The relationship with the urban context was always kept in mind: Urban force fields, passageways, path connections, and sight lines were essential criteria in the planning. In combination with the different buildings they yield places with identity on the campus. Accounting for the conduct of the students, teachers, and neighboring residents and the attempt to anticipate their needs informed the design process. It led to the idea of a "walking along park" that traverses the entire area in a slightly hinged diagonal and is crossed by paths and opens up onto various open spaces. They form a stage for the architecture – a built topography of passageways, terraces, ramps, enclosing and defining walls, incised window openings, platforms, and cantilevered components that integrates into the urban landscape of the WU Campus. In essence, all buildings are drawn, almost magnetically, around the Library and Learning Center and its central plaza. The campus is conceived as a succession of paths and squares with varying degrees of publicness and activity, which flow around the built volumes in equal measure. They develop sequences, generate references, create panoramas and horizons – and therewith identity. BUSarchitektur consistently pursued this approach, from the urban scale to the organization of study zones. In order for this concept to function, a decisive move was to designate the campus as a pedestrian zone: No cars or bicycles are permitted in the inner zone of the entire area.

Bewegung ist wesentlicher Bestandteil von ganzheitlichem Lernen: Basketballplätze und andere Sportmöglichkeiten flankieren die Ränder des WU Campus
Movement is an essential part of holistic learning: Basketball fields and other sport facilities flank the borders of the WU Campus

Planen mit unbekannten Größen

Nach einer zweiten Überarbeitungsphase kürte die Jury unter dem Vorsitz von Wolf D. Prix am 9. Mai 2008 das Projekt von BUSarchitektur zum Sieger: Damit begann die wahre Bewährungsprobe. Das Wiener Büro wurde mit General-, Master- und Freiraumplanung, sowie als Fixstarter mit der Gestaltung des Hörsaalszentrums beauftragt. Für die Architektur der anderen definierten Baufelder auf dem Areal hielt man einen zweiten Wettbewerb ab. Der Bauherr erhoffte sich davon größere Vielfalt – außerdem bot sich so die Möglichkeit, gleich mehrere international renommierte Büros ins Boot zu holen. Stararchitektur ist in einer Zeit des globalen Wettbewerbs der Universitäten ein gut vermarktbares Alleinstellungsmerkmal. BUSarchitektur nahm die Herausforderung an, den Masterplan mit mehreren zu diesem Zeitpunkt noch unbekannten Architekturgrößen umzusetzen. Vorausblickend wurden die Weichen so gestellt, dass der Freiraum als verbindendes Fluidum zwischen den Bauten fungieren konnte. „Wir haben versucht, so viel Innovation wie möglich zuzulassen", so Laura P. Spinadel, die charismatische Chefin von BUSarchitektur. „Die internationalen Architekten und die künftigen Nutzer sollten miteinander in Kommunikation treten." Das Planungskollektiv entwickelte einen integralen Masterplan, der garantieren sollte, dass bestimmte identitätsstiftende Blickverbindungen, Bezugspunkte und ein menschlicher Maßstab erhalten blieben.

Die Vorgaben der Bauordnung waren klar: sie schrieb an der Grenze zum Prater eine maximale Höhe von 25 Metern vor, die auch das Library and Learning Center in der Mitte nicht überschreitet. Die maximal zulässige Höhe der Bebauung am Gelän-

Designing with Unknown Stars

On May 9, 2008, following a second phase of revisions, the jury chaired by Wolf D. Prix selected the project by BUSarchitektur as the winner: Now the real challenge started. The Viennese office was commissioned with the general, master, and open space planning, as well as the design of the Teaching Center. A second competition would be held for the architecture of the other building plots set out on the site; a measure that the client hoped would generate more diversity. Moreover, it provided an opportunity to get several internationally renowned offices on board. In times of global competition among universities, star architecture can be an effective unique selling point. BUSarchitektur took on the task of implementing the master plan with a number of gifted architects who, nevertheless, were still unknown at that point in time. Thinking ahead, the course was set in such a way that the open space could function as a binding fluid between the buildings. "We tried to create space for as much innovation as possible," says Laura P. Spinadel, the charismatic head of BUSarchitektur. "The international architects and the future users should engage in communication with each other." The planning collective developed an Integral Master Plan that should ensure the preservation of certain identity-constituting sight lines, reference points, and a human scale.

The specifications in the building regulations were clear: On the edge to the Prater it stipulated a maximum building height of 25 meters, which also the Library and Learning Center at the center does not exceed. The maximum building height for the overall terrain was set at 33 meters. Department Building D1 for Global Business and Trade by BUSarchitektur reaches this

MASTERPLAN

**Am Eingang im Westen erhebt sich die Hügellandschaft der „Lounge"
aus grünem EPM-Sportbelag, dazu orange Blumen und Ginko-Bäume**
At the western entrance emerges the playful hilly landscape of green EPDM
sports flooring. This "Lounge" is cropped with orange flowers and Ginko trees

de betrug 33 Meter. Sie wird vom Departmentgebäude D1 für Welthandel von BUSarchitektur erreicht. Der Masterplan zielte darauf ab, unterschiedlichste Architekturhandschriften in die übergeordnete Vision eines offenen, durchwegbaren Universitätscampus zu integrieren. „Wir sind von einem Prozess ausgegangen", so Laura P. Spinadel. „Unser Masterplan legte Parameter und Spielregeln fest, innerhalb derer sich die Architekten bewegen konnten." Vorbild dafür waren Wiener Marksteine wie der Masterplan für das Flugfeld Aspern von Rüdiger Lainer (1989) oder „dyn@mosphere", die ursprüngliche Planung für das Stadtentwicklungsgebiet Kabelwerk der ARGE Rainer Pirker ARCHItexture and the Poor Boy's Enterprise (1998). Für jedes Baufeld wurden Fluchtlinien, maximale Kubaturen und obligatorische Freiräume definiert. Außerdem verfasste BUSarchitektur Handbücher mit Handlungsanweisungen, die auch Lichtverhältnisse, Beschattung und Windströme zu diversen Tages- und Jahreszeiten, Sicherheitskonzepte und mehr umfassten. Selbst Leitdetails und Fassadenanschlüsse waren darin festgehalten, außerdem gab es Empfehlungen für durchgängige Verbindungen und Sichtbeziehungen zum Prater.

Ein Ensemble bilden

Pro Baufeld wurden bis zu sechs Projekte ausgearbeitet. Um das Zusammenspiel der Entwürfe im Ensemble besser veranschaulichen zu können, legte BUSarchitektur obligatorische Schnittstellen in der 3D-Darstellung fest. Damit konnten die 3D-Modelle der Projekte in die Umgebung eingebettet werden. Diese wurden in verschiedenen Kombinationen auf das Gelände gesetzt und mit Kamerafahrten dargestellt. So ließen sich die Qualitäten

height. The objective of the master plan was to integrate diverse architectural styles into the greater vision of an open, traversable university campus. "We assumed a process," tells Laura P. Spinadel. "Our master plan determined certain parameters and guidelines within which the architects could move." Viennese cornerstone concepts such as the master plan for the Flugfeld Aspern by Rüdiger Lainer (1989) or "dyn@mosphere", the original plan for the Kabelwerk urban development zone by ARGE Rainer Pirker ARCHItexture and the Poor Boy's Enterprise (1998), served as precedents. Alignments, maximum cubage, and obligatory open spaces were defined for each building plot. Furthermore, BUSarchitektur also compiled handbooks with instructions, which included lighting and shading conditions as well as wind currents at various times of day and seasons, security concepts, and more. Even details about the guidance system and façade connections were documented therein, along with recommendations for continuous passageways and visual connections to Prater.

Forming an Ensemble

Up to six project designs were elaborated for each building plot. In order to better depict the interplay of the various designs in the ensemble, BUSarchitektur defined required connection points in the 3D visualization. In this manner, the 3D models of the projects could be embedded in their surroundings. They were placed on the terrain in different combinations and also displayed in camera tracking shots, which allowed the qualities of various constellations to be visualized, examined, and compared. In the end, the following team members were cho-

unterschiedlicher Konstellationen zeigen, überprüfen und vergleichen. Schließlich fiel die Entscheidung für folgende Mitspieler: NO.MAD Arquitectos aus Madrid planten den raffiniert verschränkten, geheimnisvoll spiegelnden, dunklen Baukörper der Executive Academy auf Baufeld W1-EA am nördlichen Spitz des Geländes. Wie ein dunkler Kristall markiert das prägnante Punkthaus den Eingang im Westen. Gegenüber breitet sich am Beginn des „Walk Along"-Weges die sogenannte „Lounge" aus, eine fröhliche Hügellandschaft aus grünem EPDM-Sportbelag mit Gräsern und orangen Blumeninseln, zwischen denen Ginko-Bäume hochragen. Ihre Blätter verfärben sich im Herbst leuchtend gelb. Ginkos finden sich überall an der osmotischen Grenze zum Prater, wo traditionell Kastanien und Ahornbäume wachsen. „Dadurch unterscheidet sich der Campus", so Bernd Pflüger, der gemeinsam mit boa/Büro für offensive Aleatorik und Landschaftsarchitektur Hannes Batik & Stefan Schmidt den Freiraum plante. „Wir wollten einen Landschaftspark kreieren, der das ganze Jahr unterschiedliche Farben zeigt." Daher wurden viele Gräser ausgesucht, die auch im Winter grün sind. „Außerdem war es wichtig, dass es mehrere Ebenen gibt, auf denen sich der Freiraum erfahren lässt." BUSarchitektur konnte etwa 55.000 Quadratmeter öffentlich zugänglicher Fläche realisieren. Darum wurden unter anderem 9.900 Quadratmeter Sträucher, Stauden und Blumen gesetzt, 1.659 Quadratmeter Liegewiesen angelegt, 232 Bäume gepflanzt, 83 Sitzplätze geschaffen, neun Trinkbrunnen gebaut und Parkplätze für 998 Fahrräder geschaffen. Diese sind – so wie die Zugänge zur politisch und gestalterisch korrekten, angstfrei hellen Tiefgarage mit 411 Stellplätzen – vorbildlich in die Anlage integriert.

sen: NO.MAD Arquitectos from Madrid planned the masterfully interlocking, mysteriously reflective building for the Executive Academy on building plot W1-EA at the northwestern tip of the site. The prominent corner house marks the western entrance like a dark crystal. Opposite, at the beginning of the walk along path, the so-called WU Lounge unfolds: a playful hilly landscape of green EPDM sports flooring with grass and orange flower islands between which Ginko trees sprout up. In autumn their leaves take on a bright yellow tint. Ginkos are omnipresent along the osmotic border to the Prater, where traditionally chestnut and maple trees grow. "The campus is different in this respect," says Bernd Pflüger, who designed the open space together with boa Büro für offensive Aleatorik and landscape architects Hannes Batik & Stefan Schmidt. "We wanted to create a landscape park with different colors all year round." To this end, many types of grass were chosen that also stay green in the winter. "Additionally, it was important that there are several levels on which one can experience the open space." BUSarchitektur was able to facilitate around 55,000 square meters of publicly accessible surface area. Hence, it was possible to plant, among other things, 9,900 square meters of bushes, perennials, and flowers, to lay out 1,659 square meters of lawn, plant 232 trees, create 83 seating places, install nine drinking fountains, and arrange parking facilities for 998 bicycles. They are – like the access roads to the politically and aesthetically correct, anxiety-free brightly lit underground garage with 411 parking places – exemplarily integrated into the overall master plan.

The main paths are paved with 18-centimeter-thick, broad concrete slabs, which are colored with ocher and light or dark

Freiraum generiert Urbanität: Begrünte Hochbeete mit Sitznischen und Stufen animieren zum Verweilen, Reden, Lesen und Lernen
Open space generates urbanity: Elevated plant beds with seating niches and steps encourage one to linger, talk, read, and learn

Die Hauptwege sind mit 18 cm dicken, breiten, befahrbaren Betonplatten gepflastert, die mit verschiedenen Pigmenten in Ocker, hellem oder dunklem Grau eingefärbt wurden. Auch die Freiräume bilden hier Sequenzen, die den Charakter der umgebenden Gebäude betonen und bestimmte Aktivitäten unterstützen. So breitet sich vor den langgestreckten, schmalen Riegeln des Department 4-Gebäudes vom Estudio Carme Pinós die „Relax"-Zone aus. In einem langen Wasserbecken aus blaugrünem Carat spiegeln sich hier der Himmel und das Gebäude. Wie ein Stempelkissen drückt sich in der Mitte eine Plattform mit handgefertigten Liegestühlen von Graulicht aus der seichten Wasserfläche. Hier kann man wunderbar chillen und das rege Treiben am Campus beobachten. Hinter dieser exponierten Zone gibt es einen weiteren Platz mit Bäumen, Bänken und Pflanztrögen. All diese Möbel und die Beleuchtungskörper aus verzinkten, beschichteten Formrohren mit steuerbaren LED-Lampen wurden von BUSarchitektur und boa entworfen. Die Lampen passen sich an die Helligkeit der Umgebung an und erhöhen so rund um die Uhr das Sicherheitsgefühl. Das Gelände ist leicht modelliert: das Gebäude vom Estudio Carme Pinós ist auf einen Hügel gesetzt und bildet mit seinem V-förmig geöffneten zweiten Flügel einen intimeren, geschützten Innenhof aus.

Kosmopolitisch
„Die Architekten gingen mit dem Instrumentarium unseres Masterplans unterschiedlich um", so Laura P. Spinadel. Sicherheitshalber gab es für jeden Bauplatz einen gemeinsamen Workshop vor Ort. „Peter Cook hat sich sehr genau daran gehalten." Der organisch geformte, in bunten, horizontalen Streifen gestriche-

gray pigments and are fit for service traffic. Here the open spaces are structured into sequences that emphasize the character of the adjacent buildings and encourage different activities. The WU Relax zone, for example, stretches out in front of the elongated, narrow blocks of Department Building D4 by Estudio Carme Pinós. The sky and the building are reflected in a long water basin made of blue-green carat. A platform with hand-made deck chairs by Graulicht protrudes in the middle like an inkpad above the shallow water surface. It's a great place to chill out and watch the bustling activities on campus. Behind this more exposed zone there is another square with trees, benches, and planted troughs. All of the furniture and the lighting fixtures made of galvanized form tubes with remote control LED lamps were designed by BUSarchitektur and boa. The lamps adapt to the lighting conditions of their surroundings and thereby enhance the feeling of security around the clock. The terrain has a slight modulation: For example, the building by Estudio Carme Pinós sits atop a small hill, where its V-shaped wings form a more intimate, protected courtyard. Sport facilities also flank the wall along the Messe Wien parking garage.

Cosmopolitan
"The architects found different ways to use the set of tools provided in the master plan," says Laura P. Spinadel. To be on the safe side, a joint workshop was held for each building plot on site. "Peter Cook strictly adhered to these options." The organic design by his British CRAB studio, painted with its colorful, horizontal stripes and stepped elevations, polarizes the most. Architects and trade journalists are irritated by the raw, untreated

„Stage": Der Platz vor dem LC ist eine Bühne für das Bauwerk und die Menschen. Die abgetreppte Piazza dient als Forum für öffentliche Meinung
"Stage": The urban space in front of the LC is a stage for the building and the people; the stepped plaza serves as platform for public opinion

ne, in den Höhen abgestufte Gebäudekomplex seines britischen CRAB studio polarisiert am stärksten. Architekten und Fachjournalisten stoßen sich an den rauen, unbehandelten Holzlatten vor der grellen Vollwärmeschutzfassade, an den vielen Farben, Formen und groben Details. Nutzer und Laien lieben die Gebäude. Ihre von Terrassen übersäten Dachlandschaften, die gedeckten Durchgänge zum Prater, die vielen Sitzbänke und anderen beiläufig integrierten Gebrauchsmöglichkeiten der Architektur verraten, dass den Planern die künftigen Nutzer wichtig waren. Maßstäblich fügt sich das Gebäude gut ins Ensemble, zwischen den geschwungenen Wänden sind unter anderem auch Tischtennistische zu finden. Sportmöglichkeiten flankieren auch die Mauer zum Parkhaus der Messe.

Das repräsentative Zentrum des Campus bildet das Library and Learning Center (LC) von Zaha Hadid Architects. Der stromlinienförmige, imposante Bau mit der weit auskragenden Bibliothek wird von drei Freiräumen flankiert: Die „Relax-Zone", eine Anordnung begrünter Hochbeete aus gespitztem Beton mit eingekerbten Sitznischen aus Holz bildet den Vermittler zwischen dem bunten Bau von CRAB studio und dem LC,

wood slats in front of the garish thermally insulated façade, by its many colors, shapes, and coarse details. Users and lay people love the buildings. The scattered terraces on the roof landscape, the covered passageways to Prater, the many benches and other casually integrated yet practical architectural elements reveal that the future users were important to the planners. The building fits well into the scale of the ensemble. Between its curved walls one can even find ping-pong tables.

The Library and Learning Center (LC) by Zaha Hadid Architects forms the representative heart of the campus. The streamlined, imposing volume and the long cantilever of the library are flanked by three open spaces: The relax zone – an arrangement of elevated plant beds in chiseled concrete forms notched with wooden seating niches – mediates between the colorful CRAB studio building and the LC and flows into the central plaza in front of the library: the WU Stage. This stepped seating landscape serves as a contemporary arena for the students. The adjacent WU Patio leads toward the red Corten steel Teaching Center (TC) by BUSarchitektur, which incorporates the Department Building D1 and the Auditorium Center. With the parallel

MASTERPLAN

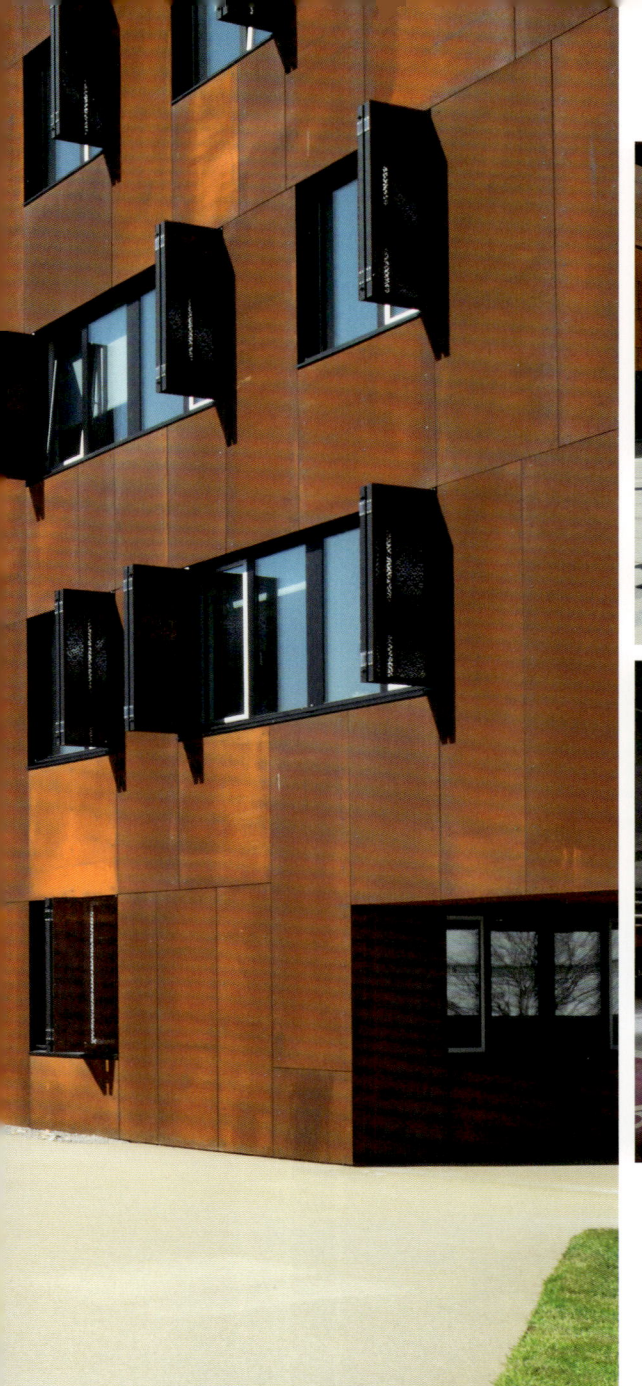

> **Gut geeignet zum Chillen: begrüntes Dach der Mensa des TC**
> Perfect place to chill: grass roof of the Mensa cafeteria of the TC

> **Der Platz vor dem TC bietet viel Bankfläche zum Besetzen**
> The square in front of the TC offers an array of benches

> **Der Grünraum dehnt sich hier bis in die Tiefgarage aus**
> The green space reaches down to the parking in the basement

vor dem sich eine große Piazza ausbreitet. Sie mündet in die „Bühne". Diese abgetreppte Sitzlandschaft fungiert als zeitgemäße Arena für die Studierenden. Der angrenzende „Patio" leitet zum cortenstahlroten Gebäudekomplex aus Departmentgebäude D1 und Hörsaalzentrum TC von BUSarchitektur über. An diesen Bauten mit ihrer innen und außen parallel verlaufenden Freitreppe, der grasgedeckten Mensa mit Oberlichtkuppeln, den vorgelagerten Terrassen und gedeckten Umgängen zeigt sich die gewünschte Verzahnung mit dem Freiraum besonders stark. Den Abschluss des Campus bilden das Departmentgebäude D2 und Student Center SC am östlichen Ausgang vom Atelier Hitoshi Abe. L-förmig windet es sich um einen offenen Platz. Die Baukörper sind geprägt vom scharfen Kontrast aus schwarz und weiß. Sie bilden langgezogene, innere Höfe und eine klare Grenze zum Prater aus. „Hitoshi Abe hat unsere Vorgaben weitgehend neu interpretiert", so Laura P. Spinadel. Konsequenzen hatte das keine, bis auf dem Umstand, dass sich darin auch eine andere Kultur im Umgang mit Öffentlichkeit und die Komplexität kommunikativer Prozesse zeigt. Experiment geglückt.

inner and outer flights of stairs, the grass roof of the Mensa cafeteria with its skylights, the protruding terraces, and protected arcades, this building is a concise demonstration of the desired interplay with the open space. The Departments and Student Center (D2 SC) by Atelier Hitoshi Abe forms the conclusion of the campus on the eastern edge. It encloses an open space in an L-shaped curve. The long building volumes, characterized by their starkly contrasting black and white pattern, create a sequence of inner courtyards and a clear border to Prater. "Hitoshi Abe largely interpreted our guidelines anew," says Laura P. Spinadel. But this has little consequence other than revealing a different culture in dealing with the public realm and the complexity of communicative processes. A successful experiment.

RAUM UND KOMMUNIKATION: REFLEXIONEN ZUR CAMPUS-PHILOSOPHIE
ALL FINE ARCHITECTURAL VALUES ARE
HUMAN VALUES, ELSE NOT VALUABLE.
(FRANK LLOYD WRIGHT)

GERLINDE MAUTNER

Der neue WU Campus bietet schon auf den ersten Blick vielfältige Möglichkeiten, Kommunikation positiv zu gestalten. Doch der Zusammenhang zwischen Raum und Kommunikation geht noch tiefer: Gebäude und der Raum zwischen ihnen sind auch sicht- und fühlbare Korrelate von organisationalen Werten, Strukturen und Prozessen. Am neuen Campus ist dieser Nexus seit den ersten Planungsschritten spürbar.

SPACE AND COMMUNICATION: REFLECTIONS ON THE CAMPUS PHILOSOPHY
ALL FINE ARCHITECTURAL VALUES ARE
HUMAN VALUES, ELSE NOT VALUABLE.
(FRANK LLOYD WRIGHT)

Even at first glance, the new WU Campus offers numerous stimuli to communication. But the relationship between space and communication goes deeper than that. The buildings and the spaces between them are visible and tangible correlates of organizational values, structures, and processes, a nexus apparent since the earliest stages of the planning process.

CAMPUS-PHILOSOPHIE / CAMPUS PHILOSOPHY

Persönlicher Hintergrund

Nach langen Jahren meiner Tätigkeit an der WU erlebe ich mit dem neuen Campus bereits den vierten Standort; nach Stationen im Haupthaus am Liechtenwerder Platz, in der Augasse 9 und dem UZA4 in der Nordbergstraße. Kolleg/inn/en vieler anderer Institute können auf ähnliche, zum Teil noch wechselhaftere Wanderschaften zurückblicken. Vom Haupthaus abgesehen, war keines der alten WU-Gebäude mit einer WU-Identität verbunden, und sie fühlten sich auch noch nach Jahren der Besiedlung sowohl in praktischer als auch symbolischer Hinsicht als Provisorien an. Nun aber sind wir als Universität in einem echten Zuhause angekommen.

Meine Reflexionen in diesem Beitrag stützen sich auf vier Säulen persönlicher Erfahrung: Als *Faculty*-Mitglied, das lehrt, forscht und in der universitären Verwaltung mitarbeitet; als angewandte Linguistin, die sich unter anderem mit *textscapes* und *organizational discourse* auseinandersetzt; als Wissenschaftlerin mit langjähriger Auslandserfahrung, insbesondere an britischen Universitäten (sowohl der *city*- also auch der *campus*-Variante); und als Mitglied des sogenannten „Sounding Board", das sich aus Vertreter/inne/n der Departments, der Verwaltungsmitarbeiter/innen und der Studierenden zusammensetzte und den Neubau vom Beginn des Planungsprozesses bis zum Umzug begleitete.

Kommunikation über den Neubau

Nach der Initialzündung – „die WU wird neu gebaut!" – folgten auf die erste Euphorie auch gleich die ersten Ängste: Vor einer „Abschiebung" in ein Wissenschaftsghetto am geschichts- und gesichtslosen Stadtrand; vor gestalterischen Modetrends, die die künstlerische Reputation von Architekten und Designern bedienen, nicht aber die Bedürfnisse der Nutzer; und vor Raumkonzepten, die Kommunikation „immer und überall" und maximale Flexibilität propagieren (Stichwort Großraumbüros und *hot desking*), statt das sachlich begründete Bedürfnis von vielen Mitarbeitern nach Ruhe und konzentrierter Abgeschiedenheit zu berücksichtigen.

Mit der Wahl des Standortes Prater war die erste Angst gebannt. Wir waren erleichtert, dass wir auch im räumlichen Sinne im Herzen dieser Stadt bleiben würden: Ein erheblicher praktischer Vorteil und zugleich ein Signal dafür, dass sich die WU um den Austausch mit ihrem gesellschaftlichen Umfeld bemüht. Diesem Konnex sollte schließlich auch durch die offene Natur des Campus – ohne Zäune und Mauern – Rechnung getragen werden. Was die Sorge bezüglich nicht funktionaler Modetrends betraf, so stand für viele die Angst vor Glasfassaden und gebäudeinternen Glaswänden ganz oben auf der Liste. Transparenz und Kommunikation in Ehren, aber einschlägige Erfahrungsberichte von „Glasopfern" anderer Neubauten verhießen nichts Gutes: Hitzekollaps, Aquariumsfeeling, *Big-Brother*-Syndrom und Umsatzsteigerung bei schützenden IKEA-Paravents. Als schließlich auch dieses Thema geklärt war, gab es neuerliches Aufatmen. Häuser und Räume mit Wänden aus Mauerwerk haben schon etwas Beruhigendes; ebenso wie Einzelbüros mit festen Türen, und Schreibtische mit Sesseln. Wenn es nach ihm ginge, meinte einmal ein Architekt im Rahmen einer WU-Veranstaltung, würde er am liebsten mit dem Laptop auf den Knien am Gang auf dem Boden sitzen und die Studenten um sich scharen. Dem Himmel sei Dank, dass es in diesem Punkt nur bei einer Vision geblieben ist.

All die genannten Bedenken und viele andere mehr konnten im Sounding Board (SB) ausführlich besprochen werden. Das SB war kein nach dem Abstimmungsprinzip funktionierendes Ent-

Personal Background

As a long-serving member of Vienna University of Economics and Business (WU), I had worked at three locations before coming to the new campus: the main building on Liechtenwerder Platz, in Augasse 9, and in the UZA4 in Nordbergstraße. Colleagues at many other institutes can look back on similar paths, some even more erratic. With the exception of the main building, none of these previous locations possessed a WU identity, and even after years of occupancy they still felt provisional both in practical and symbolic terms. But now, we as a university have finally found our home.

My reflections in this contribution rest on four pillars of personal experience: as a faculty member involved in teaching, research, and administration; as an applied linguist who deals with such things as textscapes and organizational discourse; as a scholar with extensive international experience, in particular at British universities (of both city and campus types); and, finally, as a member of the so-called Sounding Board, comprised of representatives of academic departments, administration, and students, which accompanied the building process from the start of the planning phase up to the relocation itself.

Communication about the New Campus

The starting pistol had hardly sounded – "The WU to get a new campus!" – when initial euphoria was followed by the first anxieties. Would we be "deported" to an academic ghetto to some site on the faceless urban periphery with no history behind it? Would fashionable design trends catering to the artistic reputations of architects and designers take precedence over the needs of users? Would spatial concepts promoting communication "everywhere and all the time" and obsessed with flexibility (buzzwords being "open-plan offices" and "hot desking") mean ignoring the well-founded desire of many campus users for silence and seclusion in which to concentrate?

The most urgent concerns were stilled when the Prater was chosen as the campus location. We were relieved to be remaining spatially in the heart of the city: a considerable practical advantage and, at the same time, a signal of the WU's intent to interact with its social surroundings. This intent would ultimately be reflected in the open character of a campus without fences or walls. There remained the suspicion of non-functional fashion trends, of which glass façades and interior glass walls bulked especially large for many. It wasn't that people feared transparency and communication, but that the reports from "glass victims" in other new buildings – of sweltering heat, fishbowl claustrophobia, Big Brother syndrome, and booms in the sales of IKEA privacy screens – didn't inspire confidence. When this issue was also cleared up there was another sigh of relief. After all, houses and rooms with real brick walls do have a reassuring feel, as do single offices with solid doors and desks with chairs. If he had his way, one architect averred at a WU event, he would prefer to sit on the corridor floor with a laptop on his knees and students crowded around him. Mercifully, he didn't get his way!

All these concerns and many more were thoroughly discussed in the Sounding Board (SB). This was not a decision-making body where votes were taken; it was a communication forum – nothing more, nothing less. Its existence over several years can in itself be seen as symbolizing the significance of communication for the university in general, and for the new campus project in particular. Personally, I'm convinced that the largest possible building that could be built entirely on the basis of direct democracy is an allotment hut for a small family – and then only

scheidungsgremium, sondern ein Kommunikationsforum – nicht mehr, aber auch nicht weniger. Allein seine Existenz über mehrere Jahre hinweg kann als Symbol für die Bedeutung der Kommunikation an dieser Universität im Allgemeinen und im Kontext des Neubaus im Besonderen gelten. Vollständig basisdemokratisch bauen, so bin ich überzeugt, lässt sich bestenfalls eine Schrebergartenhütte für eine Kleinfamilie (und auch nur, solange die Kinder noch nicht wort- und argumentationsmächtig sind). In einer komplexen Organisation hingegen, mit ca. 24.000 Studierenden und fast 1.600 Mitarbeiter/inne/n, lässt sich ein Bauprojekt nicht als Wunschkonzert realisieren, und erst recht nicht, wenn für einen großen Teil der Mitarbeiter (mich eingeschlossen) das rastlose Problematisieren gleichsam zum Berufsethos gehört (und deren eigene Baukompetenz bereits mit dem Aufstellen eines Zweimannzelts ausgereizt gewesen wäre). Wir Nutzer konnten bei dem Konzert nicht den Ton angeben, aber wer wollte, konnte mit kräftiger Stimme im Chor singen.

Das Sounding Board hat Meinungen gebündelt, Konsens und Dissens ans Licht gebracht und gegensätzliche Interessen in zivilisierten Wettstreit treten lassen. Es war ein Forum zum Miteinander-Reden und, noch wichtiger, zum Zuhören seitens der Projektleitung und des Universitätsmanagements. Es gab den an Baufragen Interessierten vielfältige Einblicke in die Komplexität des Projekts – Einblicke, die auch so manchen Aufreger relativierten: Während wir Nutzer hitzig über Fensterformen, Kaffeemaschinen und Möbelfarben diskutierten, dachten (zum Glück) andere daran, dass es auf einem Uni-Campus Zufahrten für Müllabfuhr, Feuerwehr und Rettung geben muss. Gewiss: Trotz SB bekam nicht jeder das, was er wollte. Aber das SB stellte sicher, dass wesentliche Aspekte berücksichtigt wurden und insgesamt jeder erheblich mehr bekam, als bei vergleichbaren Bauprojekten im In- und Ausland üblich.

Kommunikation im und durch den Neubau
Der Masterplan ist ein Geniestreich. Die „Hauptstraße", die alle Gebäude miteinander verbindet, ist nicht nur ein funktional angelegter Gehweg, sondern erwies sich schon in den ersten Tagen nach dem Umzug als eine lebendige Kommunikationsader. Die Erfahrung zeigt, dass es de facto unmöglich ist, auf dem Campus von A nach B zu gehen, ohne zufällig Kolleg/inn/en anderer Departments oder aus der Verwaltung zu treffen. Gerade die Geselligsten unter uns mussten rasch einen neuen Gesichtsausdruck lernen – jenen nämlich, der freundlich erfreutes Grüßen signalisiert, ohne jedes grundsätzlich willkommene Zusammentreffen gleich in eine prohibitiv zeitraubende Plauderei ausarten zu lassen: ein „Luxusproblem", das wir an der alten WU gerne gehabt hätten.

Auch wenn man den Wunsch nach aktiver Kommunikation verspürt, bietet der Campus eine Menge: einladende Restaurants und attraktive Freiflächen zum Flanieren und Verweilen. Dass diese auch von „externen" Besuchern angenommen werden, entspricht der WU Campus-Philosophie und ist ein besonderer Anlass zur Freude. Schließlich erdet den gestressten Wissenschaftler nichts mehr als der Anblick eines lachenden Zweijährigen auf seinem Laufrad, oder der gelassene Trott eines Golden Retrievers beim nachmittäglichen Familienspaziergang.

Im Inneren der Gebäude setzen sich die baulich gestalteten Kommunikationsmöglichkeiten fort: So gibt es zahlreiche Selbststudienzonen und Projekträume, die vom ersten Tag an von Studierenden intensiv genutzt wurden, sowie Lounges nach dem angelsächsischen *Senior-Common-Room*-Modell für das Personal. Alle Departmentgebäude sind *Department*gebäude auch im Sinne der Organisationsstruktur, d. h. die Institute sind

if the children had no say. In a complex organization with almost 24,000 students and 1,600 employees, no building project can be realized in the style of a request show. Even less so when many members (myself included) regard the constant identification of imperfections as an integral part of their professional ethos – and when their own architectural competence just about extends to putting up a two-person tent. The SB did not allow us users to set the show's playlist, but we could influence which version of a particular song we heard.

Within the Sounding Board, opinions were pooled, areas of consensus and disagreement revealed, and diverging interests allowed to compete in a civilized manner. The SB was a forum in which colleagues could converse and, more importantly, the project and university management teams could listen. For those interested in building issues, it provided a variety of insights into the complexity of the project – insights that sometimes put our own concerns into perspective. For instance, while we users indulged in heated discussions about window shapes, coffee machines, and the color of furniture, others – fortunately – remembered that a university campus needs access roads for garbage collection, the fire department, and ambulances. Of course, the SB did not give everyone everything they wanted. But it did ensure that essential aspects were taken into account and that, on the whole, everyone got considerably more than they could have expected judging by comparable projects in Austria and beyond.

Communication inside and because of the New Campus
The campus concept was a stroke of genius. The "main street" connecting all the buildings is far more than a transport route; from the day we moved in, it has also proved to be a communication artery. Experience has shown that it is impossible to walk between two points on campus without bumping into colleagues from other departments or the administration. Above all, the most sociable among us had to quickly learn a new facial expression signaling friendly greeting without turning every essentially welcome encounter into a prohibitively time-consuming chat – a "problem" we would have loved to have had at the old WU.

For those who desire it, the campus offers a host of opportunities for more active communication: inviting eateries and attractive open spaces in which to linger or stroll. The fact that these have been readily adopted by "external" visitors is in line with the campus philosophy and a source of particular pleasure. Ultimately, nothing better grounds a stressed-out scholar than the sight of a laughing two-year-old on a balance bike or a laid-back golden retriever on its afternoon family walk.

Inside the buildings, architecture continues to inspire communication, through the numerous self-study zones and project rooms – intensively used by students from day one – and the staff lounges modeled on Anglo-American Senior Common Rooms. All department buildings are true *department* buildings in that the various component institutes are no longer spatially and visually separated from one another. The old institute-based structure has become increasingly virtual in many regards – faster, more comprehensively, and more consensually in some departments than others, but always irreversibly (in the medium term) and clearly reflected in architectural terms.

Open borders to the outside world are not the only symbolic concern to have played a role in the campus design process. Another is the complex set of rules – born of intense discussion in various forums – that regulates the visual presence of sponsors on campus. It represents a workable compromise be-

nicht mehr räumlich sichtbar voneinander getrennt. Die alte Institutsgliederung wird in vielerlei Hinsicht zunehmend virtualisiert – in manchen Departments schneller, intensiver und konsensueller als in anderen, aber in jedem Fall (mittelfristig) unwiderruflich und mit einem deutlichen baulichen Korrelat.

Dass die Grenzen des WU Campus nach außen offen sind, ist nicht der einzige symbolische Akt, auf den bei der Gestaltung geachtet wurde. Ein anderer ist das komplexe Regelwerk – entstanden nach intensiven Diskussionen in verschiedenen Gremien –, das steuert, wie Sponsoren am Campus präsent sein dürfen. Das Ergebnis ist ein tragfähiger Kompromiss zwischen den PR-Anliegen von Unternehmen und dem Bedürfnis der Universität, ihren Raum und über den Raum ihre Identität nicht zu „verkaufen". Nach den Richtlinien gibt es in Lehrräumen keine Werbebotschaften; das Audimax als besonders symbolträchtiger Ort bleibt vom „*sponsored naming*" ausgeschlossen, und die Firmenschilder vor gesponserten Räumen (die in jedem Fall auch ihre neutrale Raumnummer behalten) sind in einer diskreten, nicht raumgreifenden Größe genormt. Im Learning Center schließlich erinnert an gut sichtbarer Stelle eine große Tafel mit einem Zitat aus dem Staatsgrundgesetz 1867 daran, dass die öffentliche Finanzierung von Universitäten eine wesentliche Voraussetzung für die Freiheit von Forschung und Lehre ist.

Der neue Campus als Metapher

Der neue WU Campus ermöglicht Kommunikation nicht nur, sondern er verkörpert sie auch. Sehr unterschiedliche Elemente treten im Ensemble in eine Beziehung zueinander. Diese Beziehung lebt einerseits vom Unterschied zwischen den Elementen, andererseits von dem sie einigenden Band, der vom Masterplan definierten „Hauptstraße", die den Campus durchzieht. Die tägliche Erfahrung zeigt, dass diese Idee nicht im theoretischen Anspruch stecken geblieben ist, sondern sie im Kommunikationsverhalten der Menschen zur gelebten Realität wird. Die Gebäude am Campus stehen zwar in respektvoller Distanz, scheinen sich aber einander zuzuneigen. Sie gleichen einander nicht, aber sie passen zueinander – ganz so wie die an der WU vertretenen Wissenschaften. So wie die Harmonie im Gebäudeensemble lebt auch die akademische Kommunikation innerhalb von Disziplinen und über deren Grenzen hinweg von einer fein kalibrierten dialektischen Spannung: gering genug, um destruktive Konflikte zu vermeiden, aber groß genug, um gerade aus der Widerständigkeit Neues entstehen zu lassen.

Der WU Campus erweist sich als eine gelungene Fügung aus mehreren architektonischen Meisterwerken von anspruchsvoller Ästhetik. Sie gestalten mit ihrer individuellen Andersartigkeit und gewollten Gegensätzlichkeit eine „Avenue des Wissens", die zu Begegnung und Austausch einlädt. Uns WU-Angehörigen kommuniziert der Campus zugleich den Auftrag, uns von seiner lebendigen Offenheit und Vielfalt inspirieren zu lassen, ganz im Sinne von Winston Churchill: „We shape our buildings; thereafter they shape us."

> Die Gebäude am Campus stehen zwar in respektvoller Distanz, scheinen sich aber einander zuzuneigen. Sie gleichen einander nicht, aber sie passen zueinander – ganz so wie die an der WU vertretenen Wissenschaften.

> Although the various buildings maintain a respectful distance, they seem somehow to lean toward one another. They are not similar, but they complement each other – just like the disciplines represented at the WU.

tween companies' PR agendas and the university's desire not to "sell" its space and, with that, its identity. The guidelines permit no promotional messages *inside* lecture rooms; the company name plates in front of sponsored rooms (which also keep their neutral room number) are to be of standard size, discreet and unobtrusive; and the Audimax, with its emblematic status, cannot be given a sponsored name at all. Last but not least, a prominently displayed plaque in the Learning Center reminds us, with a quote from the Austrian Basic Law of 1867, that the *public* financing of universities is a fundamental prerequisite for the freedom of research and teaching.

The New Campus as Metaphor

The new WU Campus not only facilitates communication; it embodies it. In the ensemble, highly diverse elements enter into relationships with each other. These derive both from the differences between the elements and from the bond that unites them: the "main street" traversing the campus that was envisaged in the original concept. Daily experience has revealed that this idea is no theoretical pretense; rather it has been realized in the way campus users communicate. Although the various buildings maintain a respectful distance, they seem somehow to lean toward one another. They are not similar, but they complement each other – just like the disciplines represented at the WU. Like the harmony of the built ensemble, academic communication within and across disciplines draws on a finely calibrated dialectic tension: slight enough to avoid destructive conflicts, strong enough for opposition to generate innovation.

All in all, the WU Campus is the successful fusion of various, aesthetically sophisticated architectonic masterpieces. With their individuality and deliberate contrariety, they create an "avenue of knowledge" that invites encounters and exchange. At the same time, the campus communicates to WU members the remit to be inspired by its lively openness and diversity, very much in the spirit of Winston Churchill: "We shape our buildings; thereafter they shape us."

LC

ZAHA HADID ARCHITECTS: LIBRARY AND LEARNING CENTER

EIN NEUES LEBENSGEFÜHL
DAS LIBRARY AND LEARNING CENTER VON
ZAHA HADID ARCHITECTS

A NEW QUALITY OF LIFE
THE LIBRARY AND LEARNING CENTER BY ZAHA HADID ARCHITECTS

MATTHIAS BOECKL

Schon in den ersten programmatischen Überlegungen für den neuen Campus der WU standen die Studierenden und deren Hauptaktivität im Mittelpunkt: Das Lernen. Mit großer Symbolik sollte das Studieren neu gedacht werden, in Organisation, Form und Betrieb. Das Lernen wurde daher auch in den räumlichen Mittelpunkt des Campus gestellt. Die bauliche Realisierung dieser Idee lieferte eines der bemerkenswertesten Gebäude Wiens der vergangenen Jahre: Fließender Raum, Bewegung und Licht sind seine bestimmenden, sinnlich intensiv erlebbaren Größen.

Die Kräfte formen
Gerade in großen Kultur- und Bildungsbauten der vergangenen Jahre verdichteten und präzisierten Zaha Hadid Architects ihre charakteristische und unverwechselbare Formensprache: Geneigte Wände und Baukörper, Auskragungen schräg zugeschnittener Prismen, rund und weich fließende Kanten und Linien, organisch geformte Innenräume mit vertikal gestapelten Aushöhlungen und Canyons, Rippen und Lichtstreifen zur Betonung der Raumbewegung, schwarze und weiße Oberflächen. Bauten wie das MAXXI-Museum in Rom, das Heydar Aliyev Centre in Baku und das Broad Art Museum der Michigan State University in East Lansing wollen „eine Struktur liefern, die sich ständig ändert, während die Besucher sie durchschreiten, und damit große Neugier schaffen, aber dennoch nie alles auf einmal zeigen". Die von Zaha Hadid und ihren Mitstreitern erfundene revolutionäre dekonstruktivistische Entwurfsstrategie der späten 1980er Jahre, in der man materielle und immaterielle Strukturen eines gegebenen Kontextes aufspürte sowie deren formales System und vor allem seine Störungen im eigenen Entwurf thematisierte, ist in den nachfolgenden Jahrzehnten erfolgreicher Baupraxis in eine klarere, sinnlich für jedermann nachvollziehbare Praxis übergegangen. Gebaute Kontexte werden nun in Form sichtbarer Kraftlinien deutlich lesbar ins Haus geholt, immaterielle Kräfte werden anschaulich in raumschaffenden Aufwölbungen und Faltungen dargestellt. Neugier und Nutzerfreude entstehen aus räumlicher Vielfalt und steter Veränderung. Wien hat ein Schulbeispiel dieser avancierten zeitgenössischen Designstrategie erhalten.

Die Schräge macht's aus
Die Bedingungen des zweiten Architekturwettbewerbes, in dem sich das Hamburger Büro von Zaha Hadid Architects (ZHA) für das zentrale Library and Learning Center bewarb, kamen den Ambitionen durchaus entgegen. „Uns hat die spezielle Aufgabenstellung eines innovativen Studiengebäudes interessiert", sagt Cornelius Schlotthauer, der schon beim BMW-Zentralgebäude in Leipzig mitgearbeitet hatte und den 2007 im Zuge des Baus der Hamburger Elbpromenade gegründeten deutschen ZHA-Ableger

In the first programmatic considerations about the new WU Campus, the students and their main activity already played a central role: Learning. Charged with great symbolic power, studying would be newly defined – in terms of organization, form, and operation. Learning was placed at the spatial heart of the campus. The architectural implementation of this idea would result in one of Vienna's most remarkable buildings of the past years: fluid spaces, movement, and light are its decisive and intensely tangible features.

Giving power shape
In recent years it has been precisely cultural and educational buildings in which Zaha Hadid Architects have refined their signature and unmistakable formal language: inclined walls and volumes, cantilevered diagonally-cut prisms, fluid round and soft corners and lines, organic interiors with vertically stacked cavities and canyons, ribs and light strips to emphasize the movement of the space, black and white surfaces. Buildings such as the MAXXI museum in Rome, the Heydar Aliyev Centre in Baku, and the Broad Art Museum at Michigan State University in East Lansing "provide a structure that constantly changes as visitors stride through it, thereby provoking great curiosity yet never revealing everything at once". The revolutionary deconstructivist design strategy formulated by Zaha Hadid and her fellow colleagues in the late 1980s, which explored the material and immaterial qualities of a given context in order to articulate their formal system and, above all, their interferences in the architectural proposal, has transformed in the following decades of successful building activities into a more pronounced and easily comprehensible practice. Visible spatial reference points now lend built contexts a clearly readable form; immaterial forces manifest in vivid bulges and folds. Curiosity and user-friendliness are stimulated by spatial diversity and constant change. Vienna now has a textbook example of this advanced contemporary design strategy.

It's the slope that counts
The stipulations in the second phase of the architectural competition, for which the Hamburg-based office Zaha Hadid Architects (ZHA) submitted a proposal for the central Library and Learning Center, complied perfectly with their ambitions: "We were interested in the specific task of designing an innovative building for studying," says Cornelius Schlotthauer who already worked on the BMW Central Building in Leipzig and is the head of the German ZHA office, which was founded in 2007 for the construction of the Hamburg River Promenade. The building should not only accommodate the new central library, which consolidates many smaller former institutional units; moreover, all administrative student service entities were also to be situ-

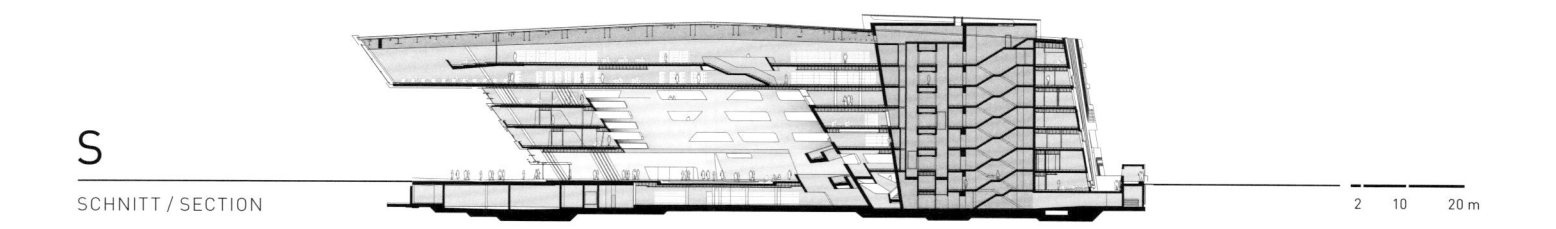

S

SCHNITT / SECTION   2 10   20 m

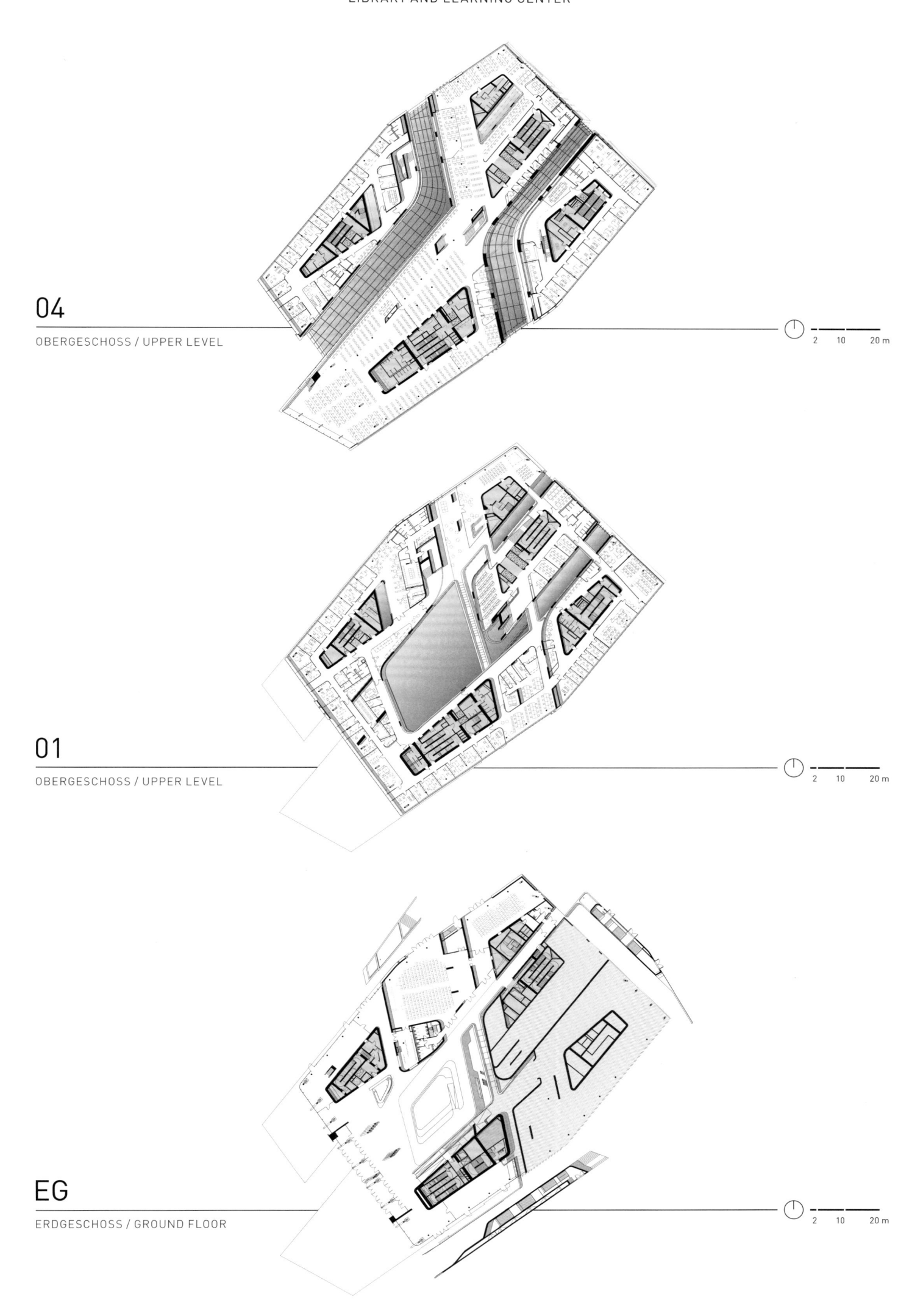

LIBRARY AND LEARNING CENTER

04
OBERGESCHOSS / UPPER LEVEL

01
OBERGESCHOSS / UPPER LEVEL

EG
ERDGESCHOSS / GROUND FLOOR

LIBRARY AND LEARNING CENTER

Der beste Platz für die Studierenden: Die Auskragung beherbergt Leseplätze mit Fernblick – wegen der Lage am Ende der Wegführung und der Größe des Atriums ragen die obersten Geschosse über die unteren hinaus
Best place for students: The cantilever offers reading places with a spectacular view – the projection of the upper floors results from the large atrium size and the position at the end of the path through the building

leitet. Das Haus sollte ja nicht bloß die neue Zentralbibliothek beherbergen, die aus vielen kleineren ehemaligen Institutseinheiten geschaffen wurde. Darüber hinaus sollten auch alle Verwaltungseinheiten, die direkten Studentenkontakt pflegen, hier angesiedelt werden, das zentrale Forum der Universität, ein Café, Sprachlabors, kleinere Hörsäle und zahlreiche Büros. Dieses Programm sorgt schon an sich für starke Frequenz, die folgerichtig auch den zentralen Entwurfsgedanken prägte. „Damit das Haus innen stets in Bewegung ist, sollte das Herz des Gebäudes oben sein", beschreibt Schlotthauer die Idee. „Deshalb legten wir die großen, zusammenhängenden Bibliotheksflächen in das vierte und fünfte Obergeschoss." Diese Grundentscheidung bestimmte letztlich alle Detailformen, auch die markante Auskragung des zweigeschossigen Lese- und Studienraums über der zentralen Plaza des Campus. Da die Grundfläche des Baufeldes für die vielfältige Landschaft an unterschiedlich von oben und der Seite belichteten Lesezonen, Bücherregalen, abgetrennten Einzel- und Gruppenarbeitsplätzen sowie Relax- und Pausenbereichen nicht ausgereicht hätte, ergab sich die Auskragung oben fast von selbst. Aber auch die schrägen Wände, erklärt Cornelius Schlotthauer: „Das komplexe Raumprogramm lässt sich nicht einfach übereinander stapeln. Wenn man die geringere Grundfläche abgetreppt nach oben hin geschossweise erweitert hätte, wäre nie-

ated here, as well as the central university forum, a café, language labs, smaller lecture halls, and numerous offices. This spatial program in itself already entailed a higher user frequency and consequently informed the centrally-oriented design idea. "In order to facilitate constant movement in the building the heart of the building should be at the top," Schlotthauer describes the idea. "That's why we positioned the big, continuous library spaces on the fourth and fifth upper floors." This underlying decision also influenced all other design details, including the prominent cantilever of the two-storey reading and study area above the central plaza of the campus. As the surface area of the building plot would not have been sufficient for the versatile landscape of reading zones interchangeably lit from above or the side, for bookshelves, separate individual and group working places, along with relaxation and break areas, the cantilever on top almost fell naturally into place. As did the inclined walls, explains Schlotthauer: "One cannot simply stack such a complex spatial program. If we had stepped the narrow plot floor by floor to expand the volume toward the top, we would have never

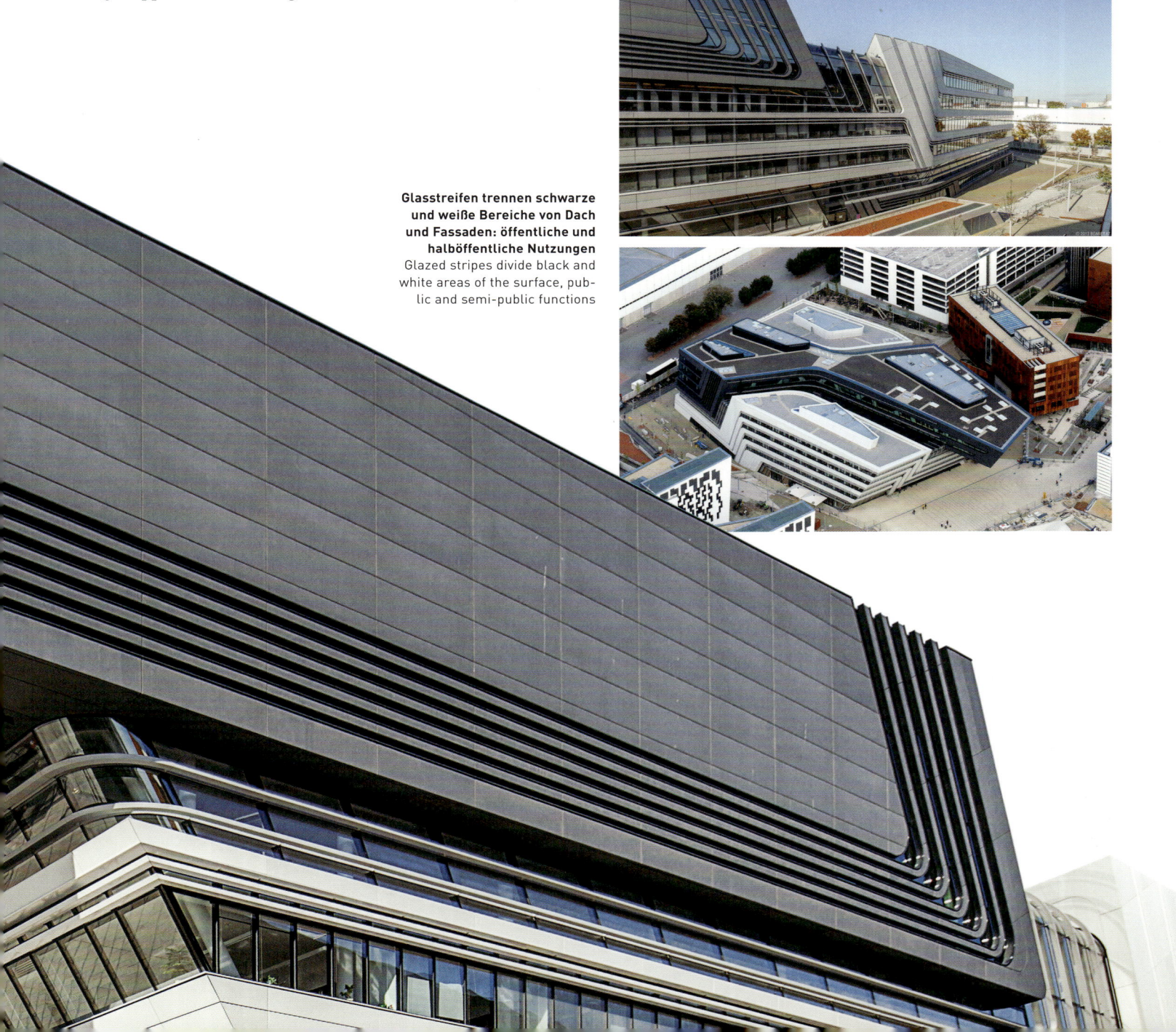

Glasstreifen trennen schwarze und weiße Bereiche von Dach und Fassaden: öffentliche und halböffentliche Nutzungen
Glazed stripes divide black and white areas of the surface, public and semi-public functions

mals die fließende Architektur entstanden, die wir wollen. Außerdem brachte die Schräge bautechnische Vorteile für das Atrium, die Kraftableitung erfolgt über bewehrte Betonkreuze in den Wänden statt über Geschossplatten und Mauern."

Wie komplex Masterplan, Hausentwurf und Konstruktion ineinandergreifen, zeigt eben dieses spektakuläre gebäudehohe Atrium. Da der Bauplatz breit und tief ist, würden ohne Belichtung von oben in der Mitte Räume ohne Tageslicht entstehen. „Also haben wir den Quader mit einer fließenden Bewegung innen ausgefräst", beschreibt Schlotthauer den lustvollen Entwurfsprozess. Das Atrium ist in der Tat eine der beeindruckendsten Raumschöpfungen Wiens im 21. Jahrhundert. Betritt man das Haus, öffnen sich auf einen Blick und in alle Richtungen hin Galerien, Schluchten, Rampen und Treppen. Fugenlos wird der anspruchsvolle Freiraum des Campus innen fortgesetzt. Tageslicht strömt zwischen den charakteristischen Lamellen im verglasten Dach ein, alle Hauptlinien und Raumkanten werden in LED-Streifen zusätzlich betont. Alles ist weiß, die Empfindungen liegen irgendwo zwischen Sakralraum, Gesamtkunstwerk und Weltraumarchitektur.

arrived at the fluid architecture we envisioned. The diagonal slant was also advantageous for the atrium in structural terms as the load is distributed via reinforced concrete crosses in the walls as opposed to floor slabs and walls."

This spectacular building-high atrium illustrates just how sophisticated the interconnection between master plan, building design, and construction is. The building plot is broad and deep, so there would have been rooms without daylight in the middle if there wasn't light from above. "We carved out the inside of a cuboid with one fluid stroke," Schlotthauer tells of the playful design process. Without question, the atrium is one of Vienna's most impressive architectural creations of the twenty-first century. Upon entering the house, galleries, canyons, ramps, and stairways open up in all directions at first glance. The elaborate open space of the campus continues seamlessly inside the building. Daylight floods the space through the characteristic louvers in the glass roof; all main lines and edges of the space are additionally emphasized with LED strips. Everything is white: The impressions oscillate between sacred space, total artwork, and outer space architecture.

LIBRARY AND LEARNING CENTER

▲
Das Atrium durchdringt das gesamte Gebäude und wird auch als Forum für über 1.000 Personen genützt
The building-high atrium can also serve as a venue for more than 1,000 people

▲
Hauptplatz des Campus: Bauten von Histoshi Abe (rechts) und BUSarchitektur (Hintergrund links)
Main square of the campus: buildings by Hitoshi Abe (right) and BUSarchitektur (background left)

▲
Platzbildung an der Rückfassade des Library and Learning Centers gegenüber der Wiener Messe
The square at the rear side of the Library and Learning Center vis-à-vis the Messe Wien fair complex complex

▲
Blick durch das Atrium zur Eingangsseite: Verglaste Decke und Fassaden bringen viel Licht ins Haus
View through the atrium to the entrance: The glazed ceiling and façades provide ample daylight in the building

LIBRARY AND LEARNING CENTER

Der Weg durchs Haus: In Laubengängen rund ums Atrium und
angrenzenden offenen Räumen liegen die Bibliotheksarbeitsplätze,
schräge Wände führen nach oben zum großen Lesesaal
The path through the house: Open reading spaces
are situated along the atrium galleries, sloped walls
lead up to the large reading hall

LIBRARY AND LEARNING CENTER

Lounge-Charakter

In schraubenden Bewegungen entlang der Rampen, Treppen und Laubengänge dieses Raumwunders wandert der Besucher nach oben und durchstreift dabei die verschiedensten Arbeitssituationen: Tische mit und ohne Screens, zwischen Bücherregalen und neben Fensterausblicken, am Rande von Vertikaleinschnitten oder mit Tageslicht durch Glasdecken. „Auch die Materialität ist von entscheidender Bedeutung", betont Architekt Schlotthauer. Die Fassaden sind in weißen und schwarzen Glasfaserbeton-Paneelen von bis zu 4,20 Meter Länge ausgeführt, wobei der weiße Baukörper administrative Zonen und der schwarze die Arbeitsbereiche der Studierenden bezeichnet. Dazwischen zieht sich als funktionale Trennlinie die markante Glasfuge mit ihren Lamellenstreifen-Band in sanften Kurven über alle Fassaden und das Dach des Hauses. Innen ist die Atmosphäre der Lernzonen dank satt-violetten, weichen Teppichböden entspannt: „Wir wollten hier einen loungeartigen Charakter und eine gewisse Lässigkeit hineinbringen. Das Haus stimuliert ein neues Lebensgefühl beim Lernen: Wir wollen Interaktion und Austausch, dies ist schließlich der Arbeitsplatz der Studierenden."

Lounge character

In a spiral movement upward along ramps, stairways, and arcades the visitor passes by an array of work stations: tables with or without screens, between bookshelves and beside views outside, at the edge of vertical incisions or with daylight from glass ceilings. "Also the materiality plays a decisive role," architect Schlotthauer points out. The façades are constructed of white and black fiber reinforced concrete panels with a length of 4.20 meters; the white components designate the administrative zones and the black the students' work areas. In-between, a prominent seam of glass with its band of louvers marks the functional divide, permeating all façades and the building's roof in gentle curves. Inside the atmosphere of the study zones is relaxed, thanks also to the deep purple, soft carpet floor: "Here we wanted to create a lounge-like and laid-back ambience. The house stimulates a new quality of life while learning. We strive for interaction and exchange – after all, it's the workplace of the students."

**Für digitale Projekte werden Arbeits-
plätze in Tribünenform angeboten**
Working places for digital projects are provided
in a tribune-like arrangement

**In den zwei obersten Geschossen liegt der große Lesesaal
mit Blick über die Baumkronen des Praters**
The large reading hall with a view above the trees of the
Prater park is situated on the two uppermost levels

LIBRARY AND LEARNING CENTER

Hinter den weißen Bereichen der Fassade liegen die Administrationsräume, schräge Stützen zeigen die dynamischen Kraftlinien des Gebäudes
Administration spaces are situated behind the white zones of the façade, inclined columns convey the dynamic forces of the building

LIBRARY AND LEARNING CENTER

> **Fließende Formen: Schon beim Empfangspult präsentiert Zaha Hadids Gebäude seine Gestaltungsphilosophie**
Total fluidity: Zaha Hadid's building presents its design philosophy already at the reception desk

Die Glasstreifen an Fassaden und Decken bringen Licht von oben und von der Seite in die Arbeitsbereiche
The glass stripes on the façades and ceilings provide much daylight in the work areas

LIBRARY AND LEARNING CENTER

> **Neben den Tageslicht- gibt es auch organisch gefasste Kunstlichtarbeitsplätze mit Blick in die Lufträume**
Besides the daylit work areas there are also artificially illuminated areas

Abgerundete Treppen, schräge Stützen: Die Kraftlinien des Hauses werden überall dargestellt
Curved stairs, inclined columns: The building's force lines are omnipresent

STATEMENTS

WAS IST EIN LEARNING CENTER? WIE FUNKTIONIERT ES?

CORDULA RAU

Das Library and Learning Center fungiert als Mittelpunkt des Campus. Es ist Haus für die Studierenden und Landmarkgebäude. Hier sind nicht nur die Bibliothek, sondern alle zentralen Services für die Studierenden angesiedelt. Der Studierende kann sich einschreiben und anschließend in die Bibliothek gehen, um sich Bücher auszuleihen. Gleichzeitig gibt es hier das Zentrum für Auslandsservices, den IT-Service, das Sprachlern-Zentrum und das Zentrum für Berufsplanung. Trotz Größe, Höhe und markanter Auskragung dominiert das Gebäude kaum. Die grauen Alu-Elemente und die dazugehörigen Glasbänder der Fassade umfassen eine dynamisch wirkende Gebäudefigur. Neben dem Atrium gibt es Lesesäle auf zwei Ebenen. Spannungsreich windet sich der Weg über Rampen, Treppen und Laubengänge mit schrägen Wänden hinauf bis ins „Cockpit". Von der spacig geneigten 25 Meter-Landmark-Auskragung ganz oben hat man einen wunderbaren Ausblick. Mehr als 1.000 Studierende können rund um die Uhr zwischen Bücherregalen, an Computerarbeitsplätzen und in kleinen Studierzellen lesen, lernen, denken. Ob ein Gebäude dieser Art gut funktioniert, misst man daran, wie gut die ausgedachte Strategie umgesetzt wurde. Hört man sich die Meinungen der Nutzer an, scheint das zur Gänze gelungen.

WHAT IS A LEARNING CENTER? HOW DOES IT FUNCTION?

The Library and Learning Center is the heart of the campus. It is both a house for the students and a landmark building. It accommodates not only the library but also all central student service units. A student can register for a course and then go directly to the library to lend books. And there is also the International Office, IT Services, the Language Resource Center, and the Career Center. Despite its size, height, and imposing cantilever the building does not overly dominate the space. Gray aluminum cladding and corresponding glass stripes envelop a dynamic architectural body. The reading rooms spread out across two stories next to the atrium. An exciting mix of ramps, stairways, and arcades with inclined walls lead up to the "cockpit". The spacey 25-meter cantilever at the very top offers spectacular views. Day and night, more than 1,000 students can read, learn, and contemplate between the bookshelves, at computer workspaces, or in small study zones. Whether a building of this kind functions properly can be measured by how well the design strategy has been implemented. According to the opinions of the users this has been achieved with great success.

NIKOLAUS BERGER
Leiter der Universitätsbibliothek
University Library Director

Cordula Rau: Zaha Hadid ist für ihre außergewöhnliche Architektur bekannt. Wie wirkt die Architektur des Library and Learning Center auf Sie?

Nikolaus Berger: Ich persönlich finde die Architektur sehr interessant. Obwohl das Gebäude nüchtern ist, was sich darin zeigt, dass es nur wenige Farben gibt – Schwarz, Weiß und Grau, auch nur zwei Lampenfarben – wird einem beim Durchgehen keinesfalls langweilig. Die Formen machen das Gebäude interessant. Das Haus weist bis in kleinste Details eine durchgängige Sprache auf. Auf mich als Mann wirkt das so formschön wie ein Maserati. Mein Team freut sich jeden Tag hier arbeiten zu dürfen. Die Architektur spielt sicherlich eine große Rolle. Sie vermittelt Freude und Spaß.

Wie war die vorherige Situation der WU?

Es hat sich sehr viel geändert gegenüber unserem früheren Domizil. Wir sind am 26. August 2013 hier eingezogen. Der Neubau der WU war Anlass, das gesamte Bibliothekssystem zukunftsorientiert auszurichten. Die ehemaligen mehr als 65 Instituts- und Hauptbibliotheken, die voneinander getrennt agiert haben, verschmolzen zu einem Bibliothekssystem. Für die Studierenden bringt das den Vorteil, dass seitdem alle Medienbestände zugänglich sind. Vorher musste man fast 70 Orte aufsuchen. Ein weiterer Vorteil ist das einheitliche System. Benutzbarkeit und Zugänglichkeit haben sich somit sehr verbessert.

Wie haben Sie das organisatorisch bewältigt?

Das ging nicht von heute auf morgen. Wir haben 750.000 Bücher im Bestand. Die Grundlage hierfür musste man zunächst auf organisatorischer, personeller und budgetärer Ebene herstellen. Beim Bau stand der Prozess des Lernens im Mittelpunkt und nicht der der Bibliothek. Das Rektorat hat vorab gründlich recherchiert. Bevor das Raum- und Funktionsprogramm entstand, befragte man die damalige Bibliotheksleitung und die Mitarbeiter. Gleichzeitig bediente man sich internationaler Bibliotheksbauexperten und Bibliotheksfachleute. Danach wurde gemeinsam mit dem Bibliotheksgremium, dem Vizerektorat für Lehre und dem Rektorat eine Strategie entwickelt. Ein Gutachten bereitete vor, wie das Bibliothekssystem geändert werden könne. Im Herbst 2007 hat sich das Rektorat für das neue Bibliothekssystem entschieden.

Cordula Rau: Zaha Hadid is known for her exceptional architecture. What effect does the architecture of the Library and Learning Center have on you?

Nikolaus Berger: Personally I find the architecture quite interesting. Although the building comes across quite sober, using only a few colors – black, white, and gray, and also only two colors for lamps – one definitely doesn't get bored while passing through it. The forms make the building interesting. The building boasts a coherent formal language down to the smallest detail. For me it's like a well-designed Maserati. My team is happy to work here every day. The architecture certainly plays a big role. It conveys pleasure and fun.

How was the situation in the previous WU?

Much has changed in comparison to our former domicile. We moved in here on August 26, 2013. We took the new WU Campus as an occasion to restructure the entire library system to be more future-oriented. Previously there were more than 65 central and faculty libraries, which operated separately from one another. Now they have merged into one single library system. The advantage for students is that all media collections are accessible now. Before you had to search in almost 70 places. Usability and accessibility have improved a great deal.

How did you manage this in organizational terms?

This didn't happen from one day to the next. We have a collection of 750,000 books. First we had to create the framework conditions on organizational, staff, and financial levels. For the planning of the building the concept of "learning" was essential, not the library itself. Before the spatial and functional program came into being, the former library director and staff were questioned. International library and library building experts were also consulted. Afterwards a strategy was developed together with the Library Committee, the Vice Rector's Office for Academic Programs and Student Affairs, and the Rector's Council. An expert report outlined how to change the library system. In autumn 2007 the Rector's Council decided for the new library system.

LEARNING CENTER — STATEMENTS

> Die Formen machen das Gebäude interessant. Das Haus weist bis in kleinste Details eine durchgängige Sprache auf. Auf mich als Mann wirkt das so formschön wie ein Maserati.

The forms make the building interesting. The building boasts a coherent formal language down to the smallest detail. For me it's like a well-designed Maserati.

Wie würden Sie das LC aus Ihrer Sicht beschreiben?
Das Library and Learning Center ist ein Haus für die Studierenden. In seiner Mitte befindet sich das Bibliothekszentrum. Bei der Planung betrachteten wir nicht nur den Ort, sondern auch das Lernverhalten der Studierenden. Es gibt beispielsweise Menschen, die lernen immer zu zweit und kommunizieren dabei ununterbrochen. Andere dagegen wollen es ruhig haben. Wieder andere wollen beim Lernen sehen und gesehen werden. Für all diese Lerntypen schufen wir passende Orte. Es gibt Lernplätze mit Solo-Arbeitsplätzen und kommunikative Lernzonen mit flexiblen Möbeln. Es gibt Teppich, um sich auf den Boden setzen zu können, und tragbare Sitzwürfel. Und es gibt Cafés – eines vor und eines in der Bibliothek. Wir bieten den Studierenden hier einen Ort an mit 70 Computern und 1.500 Lernplätzen. Das Bibliothekszentrum hat 15.000 m², das LC gesamthaft 35.000 m².

Wie ermittelten Sie die Grundlagen?
Im Vorfeld wurde der Bedarf gründlich erhoben. Die Vorbereitung, die Gespräche mit den Nutzern, Universitäten und externen Beratern dauerten zwei Jahre. Danach einigte man sich auf eine gemeinsame Strategie. Es war eine strategische Entscheidung für einen offenen Campus und diesen Stadtteil von Wien. Die Campusidee kommt aus dem Anglo-amerikanischen. Lehrende, Forschende und Studierende arbeiten gemeinsam. Gleichzeitig gehören Shops und Geschäfte auch zur Campusidee. Was uns besonders wichtig war, ist die offene Zugänglichkeit des Campus. Wir freuen uns über die internationalen Leute, die kommen. Gleichzeitig kooperieren wir gerne, beispielsweise mit der Messe Wien nebenan. Das schafft enorme Synergie.

How would you describe the LC from your point of view?
The Library and Learning Center is a house for the students. At its core is the library. In the planning process we not only considered the location but also the learning behavior of students. For example, there are people who always study in groups and constantly communicate with each other. Others, on the other hand, need silence. And then there are those who want to see and be seen while studying. We developed appropriate spaces for all these learning types. There are single-unit workspaces and communicative learning zones with flexible furniture. There are carpets for sitting on the floor and mobile seating cubes. And there are cafés: one in front and one inside the library. Here the students are offered a space with 70 computers and 1,500 learning places. The library center measures 15,000 m², the complete LC 35,000 m².

How did you assess the requirements?
The demands were carefully ascertained in advance. The preparation, the talks with the users, universities, and external advisors took two years. Then a common strategy was agreed upon. It was a strategic decision for an open campus and for this particular part of Vienna. The campus idea comes from Anglo-Saxon countries. Teachers, researchers, and students work together. But also shops and stores are part of this idea. Open access to the campus was especially important to us. We are happy about the international crowd who come to us. At the same time, we like to cooperate, for example, with the Messe Wien exhibition grounds next door. This creates enormous synergies.

UTE STEFFL-WAIS
Vizerektorat für Lehre
Vice Rector's Office for Academic Programs and
Student Affairs / Study Service Center

Cordula Rau: Wie beschreiben Sie Ihren Bereich im LC?
Ute Steffl-Wais: Das Vizerektorat für Lehre teilt sich im Wesentlichen in zwei Bereiche – einerseits in den Studierenden-nahen Bereich, der hier in der zweiten Etage angesiedelt ist, und andererseits in den Studierenden-fernen, der das gesamte Programm- und Qualitätsmanagement umfasst. Dies ist örtlich im fünften Stock bei der Vizerektorin für Lehre untergebracht. Die Idee war im neuen Study Service Center alle Serviceeinrichtungen für Studierende des Vizerektorats für Lehre räumlich zusammenzubringen. Alle Einheiten, die laufend mit Studierenden Kontakt haben, sind im gemeinsamen Frontoffice vertreten. Im alten Haus war das sehr verstreut. Die Zulassung im Erdgeschoss, die Anerkennung im vierten Stock, die Prüfungsorganisation im zweiten Stock usw. Die Studierenden mussten oft hin und hergeschickt werden. Jetzt haben wir es geschafft, den Studierenden sozusagen einen „One Stop-Shop" zu bieten. Auch alle anderen Serviceeinheiten für Studierende, die nicht dem Vizerektorat zugeordnet sind, wie beispielsweise das Zentrum für Auslandsstudien oder das Career Center sind im LC vertreten. Es war die Idee, das Haus als Herzstück des Campus zu etablieren und daher auch die Bibliothek hier anzusiedeln.

Sie sind seit Herbst 2013 hier im Gebäude. Sind sie mit der neuen Struktur zufrieden?
Im Vorfeld wurde der Raumbedarf genau erfasst. Für einige Einheiten hat sich viel geändert. Früher waren die Frontoffice-Bereiche kleiner und die MitarbeiterInnen hatten zum Teil dort ihre fixen Arbeitsplätze. Es gab keinen Backoffice-Bereich. In der Studienzulassung führte das immer wieder zu Problemen, denn man konnte nicht in Ruhe arbeiten. Da hat sich viel verbessert. Das gemeinsame Frontoffice ist trotzdem eine Herausforderung, weil sich die Studierenden mit der Orientierung noch etwas schwer tun. Aber das wird sich einspielen. Wir befinden uns momentan in einer Umgewöhnungsphase. Das betrifft nicht nur uns MitarbeiterInnen, sondern auch die Studierenden. Es bedarf an manchen Stellen noch einer kleinen Nachjustierung.

Cordula Rau: How would you describe your field of work in the LC?
Ute Steffl-Wais: The Vice-Rector's Office for Academic Programs and Student Affairs is basically divided into two units: one unit for more student-related affairs, which is located here on the second floor, and one that comprises the entire program and quality management, which has less to do with students directly. It is found on the fifth floor at the Vice-Rector's Office. The idea of the new Study Service Center was to spatially group together all student service units of the Vice-Rector's Office for Academic Programs and Student Affairs. All units involving frequent contact with the students are represented in the joint front office. In the old building this was scattered over different locations. Admissions on the ground floor, accreditation on the fourth, the examination committee on the second, and so on. Now we have managed to offer students a kind of "one-stop shop". But all other student service units, which are not associated with the Vice-Rector's Office – for example, the International Office or the Career Center – are also located in the LC. The objective was to establish the building as the heart of the campus and therefore also house the library there.

You have been working in this building since autumn 2013. Are you satisfied with the new structure?
The spatial demands were precisely evaluated in advance. Much has changed for some units. Previously the front office areas were smaller and some employees had fixed workspaces there. There were no "back office" areas. During admissions this frequently led to problems as it was not possible to concentrate on the work. This has improved significantly. Nevertheless, the joint front office poses quite a challenge because the students, at times, still have some difficulties with orientation. But things will sort themselves out. At the moment we are in a settling-in phase – not only for the staff but also the students. It is only normal that certain things still require small readjustments.

Wie empfinden Sie die räumliche Situation und die Architektur des Gebäudes?

In manchen Büros ist es etwas schwierig, mit den Säulen und den schiefen Wänden umzugehen. Ein oder zwei Büros sind davon stark betroffen. Doch im Wesentlichen ist es schon toll für uns und wir sind sehr stolz darauf hier arbeiten zu dürfen. Im Gebäude befindet sich die Bibliothek mit über 1.000 Selbstlernplätzen für Studierende, das ist eine zentrale Verbesserung im Vergleich zum alten Standort. Alle Services für die Studierenden sind in das LC integriert worden. Das ist wunderbar.

Hat sich in Ihren Augen im Vergleich zum alten Standort sehr viel geändert?

Die Zielsetzung war, mit dem LC einen zentralen Anlaufpunkt für Studierende zu schaffen. Das LC funktioniert auch als Symbol. Für uns war es wichtig, dass sich das Vizerektorat für Lehre, das letztendlich für die Studierenden zuständig ist, hier – direkt bei den Studierenden – befindet. Die Umsetzung dieser Idee ist gelungen. Das Gebäude funktioniert sehr gut im täglichen Betrieb.

How do you perceive the spatial environment and architecture of the building?

In some offices it is a bit difficult to deal with the columns and inclined walls. One or two offices are quite strongly affected by this. But all in all it is naturally great for us, and we are very proud to be able to work here. The library with over 1,000 self-study units for the students is integrated in the building – that's a significant improvement in comparison to the old location. All services for students have been incorporated into the LC, that's wonderful.

Were there other major changes in comparison to the previous location?

The aim was to create a central one-stop portal for students at the LC. The building also acts as a symbol. It was important to us that the Vice-Rector's Office for Academic Programs and Student Affairs, which is responsible for the students in the end, is found here among the students. The implementation of this idea was a success. The building functions very well in daily operations.

OLIVER VETTORI

Vizerektorat für Lehre
Vice Rector's Office for Academic Programs and Student Affairs /
Director of Program & Quality Management

Cordula Rau: Wie funktioniert das LC aus Ihrer Sicht?

Oliver Vettori: Ich glaube, das Gebäude funktioniert sehr gut, betrachtet man es als Symbol mit Zentrumsfunktion. Von außen gesehen ist es eines der spektakulärsten Gebäude auf dem Campus. Der Name und der Umstand, dass die Bibliothek hier ist, haben große Ausstrahlung. Die meisten Studierenden am Campus lernen in den Räumen der Bibliothek. Man muss ein wenig darauf achten, dass hier nicht der einzige Ort des Lernens auf dem Campus ist. Der gesamte Campus ist wichtig. Das LC bietet auch nicht alles an. Die meisten Projekträume, die Studierende selbst buchen können, sind beispielsweise im Teaching Center oder in den dezentralen Gebäuden untergebracht. Das LC ist ein wunderbarer Arbeitsplatz, schaut toll aus, die Studierenden fühlen sich wohl und es hat diese Symbolkraft. Was das Lernen angeht, funktioniert das LC sehr gut komplementär zum Teaching Center. In dem einen Gebäude ist selbstgesteuertes Lernen möglich, im anderen angeleitetes Lernen.

Cordula Rau: How does the Library and Learning Center work from your point of view?

Oliver Vettori: I think the building works very well, especially when you see it as a symbol with a hub function. From the outside, it is one of the most spectacular buildings on campus. The name and the fact that the library is situated here lend it a special charisma. The majority of the students on campus study in the library rooms. However, one must not forget that this is not the only place for studying on the campus. The campus in its entirety is important – the Library and Learning Center doesn't offer everything. For example, most of the project spaces that students can book themselves are accommodated in the Teaching Center or in the decentralized buildings. The LC is a great work place – it looks fantastic, the students feel comfortable, and it has this symbolic power. For learning it is the perfect complement to the Teaching Center. In one building self-studying is possible; the other one facilitates supervised studies.

LEARNING CENTER — STATEMENTS

„

Man wird durch Architektur geleitet. Ein schönes Beispiel dafür ist die Hauptachse des Campus. Sie ist der beste Ort für Begegnungen.

—

Architecture guides us. A beautiful example is the main axis of the campus. It's the best place for encounters.

"

Was hat sich im Vergleich zur vorherigen Wirtschaftsuniversität geändert?
Man kommuniziert anders. Vorher gab es Büros, die zehn Meter auseinander lagen, jetzt sind es drei Etagen. Umgekehrt sind Abteilungen, die vorher über mehrere Stockwerke getrennt waren und von der Logik eng zueinander gehören, jetzt viel stärker zusammen gerückt. Die Strategie sich an den Bedürfnissen der Studierenden zu orientieren wurde räumlich sehr gut umgesetzt. Von der Idee des Campus sind alle begeistert. Für die Studierenden ist ja auch der Campus in seiner Gesamtheit wichtig und nicht das einzelne Gebäude. Sie finden das Haus toll, aber es ist ihnen genauso viel wert, dass es beispielsweise auch einen Spar auf dem Gelände gibt.

Haben Sie das Raumprogramm gemeinsam erarbeitet?
Es gab mehrere Runden dafür. Wie in jedem Prozess ist manches besser, manches weniger gut gelungen. Aber gesamthaft betrachtet, funktioniert alles prima und wir sind sehr glücklich hier. Zunächst war es ungewöhnlich, dass wir in diesem Gebäude sitzen. Der größte Teil der Verwaltung ist woanders untergebracht. Für uns als Vizerektorat für Lehre ist es nicht nur symbolisch sondern auch vom Gebäude her großartig hier zu sein. Das war eine wichtige Entscheidung des damaligen Vizerektors. Er wollte dort sitzen, wo seine Leute sind. Die sollten da sitzen, wo die Studierenden sind.

Glauben Sie, dass das Gebäude und der Campus eine Aufwertung für die Gegend darstellen?
Auf jeden Fall. Der Ort wird nicht nur von uns, den Studierenden und Bewohnern des Campus genutzt, sondern von der ganzen Stadt. In Architektur manifestieren sich immer viele soziale Aspekte. Man wird durch Architektur geleitet. Ein schönes Beispiel dafür ist die Hauptachse des Campus. Sie ist der beste Ort für Begegnungen. Die Leute laufen sich spontan über den Weg, pausieren kurz und reden miteinander. Durch die räumliche Umstrukturierung hat sich viel geändert in der Kommunikation. Einige Departments berichten, erst jetzt gäbe es für sie die Möglichkeit innerhalb der Abteilung zu kooperieren. Umgekehrt wurden bestehende Beziehungen auseinander gerissen. Das schafft eine neue Realität, mit der man nicht in gewohnter Weise umgehen kann. Ich finde das positiv.

What has changed in comparison to the previous university?
You communicate differently. Previously some offices were ten meters away from one another; now it is three floors. In turn, some departments, which were formerly separated across several floors but logically belonged together, have moved much closer to each other. The strategy to account for the needs of the students has been implemented very well on the spatial level. Everyone is enthusiastic about the idea of the campus. For students the campus is important as a whole, not just the individual buildings. They love this house, but it equally matters that there is also a Spar supermarket, for example, on the premises.

Were you involved in drafting the spatial program?
This took place in several rounds. As in every process, some things turn out for the better, some less so. But seen as a whole everything works quite perfectly, and we are very happy to be here. At first it felt a bit peculiar to be sitting in this building here when the large part of administration is elsewhere. The fact that the Vice Rector's Office for Academic Programs and Student Affairs is located here is great, not only because of the building but also because of the symbolic message. This was an important decision by our former vice-rector: He wanted to sit where his people are. And we should be where the students are.

Do you think that the building and the campus represent an upgrading for the area?
Absolutely. The place is not only used by us, the students, and inhabitants of the campus but also by the whole city. Architecture always incorporates many social aspects. Architecture guides us. A beautiful example is the main axis of the campus. It's the best place for encounters. People coincidentally run into each other, take a short break and talk. The new spatial structure has caused a lot of changes in communication. Some departments report that only now is there an opportunity for them to cooperate internally. On the other hand, other existing relationships have been torn apart. This creates a new reality, which can't be dealt with in conventional ways. And I think this is a positive aspect.

D1 TC

BUSARCHITEKTUR: DEPARTMENTS 1 / TEACHING CENTER

GEBAUTE LERNLANDSCHAFT
DAS TEACHING CENTER VON BUSARCHITEKTUR

A BUILT EDUCATIONAL LANDSCAPE
THE TEACHING CENTER BY BUSARCHITEKTUR

ISABELLA MARBOE

DEPARTMENTS 1 / TEACHING CENTER

Ein wichtiger Ort am Campus der WU: Der expressive, cortenstahlverkleidete Bau beherbergt das Auditorium Maximum, rund 48 kleinere Hörsäle und Selbststudienzonen aller Art. Die Mensa mit ihrer grünen Dachlandschaft ist das Verbindungselement zum Department für Welthandel. Insgesamt ein differenziertes Gebäudekonglomerat für Forschung, Lehre und viele Kommunikationsformen dazwischen.

Drei Häuser in einem

Das Gebäude sieht bei jedem Wetter anders aus: wenn es stark regnet, wirken die leicht perforierten, vorbewitterten Cortenstahlplatten seiner vorgehängten Fassade wie schwarzer Samt, der sich mit Wasser vollgesogen hat. An den Kanten der schmalen, länglichen Lochstruktur in den Paneelen sammeln sich dann einen Augenblick die Tropfen, bevor sie sich wieder lösen. Bei Sonnenschein wirkt der Stahl wie gebürstet. Dann schimmert er in rostigem Orange, während das grelle Licht durch die feinen gelochten Ritzen fällt und scharfe Schatten malt. Dieses Haus, in dem das Hörsaalzentrum, die Mensa und einige akademische Institute aufeinandertreffen, scheint zu leben: Seine Fassade ist wie eine Haut, die sich verändert. Wer genau schaut, erkennt

An important place on the WU Campus: The striking building with Corton steel cladding is home to the Auditorium Maximum, around 48 smaller lecture halls, and a range of different self-study zones. The Mensa cafeteria with its green roof landscape forms the connecting element to the Department of Global Business and Trade. All in all, a sophisticated conglomerate for research, teaching, and all types of communication in-between.

Three Houses In One

The building always looks different depending on the weather: In pouring rain the lightly perforated, preweathered Corten steel curtain façade panels look like black velvet soaked in water. Drops collect at the edges of the long narrow slits in the panels for a moment before falling away. In the sunshine the steel seems brushed: The rusty orange shell shimmers as bright light pierces through the finely carved holes and casts sharp shadows. This house – where the Auditorium Center, the Mensa cafeteria, and a number of academic institutes meet – seems to be alive: Its façade is like a skin in constant metamorphosis. Look closely and you will see differences: The seams run horizontally in

Gebäudekonglomerat mit Charakter: Rückseite des TC, der Mensa, des Departments 1 und mit Netzen bespannte Fluchtstiegentürme
Buildings with strong character: the backside of the TC, the Mensa cafeteria, and Departments 1 with emergency escape towers covered in mesh

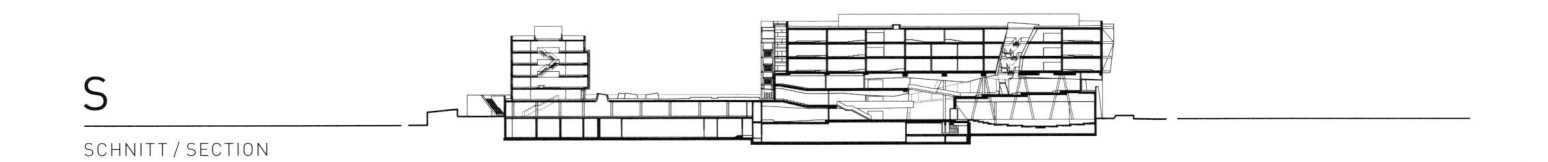

DEPARTMENTS 1 / TEACHING CENTER

S
SCHNITT / SECTION

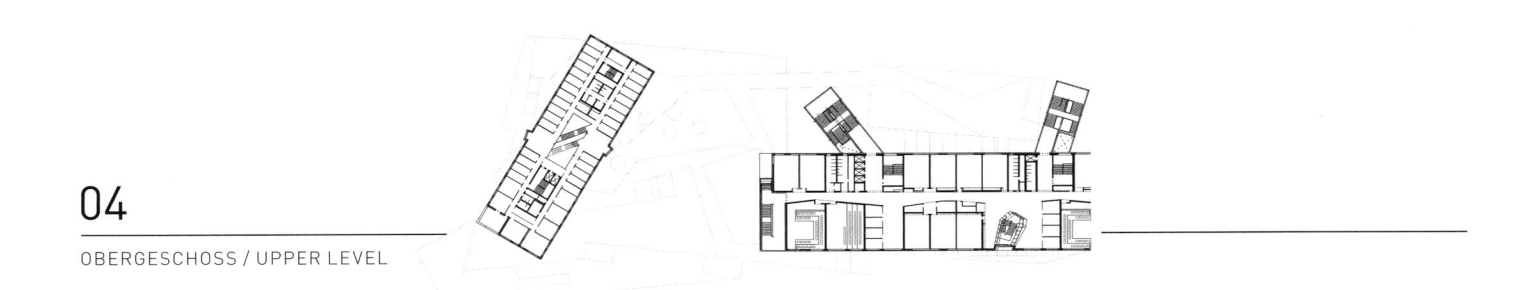

04
OBERGESCHOSS / UPPER LEVEL

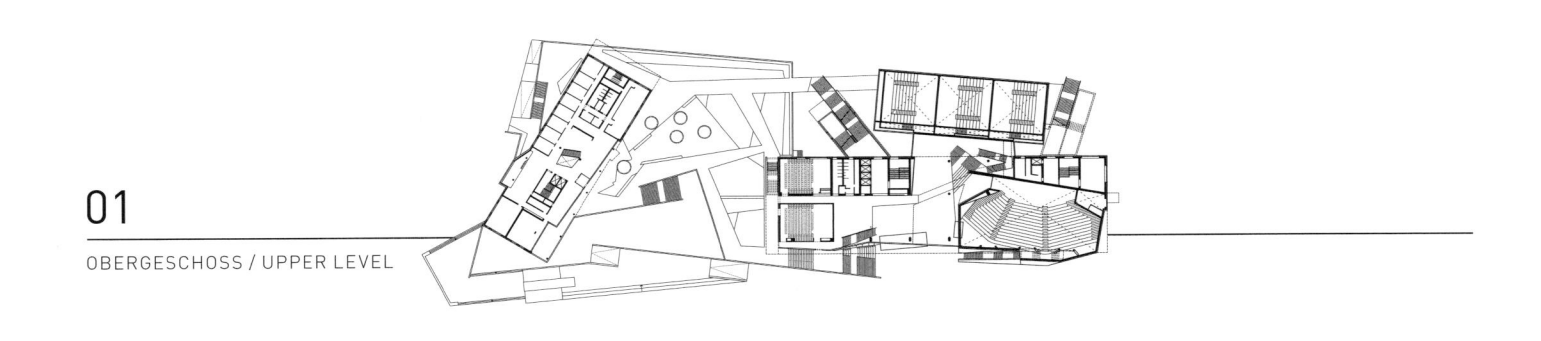

01
OBERGESCHOSS / UPPER LEVEL

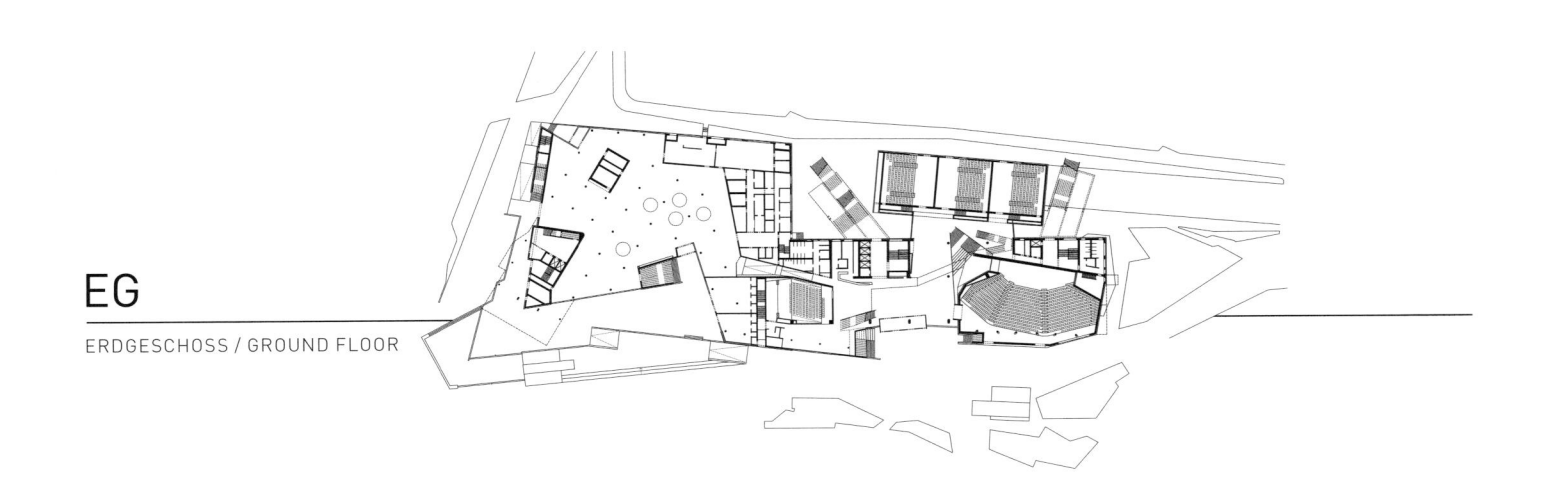

EG
ERDGESCHOSS / GROUND FLOOR

DEPARTMENTS 1 / TEACHING CENTER

Plastische Fassade: Glaseinschnitte und Beschattungselemente
Sculptural façade: glazed incisions and shading elements

Unterschiede: So verlaufen die Fugen im Bauteil des Hörsaalzentrums horizontal, auch die Sonnenschutzlamellen klappen wie Wimpern aus der Fassade. Im klar strukturierten, geradlinigen Bauteil des Departments hingegen sind alle Fugen vertikal, die schmalen, langen Beschattungselemente lassen sich verschieben und in unterschiedlichen Winkeln auffalten. Zwischen diesen beiden hoch aufragenden Baukörpern liegt die Mensa: Der Bauch in der Mitte, in dem 700 Menschen gleichzeitig essen können. „Eigentlich waren es drei Projekte in einem Haus", sagt Architekt Jean-Pierre Bolívar von BUSarchitektur. In der Mensa des Betreibers Eurest treffen sich Studierende und Lehrer, Tzou Lubroth Architekten gestalteten den Raum mit hinterleuchteten Wandpaneelen. Sie zeigen die dunklen Baumstämme mit den hellen Blatt-Tupfern eines Laubwaldes. Das vermittelt viel Atmosphäre und schafft eine Verbindung zum Außenraum. Denn das begrünte Dach der Mensa ist ein begehbarer Erholungsraum im Freien. Rampen und Treppen führen auf diesen erhöhten Garten, dessen Lichtkuppeln in der Mitte der Mensa für sonnige Momente sorgen. Schreitet man die Treppe hinab, landet man vor dem Eingang in die Aula des Hörsaalzentrums.

Parcours der Möglichkeiten

„Die Aula ist ein zentraler Punkt. Hier kommt man an, hier kann man sich orientieren, Freunde treffen und zu Vorlesungen gehen", so Architekt Jean-Pierre Bolívar. Stolz schwingt in seiner Stimme mit. Denn die Aula war im Raumprogramm des Hörsaalzentrums ursprünglich nicht vorgesehen. Doch Laura P. Spinadels Planerkollektiv BUSarchitektur konnte den Bauherrn davon überzeugen, wie wichtig sie ist. Mit offenen Armen nimmt die Aula Studierende in Empfang: Eine großzügige Eingangshalle, ein kommunikativer Treffpunkt und Verteiler an einem strategisch wichtigen Punkt. Genau genommen erweitert sie sich bis zum eingeschnittenen Lichtkeil des rundum verglasten, kompakt trapezförmig abgeknickten Treppenhauses, das von der Selbststudienzone am Dach des Auditorium Maximum bis ins fünfte Geschoss führt: Von dort hat man einen großartigen Ausblick über den Vorplatz und die umgebenden Bauten. Im Osten ragt ab dem dritten Obergeschoss ein kleiner, gläserner Erker aus der Fassade: Er gibt den Blick zur Krieau frei.

the Auditorium Center, also the sunshade louvers fold out of the façade like eyelashes. In contrast, all of the seams in the clear linear structure of the Department 1 area are vertical; the long-slim shading elements can be shifted and unfold at different angles. Between these two towering volumes rests the Mensa cafeteria: A stomach in the middle where 700 people can eat at the same time. "Actually it was three projects in one house," says architect Jean-Pierre Bolívar of BUSarchitektur. The Mensa run by Eurest is a meeting place for students and teachers. Tzou Lubroth Architects furnished the space with back-lit wall panels. They display dark tree trunks with bright dabs of leaves like a deciduous forest. It heightens the atmosphere and creates a connection with the outside world: above, the greened roof of the Mensa, an open-air leisure zone. Ramps and stairs lead up to this garden perch where the skylights in the middle deliver sunny moments down below in the Mensa. Continue back down the stairway, you land at the entrance to the Aula of the Auditorium Center.

A Path of Possibilities

"The Aula is a central point. You arrive, it is easy to orient yourself, you can meet friends and go to a lecture," says architect Jean-Pierre Bolívar with a hint of pride in his voice. Because the Aula was not specified in the original spatial program for the Auditorium Center. But Laura Spinadel's planning collective at BUSarchitektur could convince the client just how important it is. The Aula welcomes students with open arms: A spacious entrance hall, a communicative meeting and distribution point at a strategic location. More precisely, it extends over to the encarved light

Das begrünte Dach mit Oberlichtkuppeln der Mensa ist zugleich ein erhöhter Erholungsraum im Freien
The green roof of the Mensa with the skylights is at the same time an open-air leisure zone

Ein Haus voller Überraschungen: aus diesem verglasten Erker hat man einen wunderbaren Blick bis zur Krieau
A house full of surprises: This glass alcove opens up a great view to the Krieau neighborhood

DEPARTMENTS 1 / TEACHING CENTER

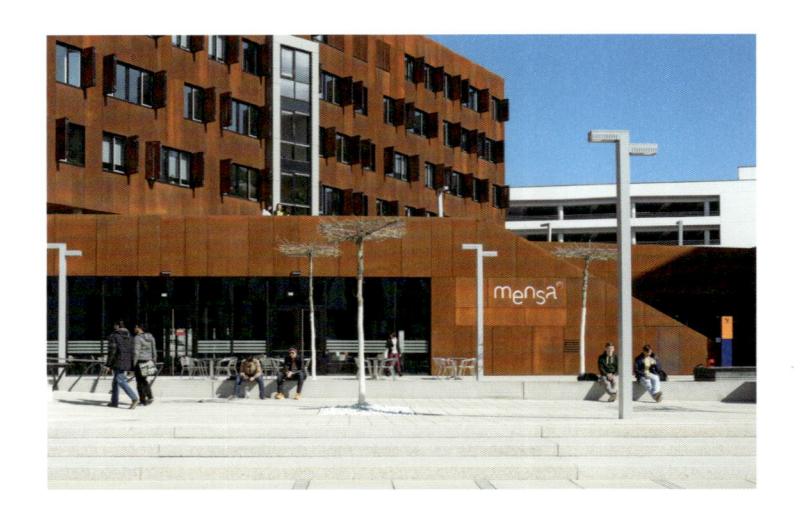

⌃
Ein Bauch, in dem 700 Menschen gleichzeitig Platz zum Essen finden: Die Mensa, die als verbindendes Element zwischen Departments 1 und TC liegt
A stomach where 700 people can eat at the same time: The Mensa is situated as a connecting element between Departments 1 and TC

24 Stunden offen für Kommunikation: Die Erweiterung des TCs in den öffentlichen Raum, der von Hitoshi Abes Bau eingefasst wird
Open 24 hours for communication: The extension of the TC in public space functions as link to the building by Hitoshi Abe

Der Weg ist das Ziel: verschiedenste Stiegen – kühn über Lufträume schwebend, ausladend breit, mit Sitztreppen wie in einer Arena oder als vergitterter, mit Netzen bespannter Fluchttreppenturm – sind ein großes Thema dieses Gebäudekonglomerats, das sich auf unzählige Arten erkunden und entdecken lässt. Es wird so zur gebauten Metapher und zum Ort des Lernens gleichermaßen: Wissen zu erwerben bedeutet Erfahrung zu sammeln, in Kontakt zu treten, sich auszutauschen oder zurückzuziehen. Die richtige Balance muss jeder für sich finden. Das räumliche Angebot des Hörsaalzentrums aber ist so vielfältig, dass es viele Optionen für Kommunikation und Austausch bietet. Von der reinen Blickbeziehung bis zum Seminarraum, in dem Gruppen gemeinsam arbeiten können.

Die Aula liegt zwischen der mit bewittertem Cortenstahl verkleideten, rostroten, freigeformten Raumkapsel des Audimax am südöstlichen Rand des Gebäudes und der kleineren, im hinteren Teil angesiedelten Hörsaalspange. Treppenkaskaden, Luftbrücken und Rampen durchmessen den bis zu 16 Meter hohen, hellen Raum. Von der Aula sieht man durch die Glasflächen über dem Eingang, die sich expressiv wie ein Streifen Himmel oder wedge of the compact trapezoidal staircase, which is glazed on all sides and leads from the self-study zones on the roof of the Auditorium Maximum up to the fifth floor: There one has a spectacular view over the square in front and the surrounding buildings. To the east, a small glass alcove juts out of the façade from the third storey on, opening up a view to the Krieau neighborhood.

The path is the goal: The range of different stairways – floating boldly in the air, sweepingly broad, with steps to sit on like in an arena, or the trellised emergency escape tower covered in mesh – is a main theme in the design, providing a myriad of ways to explore and discover the building conglomerate. In this way, it is both a built metaphor and a place of learning: Gaining knowledge means collecting experience, making contact, interaction, or retreat. Everyone must find the right balance for him or herself. In any case, the rich spatial diversity of the Auditorium Center offers abundant modes of communication and exchange: from pure visual contact to seminar rooms where groups can work together.

The Aula is situated between the free-formed Audimax with its rust-red, weathered Corten steel cladding on the southern

Licht zwischen der kluftartigen vorgehängten Fassade fräsen, auf den Vorplatz und den gegenüberliegende Bau von Atelier Hitoshi Abe. Wie durch ein Nadelöhr schlüpft man durch den Cortenstahl-gerahmten Windfang in die helle Aula mit den hohen Stahlbetonsäulen, schrägen Panoramafenstern, rostroten Wänden, Treppen, Galerien und Podesten. Die Vielzahl ihrer Wege und Zugangsmöglichkeiten erschließt sich erst nach und nach.

Lernen nach Maß
Hellgrauer, glänzender Jura-Marmor liegt am Boden mit dem markanten Leitsystem für Sehbehinderte, viele Studierende sitzen auf den bunt beschrifteten, orangen Polstermöbeln, über denen sich eine aus dreieckigen Flächen gebildete Deckenfaltung aus Gipskarton ausbreitet. Sie ist das akustisch wirksame, von Leuchtstreifen durchsetzte künstliche Firmament dieses Raumes, dessen Geometrie mit ihren hohen Lufträumen, Fensterflächen, Oberlichten, Galerien, Erkern, Treppen und Rampen ständig eine Verbindung zu seinem Umfeld und seinen Nutzern sucht. Von der Aula sieht man zum Eingang des Audimax hinunter oder zu den Selbststudienzonen hinauf, die sich auf mehreren Plattformen über das Dach des großen Hörsaals ergießen. Hier können sich Studierende ungezwungen untereinander austauschen. Es gibt freies WLAN, Automaten mit Getränken und Snacks. Eine schräg ansteigende Lufttreppe führt zum Eurest-Café gegenüber. Die Selbststudienzonen werden von kleinen Räumen mit Glaswänden flankiert, wo Gruppen ungestört arbeiten können. Das Audimax hingegen bietet 650 Hörern mit ansteigenden Sitzreihen, roten Polstersesseln, dem hellen Jura-Marmorboden, der Decke aus schmalen Holzbändern mit den Lichtstreifen, cortenstahlverkleideten Innenwänden, der

edge of the building and the smaller lecture hall tract on the back side. Cascading stairways, bridges floating in the air, and ramps traverse the bright, up to 16-meter-high space. From the Aula one views through the glass surfaces above the entrance – an expressive cut in the crevice-like steel façade, like a strip of sky or light – to the forecourt and the opposite building by Atelier Hitoshi Abe. As if through the eye of a needle, one slips through the Corten steel frame of the vestibule into the bright Aula with its towering reinforced concrete columns, inclined panorama windows, rust-red walls, stairways, galleries, and podiums. Only gradually does one learn all of its paths and access points.

Customized Learning
Lustrous light gray Jura marble lines the floors along with a distinctive guidance system for the blind and partially-sighted; students sit on the orange, colorfully labeled upholstered seating; a ceiling of triangular gypsum surfaces unfolds above them. The artificial firmament of this space is acoustically effective, punctuated by strips of light; its geometry is constantly generating connections with its surroundings and its users through voluminous airspaces, window surfaces, skylights, galleries, alcoves, stairways, and ramps. One looks down from the Aula to the entrance of the Audimax or up to the self-study zones, which flow over numerous platforms on the roof of the large auditorium. Students can informally exchange with each other here. There is free WLAN, vending machines with drinks and snacks. A slanted floating stairway leads to the Eurest Café across the way. The self-study zones are flanked by small rooms with glass walls where groups can work undisturbed. Whereas the Audimax – a space for 650 students with ascending rows of red upholstered

‹ Eine Stiege als Zugang, Treffpunkt und informelles Diskussionsforum vor dem Auditorium Maximum
A stairway as access, meeting point, and informal discussion forum in front of the Auditorium Maximum

⌃ Eine vielseitige Bühne für die Möglichkeiten von Architektur: Das TC bietet spektakuläre Raumerlebnisse
A multifaceted stage for the potentials of architecture: The TC offers spectacular spatial experiences

Kristalline Treppe an die Spitze: Dieses Stiegenhaus schraubt sich in den Selbststudienzonen bis zum Himmel überm Glasdach in den fünften Stock hinauf
Crystalline flight of stairs to the top: This transparent staircase in the self-study zones leads up to the sky over the glass roof in the fifth floor

DEPARTMENTS 1 / TEACHING CENTER

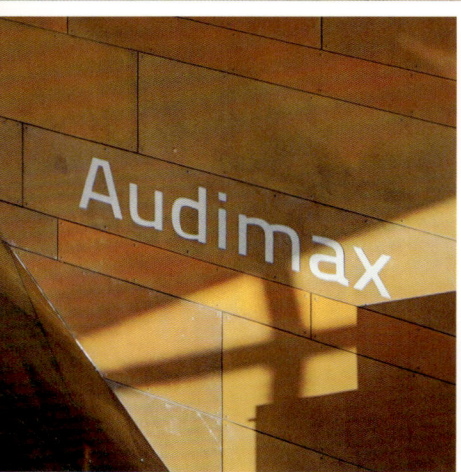

Die markanten perforierten, vorbewitterten Cortenstahlplatten der Außenhaut prägen auch das Audimax
The perforated, preweathered Corten steel of the building's outer skin can be also found on walls of the Audimax

Ein großzügiger, fließender Raum für Inspiration und Austausch: Rampe und Stiege in Selbststudienzone
A generous, fluid space for inspiration and exchange: ramp and stairs in the self-study zones

Das TC bietet verschiedene räumliche Angebote zur Wissensvermittlung: einer der kleineren Hörsäle
The TC offers different kinds of spaces to impart knowledge: one of the smaller lecture halls

Im Audimax gibt es eine tolle Akustik, 650 Sitzplätze und eine Projektionsfläche von zwei mal sechs Metern
In the Audimax there are great acoustics, 650 seats, and a projection surface two by six meters

Schiefertafel und den Projektionsflächen von zwei mal sechs Metern an der Stirnseite das perfekte, abgeschlossene Umfeld zur Konzentration. Es würde sich auch als Kino und Veranstaltungssaal wunderbar eignen.

Parallel zur Außentreppe aufs Dach der Mensa führt gegenüber im Inneren eine Freitreppe mit Bambus-Stabparkett am Glas entlang zur Galerie mit den Selbststudienzonen, die sich um die kleineren Hörsäle gruppieren. Man findet sie in unterschiedlichen Größen im ganzen Haus: vier für 180 und vier für 120 Menschen, dreizehn für 60 und 24 für dreißig Personen. Dazwischen fließen die offenen Räume der Selbststudienzone. Das wissenschaftliche Personal des Departments 1 für Welthandel wünschte sich eine rigide Zellenstruktur: Sie ist dem Nutzerwunsch geschuldet und gehorcht einem strengen Rastermaß von 2,40 Meter mal 4,95 Meter. Allerdings gibt es auch hier im zweiten Obergeschoss noch offene Kommunikationsräume und eine spektakuläre Doppeltreppe, die sich im Luftraum zwischen den umlaufenden Gängen gegenläufig überkreuzt und so zur Kommunikation animiert. Austausch als Basis für Studium, Lehre, Forschung und nicht zuletzt: den Welthandel.

seats, with Jura marble flooring, a ceiling of narrow wooden boards with light strips, Corten steel inner walls, with the chalkboard and a projection surface of two by six meters at the front – provides the perfect self-contained environment for concentration. It's perfectly suited for a movie theater or event hall as well.

Parallel to the outdoor stairway to the roof of the Mensa, inside an open stairway with bamboo strip parquet leads along the glass to the gallery with the self-study zones, grouped around smaller lecture halls. One finds these halls in different sizes throughout the house: four for 180 and four for 120 people, 13 for 60 people, and 24 for 30. The open space of the self-study zones flows in-between. The scientific staff of the Department of Global Business and Trade wanted a rigid cell structure: This space is a product of the users' wishes and follows a strict grid of 2.40 by 4.95 meters. Albeit, here on the second floor are also open communication rooms and a spectacular twin stairway that cuts across the airspace between the circulation paths and encourages communication. Exchange as the basis for studying, teaching, research, and last but not least: global trade.

INTEGRATION ARCHITEKTONISCHER UND STRUKTURELLER KOMPLEXITÄT
KONSTRUKTIONS-HIGHLIGHTS AM WU CAMPUS

ANDREI GHEORGHE

Der neue WU Campus hat in städtebaulicher, landschaftsplanerischer und architektonischer Hinsicht neue Akzente gesetzt. Qualitätsvolle Architektur definiert sich auch über das erfolgreiche Integrieren mehrerer Disziplinen und Baufachbereiche in Konzeption und Ausführung. Ein ambitionierter Architekturentwurf verlangt auch eine komplexe Handhabung in der Ausführung, im Besonderen im Hinblick auf das Design der Baukonstruktion. Eine Herausforderung liegt in diesem Zusammenwirken von konstruktiven mit architektonischen Konzepten, in welchem den Entwerfern und Ingenieuren idealerweise eine Symbiose dieser zwei Disziplinen gelingen kann. Das Wiener Büro Vasko+Partner (V+P) war in einer Arbeitsgemeinschaft mit BUSarchitektur der verantwortliche Generalkonsulent für den WU Campus.

THE INTEGRATION OF ARCHITECTURAL AND STRUCTURAL COMPLEXITY
CONSTRUCTION HIGHLIGHTS ON THE WU CAMPUS

The WU Campus has broken new ground in urban planning, landscape design, and architectural regards. High-quality architecture is the product of the successful integration of numerous disciplines and specialist construction fields in its conception and realization. Realizing an ambitious architectural design involves complex processes, especially in terms of planning the building's construction. The interplay between constructive and architectural concepts is a challenge where ideally the designer and the engineer can achieve a symbiosis between these two disciplines. For the WU Campus the Viennese firms Vasko+Partner (V+P) and BUSarchitektur collaborated as the responsible general consultants.

STRUCTURAL DESIGN HIGHLIGHTS

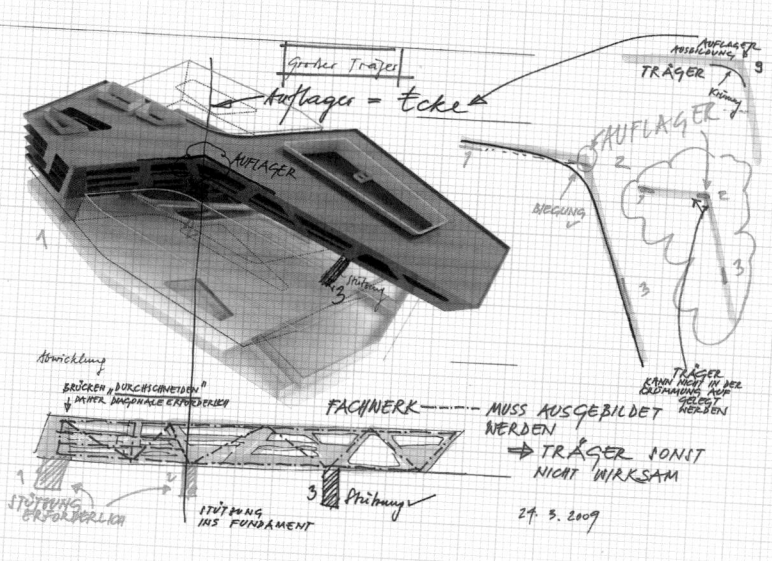

Vasko+Partner: Library and Learning Center, Konstruktionsentwurf
Structural design process

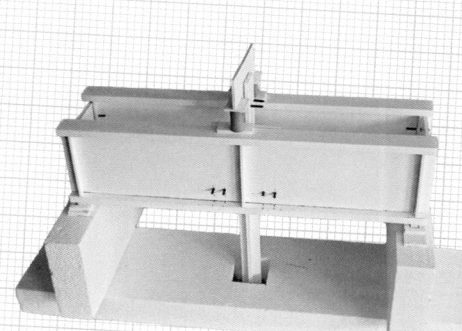

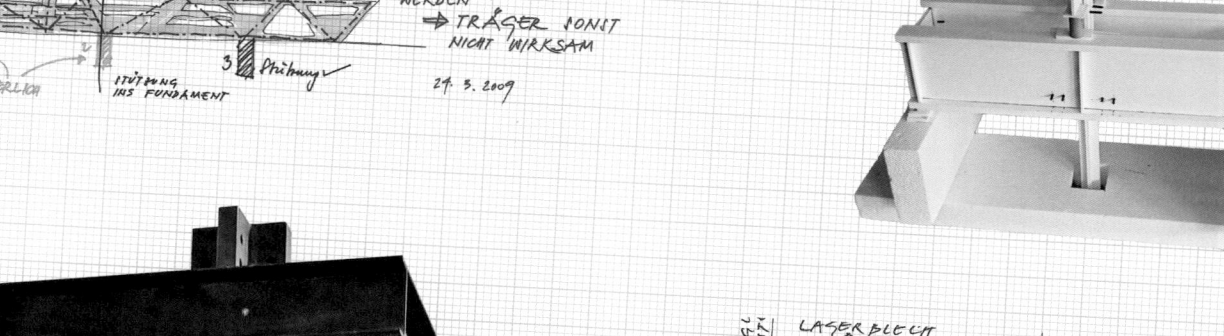

Library and Learning Center: Hängestütze
Suspension column

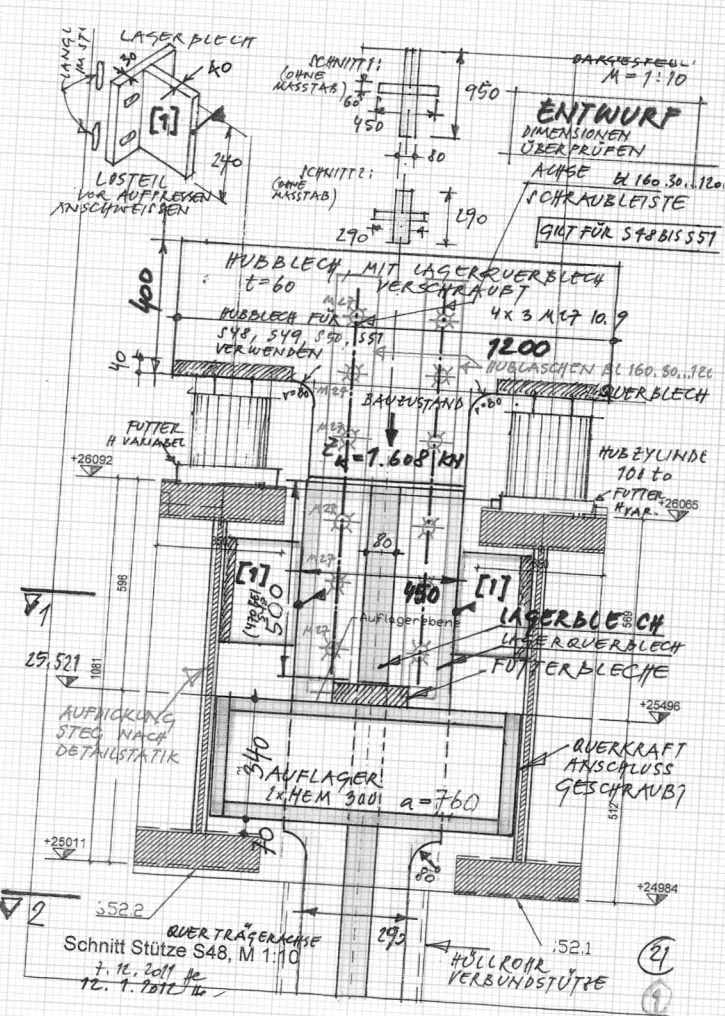

Vasko+Partner: Library and Learning Center, Modell und Zeichnung der Lasteinbringung der Hängestützen
Model and drawing of soft loading process of the suspension columns

Library and Learning Center:
Einheben des Hauptstahlfachwerkes
Hoisting the steel frame

Das Library and Learning Center von Zaha Hadid Architects (Entwurf) mit Vasko+Partner (Statik)

Die komplexe Raumgeometrie des Library and Learning Center stellte sehr hohe Ansprüche an die Tragkonstruktion des Gebäudes. Im Rahmen der Entwurfsplanung wurde von den Architekten ein exaktes dreidimensionales Modell der Gebäudehülle vorgegeben, welches in weiteren Planungsschritten für die Konstruktion adaptiert und verfeinert wurde. Aus der Integration der Konstruktion ergab sich durch eine Verfeinerung der Schräge der Fassade im Eingangsbereich von einem Winkel von 40° auf 35° zur Lotrechten das Vergrößern der statisch wirksamen Fläche der Stahlbetonkerne und Materialänderungen von Beton auf Stahl, besonders im Bereich der großen Auskragung über dem Vorplatz.

Im Rahmen der Fundamentherstellung wurde die Baugrube mit Schmalwänden abgesichert und die Fundamentplatte als „braune Wanne" ausgeführt. Aufgrund der weiten Auskragung über dem Eingangsbereich mussten diese Kräfte über die bis zu 3,50 m starke Betonfundamentplatte mittels Zug- und Brems-Ankerpfählen in den Untergrund eingebracht werden. Der frei auskragende Gebäudeteil wurde über schräge Stahl/Beton-Verbundstützen abgeleitet, welche einen Vollstahlkern und Betonummantelung in einem Rohrdurchmesser von 400 mm aufweisen. Als Ausgleich wurde das Gebäude im hinteren Bereich zurückverhängt. Die Regelgeschosse wurden in Stahlbeton (ca. 30 cm) ausgeführt, besonderes Augenmerk musste hier auf eine ausreichende Durchstanzbewehrung gelegt werden.

The Library and Learning Center by Zaha Hadid Architects (design) with Vasko+Partner (engineers)

The complex spatial geometry of the Library and Learning Center placed great demands on the load bearing structure of the building. In the framework of the design planning phase an exact three-dimensional model of the building shell was provided by the architects, which was adapted and refined for the construction in further planning stages. The integration of the constructive elements led to a fine-tuning of the inclination of the façade in the entrance area from 40° to 35° to vertical, the enlargement of the statically effective surface of the reinforced concrete cores, and material changes from concrete to steel, especially in the area of the substantial cantilever over the central plaza.

During the foundation work the excavation pit was secured with diaphragm walls and the foundation plate was put in place in the form of a "brown tub". Due to the broad cantilever over the entrance area, these forces had to be transferred through the up to 3.50-meter-thick concrete foundation plate by means of tension and compression anchor columns in the underground. The load of the cantilevering building component is channeled through diagonal steel-concrete composite columns, which have solid steel cores with a concrete casing in a pipe diameter of 400 mm. The rear of the building is anchored into the ground as a balancing measure. The standard floors are reinforced concrete slabs (circa 30 cm), whereby special attention had to be paid to sufficient punching shear reinforcement.

STRUCTURAL DESIGN HIGHLIGHTS

Die Auskragung von ca. 25 m über die Campusplaza wurde mit einem Stahlfachwerk realisiert. Obwohl ursprünglich in Beton geplant, entschied man sich im Rahmen der Ausführung für eine Stahlkonstruktion: „Diese Entscheidung ermöglichte ein schnelleres und einfacheres Herstellen ohne Schalungsaufwand bei größtmöglicher Transparenz der Fassade", erklärt Lothar Heinrich von V+P. Der Architekturentwurf wurde adaptiert und die Lage der Fenster in ein Fachwerk integriert. Dieses schließt an die Hauptgebäudekonstruktion über einbetonierte Stahleinlagen an. Extrem kleine Toleranzvorgaben im Millimeterbereich konnten bei der Ausführung durch die Berücksichtigung der Formänderungen eingehalten werden. Insgesamt wiegt das Fachwerk ca. 320 Tonnen, dieses wurde in acht Stücken bis 90 Tonnen Gewicht eingehoben und an der Einbaustelle eingeschweißt. Da das Fachwerk auch eine Querneigung von 15° aufweist, musste für das Einheben eine Hilfskonstruktion zum vertikalen Einhängen entwickelt werden. Das Einheben selbst erfolgte mit Hilfe eines Raupenkrans in der Nacht. Die Dimensionen der Unter- und Obergurte sind extrem schlank (300 mm breit) und bis 3.000 mm hoch, die Stahlbleche von 80 bis 100 mm sind entsprechend keilförmig zugeschnitten und durchgeschweißt. Das Stahlfachwerk wurde auf den Köpfen der Verbund-Schrägstützen aufgesetzt, zur Aufnahme der großen lokalen Spannungen wurden nach Naturmaß gefräste Vollstahlblöcke (300 × 500 mm) vorgesehen. Oberhalb dieses Fachwerks wurden die Geschosse des auskragenden Gebäudeteils von ei-

The cantilever of approximately 25 meters over the campus plaza was achieved with a steel framework. Although it was originally planned in concrete, the decision for a steel structure was made in the design process: "This decision enabled faster and simpler construction without the need for extensive formwork and the greatest possible transparency of the façade," explains Lothar Heinrich from V+P. The architectural design was adapted and the positions of the windows were integrated into the framework. It is connected to the construction of the main building via steel inserts embedded in the concrete. Extremely small tolerances in the millimeter range could be maintained in the construction process by taking material deflection into consideration. The framework weighs a total of 320 tons. Eight constituent pieces weighing up to 90 tons were lifted and welded into place. As the framework is also skewed laterally by 15° a special construction had to be developed to hoist and vertically mount the structure. The mounting process itself was accomplished overnight with the help of a crawler crane. The dimensions of the lower and upper chords are extremely thin (300 mm wide) and up to 3,000 mm high; sheet steel was then cut with a corresponding wedge shape and welded in place. The steel framework was anchored on the heads of the diagonal composite columns; solid steel ingots (300 × 500 mm) were employed to absorb the high local tensions and milled on site. The floors in the cantilevered part of the building were hung from a steel girder grillage on the upper part of the framework em-

Library and Learning Center:
Stahlträgerrost im Bereich der Auskragung
Structural steel grillage in the cantilever area

Library and Learning Center:
Element des Hauptstahlfachwerkes
Element of the main steel frame

nem Stahlträgerrost abgehängt. Dieser wurde mit Zwillingsträgern ausgeführt, welche auf dem auskragenden Fachwerk aufgelegt wurden. Besondere Sorgfalt musste beim Einhängen der Hängestützen in die Zwillingsträger aufgewendet werden. Die Idee war, „eine sanfte Lasteinbringung der Hängestützen in die Zwillingsträger durch hydraulisches Aufpressen zu ermöglichen", erläutert Lothar Heinrich. Jeder Einhängepunkt wurde somit in der richtigen Reihenfolge in die errechnete Endzustandslage gebracht, mit Stahlplatten die Position fixiert und anschließend der Hängestützenkopf am Querträger befestigt.

Für die Umsetzung der ambitionierten Architektur waren spezifische Herausforderungen im Teamwork und Projektablauf zu bewältigen. Die exakte 3D-Vorgabe als Arbeitsgrundlage für das Team der Ausführungsplanung wurde vom Entwurfsteam zur Verfügung gestellt. Eine direkte, persönliche Kommunikation zwischen dem verantwortlichen Statiker und den Konstrukteuren wurde im Rahmen der Stahlbaudetailplanung eingeführt und als sehr erfolgreich befunden, um einen effizienten Planungsablauf zu garantieren. Gemeinsame Begriffsbestimmungen wie etwa der Unterschied zwischen Schräge und Neigung wurden definiert und festgelegt. Um spezielle Bereiche zu entwickeln und zu diskutieren (z. B. den Einhängepunkt der Stützen in den Zwillingsträgern), wurde mit physischen Modellen gearbeitet. Aufgrund der komplexen Geometrie wurden neue Plankonventionen verwendet, um z. B. in einem Schalungsplandokument verschiedene Schnittführungen durch unterschiedliche Farbko-

ploying twin girders. Special care was taken in mounting the suspension columns in the twin girders. The idea was "to facilitate a soft loading of the suspension columns in the twin girders through hydraulic pressure," says Lothar Heinrich. To this end, each mounting point was put in the right order in the calculated end position, fixed in position with steel plates, and then the head of the suspension column was attached to the cross girder.

In order to construct this ambitious piece of architecture, specific challenges in the teamwork and project structure had to be tackled. The exact 3D model was made available by the design team as a working basis for the construction planning team. In the steel construction detail planning phase direct personal communication between the responsible structural engineer and the builders was introduced as a measure and was found to be quite successful in order to guarantee an efficient flow in the planning. A shared understanding of terms – such as the difference between slant and tilt – was defined and set. Physical models were used to develop and discuss special areas (e.g. the mounting point of the columns on the twin girders). Given the complex geometry, new plan conventions were employed: for example, using various color codes in a formwork plan to indicate different cutting paths. The high standards of quality – also for the visible concrete – were set in advance with 1:1 pattern samples. There were also special challenges in the reinforcement configuration inside the concrete components, hence bolted connections were used to a large extent.

Library and Learning Center:
Stahlfachwerk im Bereich der Auskragung
Steel frame in the cantilever area

tierungen anzugeben. Die hohen Qualitätsvorgaben – auch an den Sichtbeton – wurden über 1:1-Musterabnahmen vorab festgelegt. Besondere Herausforderungen wurden ebenfalls an die Bewehrungsführung in den Betonbauteilen gestellt, daher wurde in hohem Masse auch mit Schraubverbindungen gearbeitet.

**Das Department 1 & Teaching Center von
BUSarchitektur (Entwurf) mit KPPK ZT GMBH (Statik)**
Das Wiener Büro BUSarchitektur entwarf den Masterplan für den Campus und konnte daher bei Entwurf und Realisierung des Hörsaalzentrums auch im Besonderen auf das Zusammenwirken von Außen- und Innenraum eingehen. Das Gebäude wurde als ein Teil der erlebbaren Landschaft entlang einer Sequenz öffentlicher Bereiche konzipiert.

Die Fluchtwegproblematik spielte aufgrund der hohen Nutzerfrequenz eine wichtige Rolle, auch aus diesem Grund sind die großen Hörsäle im unteren Bereich mit direktem Zugang nach außen situiert. Grundsätzlich ist das Teaching Center mit der Mensa und den Departments als Skelettbau mit aussteifenden Wandscheiben und Zirkulationskernen in Stahlbeton ausgeführt. Im Untergeschoss wurde der Stützenraster aufgrund der funktionellen Gegebenheiten teilweise über die Stahlbetondecke auf Wandscheiben umgelagert. Die notwendigen Fluchtstiegenhäuser wurden als Stahlkonstruktionen an den Gebäudekörper angelegt, teilweise wurde die perforierte Corten-Fassade hier fortgesetzt, um einen einheitlichen Gebäudekörper zu erreichen.

**The Department 1 & Teaching Center by
BUSarchitektur (design) with KPPK ZT GMBH (engineers)**
The Viennese architecture office BUSarchitektur was responsible for the design of the campus master plan. Hence, they could especially focus on the interplay between indoor and outdoor spaces in the design and realization of the Teaching Center. The building was conceived as a part of an experiential landscape along a procession of open spaces.

Due to the great number of users, emergency escape routes played an important role. For this reason, the large auditoriums were situated in the lower part of the building with direct access to the outside. In principle, the Teaching Center with the Mensa cafeteria and department offices was built as a frame construction with supporting walls and reinforced concrete circulation cores. Given the layout of the functions, the column grid in the basement was partially repositioned on wall segments above the reinforced concrete floor. The required emergency exit stairways were designed as steel constructions attached to the building volume; in certain areas the perforated Corton steel cladding is uninterrupted to give the building a uniform appearance. The public areas are designed as a meandering three-dimensional landscape, which offers various ways to discover the building at different speeds. One never has a complete overview of the building; the spatial arrangement only unfolds by using it.

The outdoor stairways were conceived as elements of the campus landscape that pervade into the building. The large vol-

Teaching Center:
Auskragendes Stiegenhaus als Stahlkonstruktion
Cantilevering steel stair construction

Der öffentliche Bereich ist wie eine mäandrierende, dreidimensionale Landschaft angelegt und bietet Wege an, um das Gebäude in verschiedenen Geschwindigkeiten zu entdecken. Man hat nie den ganzen Raum gleichzeitig im Blick, erst in der Nutzung entfaltet sich die Raumabfolge.

Die äußeren Treppenlandschaften, die auch als Fluchtwege angelegt sind, wurden als Bestandteil der Campuslandschaft konzipiert, die sich weiter ins Gebäude erweitern. Die großen Volumen der Hörsäle wurden in der Sockelzone auseinandergeschoben, um Sichtbeziehungen zu schaffen. Man entdeckt das Gebäude in Sequenzen, und die Konstruktion reagiert kompromisslos auf dieses Konzept, um Durchblicke und Durchwegungen zu schaffen. Die frei spannende Decke des größten Hörsaals im Erdgeschoss (Auditorium Maximum, Audimax) wird ermöglicht, indem ein „Betonbock" die darüberliegenden Geschosse abfängt. Diese Konstruktion stützt sich einerseits am Kern ab, andererseits durch schräge Doppelstützen in Stahlbeton entlang der freigespielten Glasfassade.

Die Stahlbetondecken sind für ein innenliegendes, an die Fassade anschließendes Glasstiegenhaus ausgeschnitten. An dieser Stelle ist die brandabschnittsbildende Verglasung über mehrere Geschosse durchgezogen. Um dies zu ermöglichen und die Durchbiegung zu minimieren, sind die Ränder der Betondecken mit einbetonierten I-Profilen versteift. Die Läufe der Stahlstie-

umes of the auditoriums are interspersed in the plinth to create multifarious visual relationships. One discovers the building in sequences, and the construction responds to this concept without compromise, creating different vistas and passageways. The free-standing roof of the largest auditorium on the ground floor (Auditorium Maximum, Audimax) was built as a concrete "trestle", which carries the load from the floors above. This construction, in turn, is supported by the building's core and by diagonal reinforced concrete double columns along the unobstructed glass façade.

The concrete floors were cut out to accommodate an inner glass-lined staircase that connects to the façade. Here the fire compartment glazing is continuous over numerous storeys. To this end, the edges of the concrete floor are stiffened with embedded I-profiles, which also minimizes deflection. The elegantly constructed steel stairways and landings were designed to freely project out of the respective floor without any form of vertical support. This effect underscores the visual separation of the large volumes, which can also be read on the façades.

Structural elements and constructions were strategically used in order to create voids in the architecture in keeping with the open space design. This can especially be seen on the cantilevered eastern corner of the building, which facilitates views along the main circulation axis of the campus.

genkonstruktion sind gemeinsam mit dem Podest pro Geschoss aus der jeweiligen Geschossdecke frei auskragend konzipiert, und hier ohne vertikale Unterstützung in jeder Hinsicht elegant ausgeführt. Dieser Effekt unterstützt die visuelle Trennung der großen Volumina, die sich auch auf der Fassade abzeichnet.

Statische Elemente und Konstruktionen wurden bewusst eingesetzt, um auf die Freiraumplanung abgestimmte Freistellungen in der Gebäudetektonik zu ermöglichen. Dies wird im Speziellen am ostseitig frei auskragenden Gebäudeeck sichtbar, dadurch wurden Durchblicke entlang der Hauptzirkulationsachse des Campus geschaffen.

Die Executive Academy von NO.MAD Arquitectos (Entwurf) mit Vasko+Partner (Statik)

Das Gebäude ist als „Schachtel" mit drei aussteifenden Kernen konzipiert. Die verschiedenen Auskragungen wurden durch teils ineinander verschachtelte Wandscheiben bewerkstelligt. Die dichte Bewehrungsführung erforderte den Einsatz von selbstverdichtendem Beton, wodurch erst der hohe Perforationsgrad für Fensteröffnungen ermöglicht wurde. Aufgrund der hohen Belastung im Bauzustand wurden für das Betonieren der Wandscheiben temporäre Stahlbetonstützen eingezogen, die nach der Fertigstellung der Konstruktion entfernt wurden.

Das Institutsgebäude von Carme Pinós (Entwurf) mit Vasko+Partner (Statik)

Es wurde eine Stahlbetonkonstruktion mit punktgestützten Flachdecken ausgeführt. Ein besonderes architektonisches Merkmal ist die aus verschobenen vertikalen Glasbändern bestehende Fassade, im konstruktiven Fassadenraster wurden Füllelemente mit ausgesparten Fensteröffnungen eingesetzt. Die davor liegende Fassadenkonstruktion betont die geschossübergreifenden Fensterbänder.

Institutsgebäude und Student Center von Hitoshi Abe (Entwurf) mit Vasko+Partner (Statik)

Das Bauwerk wurde in Stahlbeton mit Flachdecken und Punktstützen geplant. Die Aussteifung erfolgt über Stahlbetonkerne und einzelne Wandscheiben, dadurch konnte eine größtmögliche Flexibilität in der architektonischen Fassadengestaltung gewahrt bleiben. Funktionell notwendige größere Spannweiten wie im Bereich des Sportsaals wurden über 1,50 m hohe Querträger erreicht. Um auch einen freien Durchblick und eine architektonische Sichtbeziehung zum öffentlichen Bereich zu ermöglichen, wurden diese Träger im Fassadenbereich durch einen Längsträger abgefangen und seitlich umgelagert.

Instituts- und Verwaltungsgebäude von CRAB studio (Entwurf) mit Vasko+Partner (Statik)

Das Stahlbetontragwerk, inklusive der dominanten Rundungen, wurde in Ortbetonbauweise hergestellt. Die Ästhetik wird geprägt durch die vorgesetzten Lamellen aus naturbelassenem Lärchenholz, welche am Gebäude mittels kreuzförmigen Stahlkonsolen befestigt sind.

The Executive Academy by NO.MAD Arquitectos (design) with Vasko+Partner (engineers)

The building is conceived of as a "cube" with three reinforcing cores. The different cantilevers are achieved through partially interlocking wall panels. The dense reinforcement required the use of self-compacting concrete, a measure that also facilitates the numerous perforations in the building shell for windows. Due to the high level of load distribution during the construction process, provisional reinforced concrete columns were inserted for the pouring of the concrete walls and then removed upon completion of construction.

The Department Building by Carme Pinós (design) with Vasko+Partner (engineers)

The Department Building is a reinforced concrete construction with point-supported flat slabs. A special architectural feature is the shifted vertical glass strips on the façades. Infill elements with recessed window openings were placed in the construction of the façade grid. The covering façade construction emphasizes the multi-storey strips of windows.

The Department Building and Student Center by Hitoshi Abe (design) with Vasko+Partner (engineers)

The building was also designed as a reinforced concrete structure with point-supported flat slabs. Reinforcement is provided by the concrete cores and individual walls, ensuring the highest level of flexibility in the architectural design of the façades. Broader spans informed by functional requirements – in the area of the sports hall, for example – were achieved through 1.50-meter-thick cross members. In order to create free vistas and an architectural-visual connection with the public space, these girders are supported by a longitudinal beam integrated in the façade.

The Department and Administration Building by CRAB studio (design) with Vasko+Partner (engineers)

The reinforced steel structure, including all its prominent curves, was built with in-situ concrete. Untreated silver fir slats mounted to the façade via steel cruciform brackets give the building its unique aesthetic.

Teaching Center:
Freigespielte Gebäudekörper entlang der Hauptfassade
Dispersed building volumes in the plinth area

D2 SC

ATELIER HITOSHI ABE: DEPARTMENTS 2 / STUDENT CENTER

DEPARTMENTS 2 / STUDENT CENTER

SCHICHTEN UND FÜLLUNGEN
DAS DEPARTMENTGEBÄUDE UND STUDENT CENTER VON ATELIER HITOSHI ABE

LAYERS AND FILLING
THE DEPARTMENTS AND STUDENT CENTER BY ATELIER HITOSHI ABE

MATTHIAS BOECKL

DEPARTMENTS 2 / STUDENT CENTER

Ein schlankes Haus, das sich in mehreren Schichten entfaltet und in sanften Schwüngen über eine beträchtliche Länge erstreckt. Ein Haus, das Wege und Plätze zu seinem Hauptthema macht. Ein Haus, das dem Campus höchst kontemplative Innen- und Außenräume hinzufügt. Ein fernöstlicher Ausgleich der Gegensätze. Hart und weich, öffentlich und nichtöffentlich, schwarz und weiß verbinden sich darin zu einer Synthese.

Programm und Masterplan

Masterplan und Raumprogramm des neuen Campus der Wirtschaftsuniversität sahen für das südöstlichste Baufeld eine Vielfalt verschiedenster Funktionen vor. In urbanistischer Hinsicht sollte hier die sensible Grenz- und Übergangssituation zwischen Campusgelände und den unmittelbar angrenzenden weiten Grünflächen des Praters formuliert werden. Und funktional gab es mit öffentlichen, halböffentlichen und nicht öffentlichen Räumen ein heterogenes Spektrum zu bedienen, bei dem die in sich ruhenden Bürobereiche mehrerer akademischer Abteilungen quantitativ dominieren.

Die öffentlichen Funktionen sind besonders relevant für das Leben am Campus und liefern hier beachtliche Basis-Frequenz: Ein Student Center bietet Raum für alle studentischen Einrichtungen der Universität, vor allem Beratungsstellen der Hochschülerschaft, und für drei Sporthallen, die von einem interuniversitären Institut betrieben werden. Ein Lebensmittelmarkt versorgt nicht nur die Uniangehörigen, sondern auch Bewohner der Stadtquartiere rund um den Campus. Der Kindergarten verkörpert schon in seiner Aufgabe das Leben an sich. Auch ein beliebtes Café sorgt für lebensnahe Momente. Die Buchhandlung „Management Book Service" bietet wissenschaftliche Medien zum Kauf an und eine akademische Fachbibliothek stellt die Lektüre kostenlos zur Verfügung.

A slender house unfolding in several layers and stretching a considerable length in gentle waves. A house that declares paths and plazas its central motif. A house that complements the campus with highly contemplative inner and outer spaces. A Far Eastern balance of contrasts: hard and soft, public and non-public, black and white unite in a synthesis.

Program and Master Plan

The master plan and spatial program specified a variety of different functions for the building plot on the southeastern edge of the new campus for the University of Business and Economics. From an urbanistic perspective, the sensitive border and transition situation between campus terrain and the immediately adjacent, green expanse of Prater park was to be formulated on this site. On the functional level, public, semi-public, and non-public spaces should serve a heterogeneous spectrum with the reposed office areas of several academic departments dominating quantitatively.

The public functions are especially important for life on campus and are continually frequented: A Student Center accommodates a range of student-related facilities – above all, the coun-

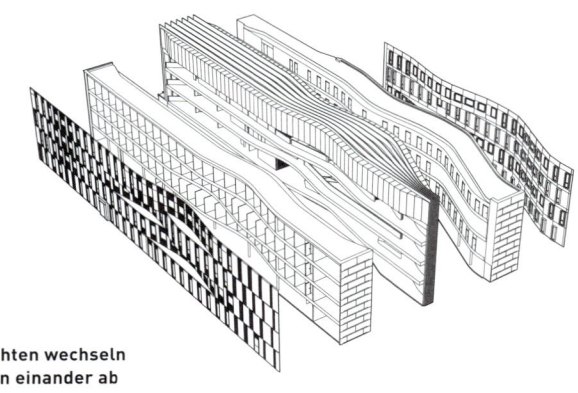

In Wellenbewegungen wird der Übergang ins Wald- und Wiesengebiet des Praters formuliert
Transition of the campus to the Prater park in softly ondulating waves

Millefeuille-Konzept: In fünf Schichten wechseln Fassade, Büros und zentrale Atrien einander ab
Millefeuille concept: five spatial layers of façades, offices, and central atriums

DEPARTMENTS 2 / STUDENT CENTER

S 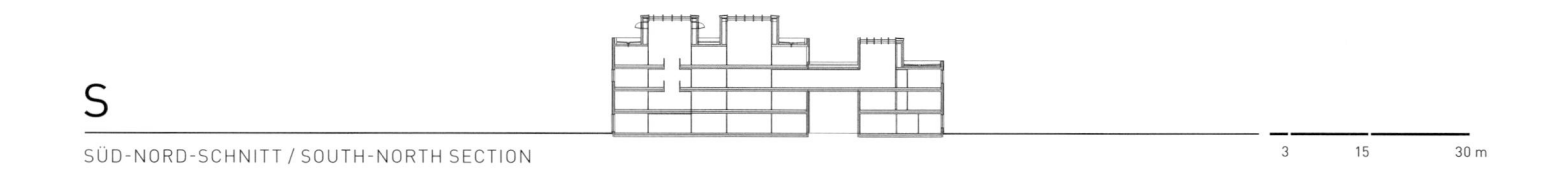
SÜD-NORD-SCHNITT / SOUTH-NORTH SECTION

3　15　30 m

S 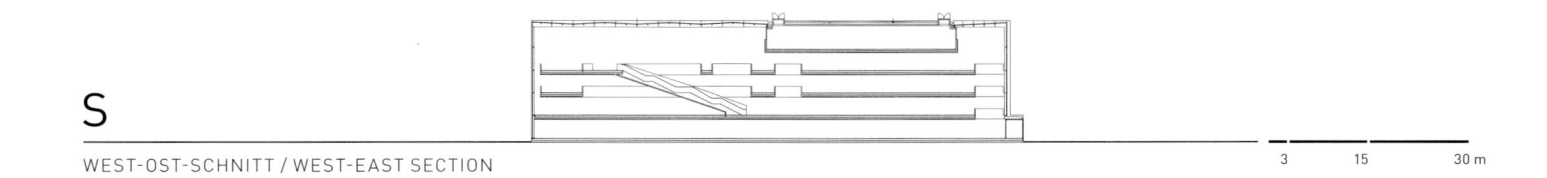
WEST-OST-SCHNITT / WEST-EAST SECTION

3　15　30 m

DP 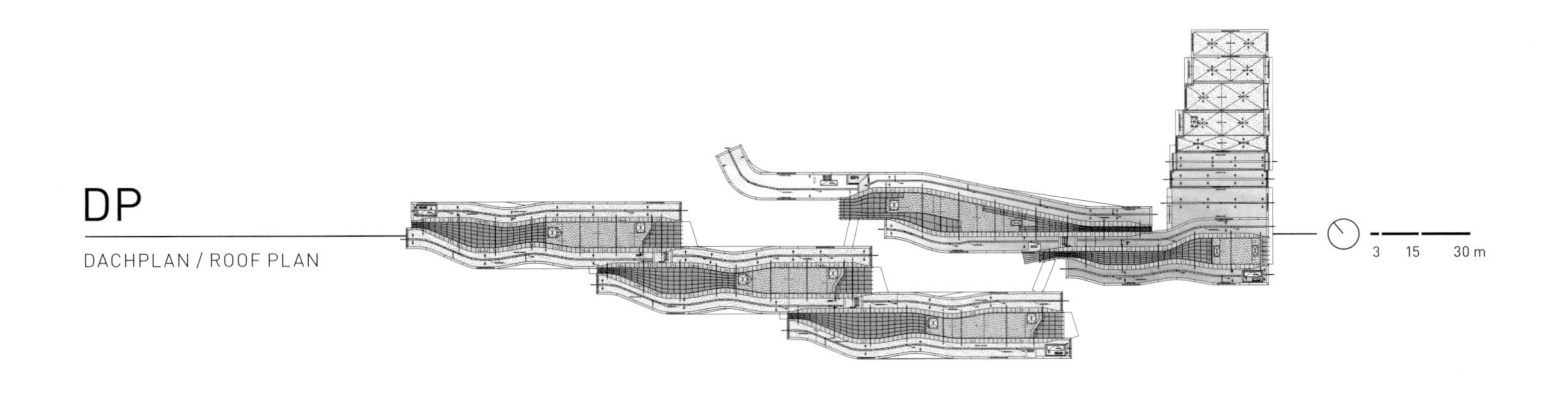
DACHPLAN / ROOF PLAN

3　15　30 m

EG 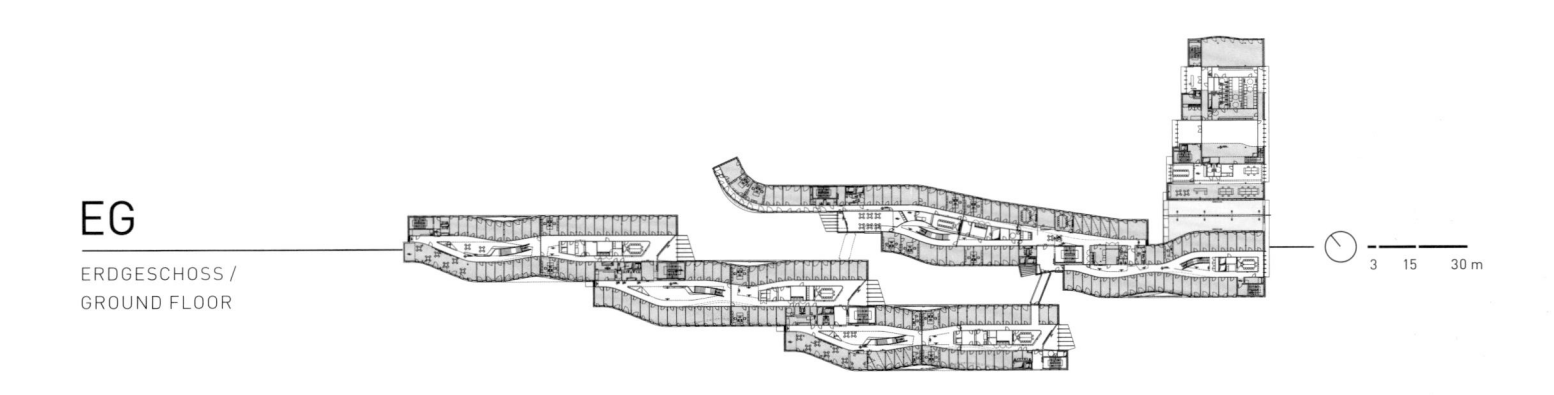
ERDGESCHOSS /
GROUND FLOOR

3　15　30 m

Die beiden langgezogenen Trakte sind auf Höhe des ersten und zweiten Obergeschosses mittels Skybridges verbunden
The two parallel wings of the complex are connected via skybridges on the first and second floors

Neben den stark frequentierten Seminarräumen und Hörsälen einer Universität gibt es in Hochschulen auch die wichtigen Bereiche der Forschung und konzentrierten Arbeit in Kleingruppen. Im Feld der Wirtschaftswissenschaften erfordert dieser Kernbereich akademischer Produktion keine hochgerüsteten Labors oder Maschinenhallen, sondern vor allem Büros und Besprechungsräume, in denen Wissenschaftler und ihre Mitarbeiter relativ abgeschirmt vom Studienbetrieb ihre Projekte bearbeiten können. Für eine ambitionierte Planung ist dieser Bereich eine besondere Herausforderung – relativ konventionelle Büroeinheiten sollen auf der Höhe räumlicher und ästhetischer Möglichkeiten in einem lebenswerten Ambiente mit Lounges und anderen Begegnungszonen organisiert werden.

seling services of the Austrian Students' Union – and three sports halls run by an inter-university institute. A supermarket caters to members of the university but also to residents of the neighboring city quarters as well. The kindergarten, already in its assignment, is a manifestation of life itself. Also the café is a popular place for lively moments. The bookstore "Management Book Service" has scientific media for sale while an academic specialist library provides reading material free of charge.

Apart from bustling seminar rooms and auditoriums, a university also comprises important areas for research and focused work in small groups. In the field of economic sciences, however, this central realm of academic production does not require high-end laboratories or machine halls; foremost it is offices and

Das Student Center am Ostrand des Campus: Hier liegen soziale Zentren wie der Kindergarten und die Sporthallen
The Student Center at the eastern edge of the campus with social centers such as the kindergarten and gyms

An der Innenseite bilden sich Stadtplatz-Situationen, rechts die Trakte für Departments, hinten das Student Center
Inner side with urban square-like situations, departments in the wings to the right, Student Center in background

Wege und Räume

Die Architekten interpretierten den Bauplatz mit einer L-förmigen Anlage, in der ein kurzer hoher Trakt das Student Center birgt und die Auftakt-Situation am Ostrand des Campus schafft. Im rechten Winkel dazu wurden zwei langgezogene Paralleltrakte positioniert, von denen einer in zwei, der andere in drei parallele und gestaffelte Scheiben unterteilt wurde. Die Planer berichten von der Entwurfs-Herausforderung: „Das Ziel dieser programmatisch komplexen akademischen Anlage war es, eine klare organisatorische Strategie zu entwickeln, die maximale Flexibilität bietet, Interaktion zwischen den verschiedenen akademischen Abteilungen stimuliert und einen hohen Grad an Durchlässigkeit am Bauplatz schafft. Um dies zu erreichen, wurde eine Reihe schlanker, einander überlappender Baukörper an der Längsseite des Baufeldes positioniert." Damit diese langen Trakte den Campus nicht vom angrenzenden grünen Prater abschotten, wurden zwei Querdurchgänge geschaffen – einer durchsticht als Korridor den inneren der beiden Längstrakte, während der andere im Zickzack-Kurs durch den Freiraum zwischen den beiden Trakten führt. Auf der Höhe des ersten und des zweiten Obergeschosses sind diese per Skybridges mit-

meeting rooms where scientists and their teams can work on their projects in relative seclusion from other campus activities. Hence, this area poses a special challenge for an ambitious design – state-of-the-art spatial and aesthetic solutions must embed relatively conventional office units in a livable ambience with lounges and other zones for social encounters.

Paths and Plazas

The architects interpreted the building site in the form of an L-shaped complex with a short, high volume that houses the Student Center and creates a prelude scenario on the eastern edge of the campus. Two parallel tracts stretch out at a right angle from this volume, one divided into two, the other into three parallel and staggered slabs. The planners report on the design challenge: "The goal for this programmatically complex academic facility was to develop a clear organizational strategy that would maximize flexibility, promote interaction between the various academic departments and allow for a high degree of permeability across the site. In order to accomplish this, a series of slender overlapping volumes were arranged along the length of the site."

einander verbunden. Der Raum zwischen den Häusern mit ihrer schwarz-weiß-Wellenfassade bildet kleine Stadtplätze, die in ihrem unregelmäßigen Zuschnitt an historische Innenstadtsituationen erinnern und einen anderen Charakter besitzen als die übrigen Plätze am Campus: Dieser ruhige Studienbezirk verströmt eine fast fernöstlich anmutende Kontemplation.

Sanfte Rhythmen
Während quer verlaufende Kraftlinien des Campus die langgestreckten Baukörper von simplen Quadern zu ondulierenden Fassadenschwüngen verformen, entfalten die Innenräume anschaulich Hitoshi Abes „Millefeuille"-Konzept. Er benützt das Bild der französischen Süßspeise, weil deren Blätterteig-Schichten im Inneren eine Füllung und oft auch eine Frucht bergen. So ist auch das Haus aufgebaut. Auf die gewellte äußere Fassadenschicht folgt eine Lage mit Büroräumen, ganz innen liegt die „Füllung" gebäudehoher, großzügiger Atrien, die mit sanft geschwungenen Treppen und Laubengängen die einzelnen Bürogeschosse erschließen. An die zentralen Atrien sind die Frontdesks der Institute und Lounges mit Teeküchen und Sitzecken angelagert, gegen die Enden der langgestreckten Trakte hin verjüngen sie sich zu Kernzonen, die Serviceräume und kleine verglaste Sitzungssäle bergen. Eine weitere Schicht Büroräume und die Rückfassade spiegeln das System entlang der Mittelachse.

Two lateral passageways were designed to prevent these long tracts from sealing off the adjacent green Prater park – one punctures through the tracts as a corridor while the other traces a jagged path along the open space between them. Sky bridges connect the first and second storeys. The space between the buildings with their black-and-white wave-like façades forms little city squares. The irregular layouts of these plazas are reminiscent of situations in old city centers and thereby take on a different character than the other squares on campus: This quiet study district almost exudes an air of Far Eastern contemplation.

Gentle Rhythms
While the criss-crossing movement lines of the campus transform the elongated building volumes from simple cuboids into undulating façade patterns, the interior is a vivid demonstration of Hitoshi Abe's "millefeuille" concept. He employs the image of the French pastry as their flakey layers alternate with a filling and often fruit inside. The construction of the house follows this metaphor: The wavy outer shell coats a layer of office spaces; at the center is the "filling" – generous, building-height atriums with gently curving stairways and arcades that provide access to the individual office floors. The front desks of the institutes and lounges with tea kitchens and sitting areas surround the atriums; the long tracts taper at their ends to form hubs with service

Bibliothek und Erschließungszonen sind in asketischem Schwarz-Weiß-Kontrast gehalten
Library and circulation zones in strict black-and-white contrast

Die Wellenbewegung der Fassaden setzt sich im Inneren an Decken und Böden fort
The wave movements of the façade are continued inside on the ceilings and floors

Im Kern der Department-Trakte liegen mehrere gebäudehohe Atrien mit spektakulären Kaskadentreppen
Spectacular cascading stairways in the building-high atriums of the deparment wings

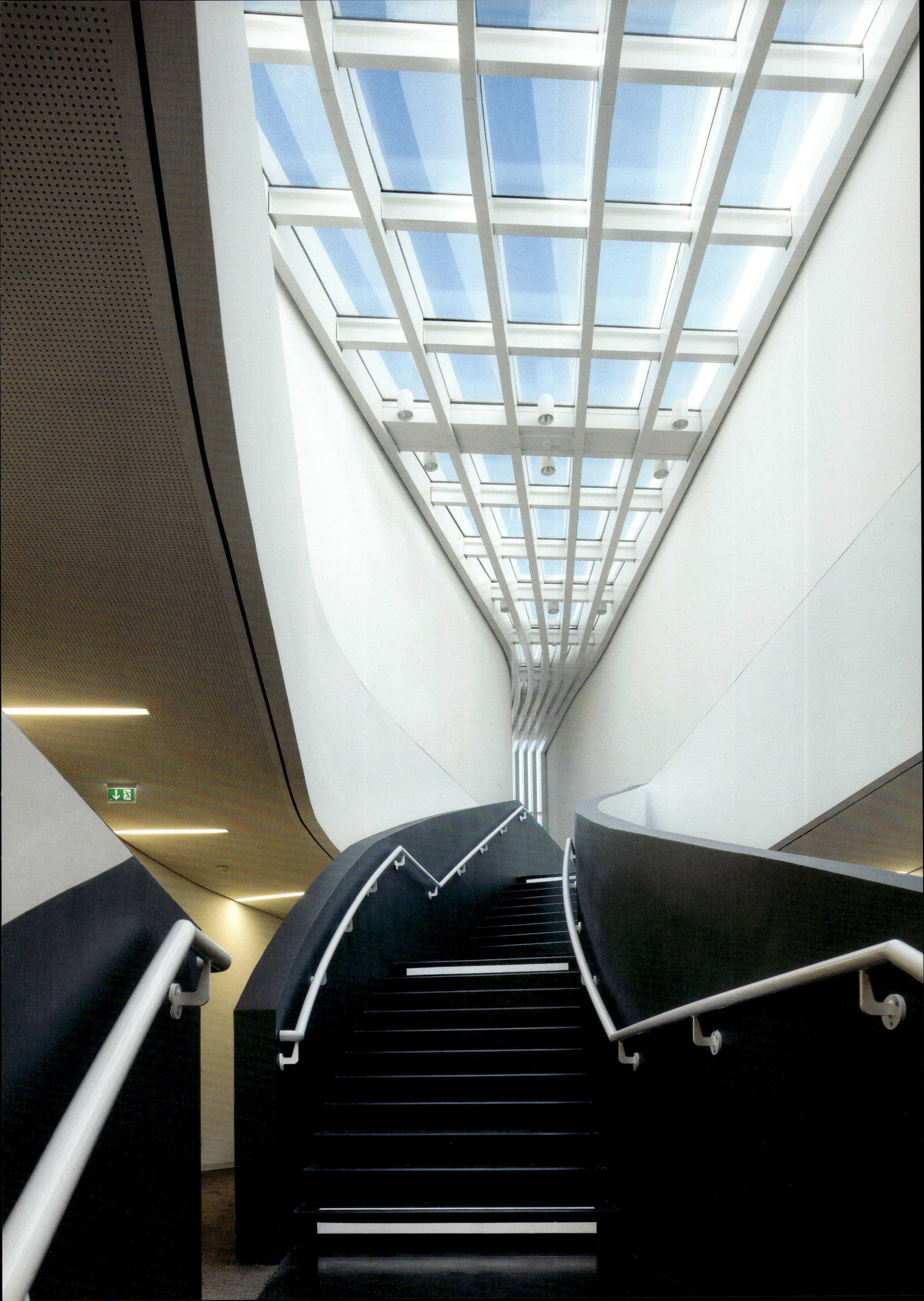

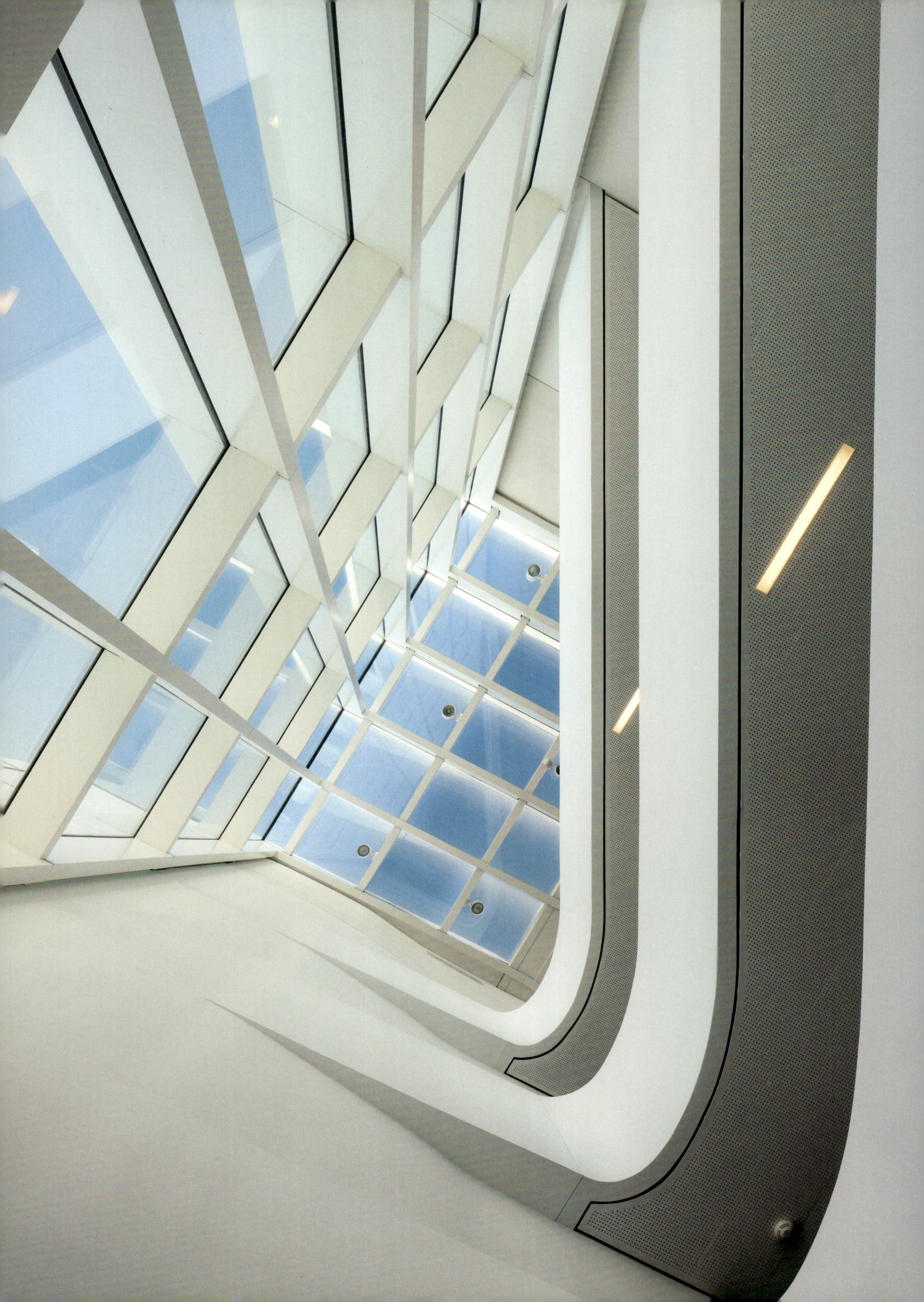

Das Thema des Natur-Deckenlichts im Gebäudekern beschränkt sich aber nicht auf die Atrien. Auch die kurzen Fassaden der fünf langen Teiltrakte sind mit vertikalen Glasstreifen versehen, die über die Oberkante ein Stück weit auf das Flachdach gezogen und mit Lamellen gegliedert sind. So stellt sich ein angenehmer Belichtungs- und Wiedererkennungsrhythmus ein: Man betritt das Haus an der Stirnseite, wo der gebäudehohe Luftraum über dem Eingang Tageslicht in die Kernzone bringt. Dann passiert man einen der beiden kurzen, künstlich belichteten Flure links oder rechts des Servicekerns, um gleich darauf das lichtdurchflutete zentrale Atrium mit seinen fließenden Raumkaskaden zu bestaunen. Links und rechts begleiten Büroräume mit Lochfenstern den Weg. Am anderen Ende wiederholt sich diese Abfolge umgekehrt, sodass die Schichtenstruktur auch in Längsrichtung erlebbar wird.

Die Farben-, Formen- und Materialsprache verströmt klare Gelassenheit: Außen und innen ist alles in Schwarz-Weiß-Kontrasten gehalten, von den Fassadenpaneelen über die Teppichböden bis zu Wand- und Deckenfarben. Auch die großzügigen Lounges im Kern ordnen sich diesem Raster ein, der von sanft geschwungenen Fluchten und Kanten angenehm gebrochen wird. Gelbe und rote Sitzmöbel setzen stark wirksame Farbakzente in die abstrakte Komposition.

zones and small glazed conference rooms. Another layer of offices and the back façade mirror the system along its central axis.

The presence of natural light from above, however, is not restricted to the atriums at the core. Also the short end façades of the five tract segments are furnished with vertical glass strips that protrude a bit above the upper edge onto the flat roof and are structured with louvers. This creates a pleasant and recurring rhythm of light: One enters the building on this glass front face, where the building-high airspace above provides daylight for the entrance area. Then one proceeds down one of the two artificially lit corridors to the left or right of the service zone only to marvel but a moment thereafter at the light flooded central atrium with its fluid spatial cascades. Offices with window holes accompany the path on the respective outer side. This succession is repeated at the other end in reverse, providing an experience of this layer structure in the longitudinal direction as well.

The vocabulary of colors, forms, and materials radiates pure serenity: Inside and outside are kept in black and white contrasts, from the façade panels and carpet floors to the colors of walls and ceilings. Also the generous lounges in the center comply with this grid, which is pleasantly interrupted by the gently curved corridors and edges. Yellow and red seating elements add a highly effective color accent to the abstract composition.

Verglaste, gebäudehohe Eingangshallen bilden die Stirnseiten der Längstrakte
Glazed entrance halls at the narrow sides of the long wings
<

Sporthalle im Student Center
Gym in the Student Center
>

Nüchterne Seminarräume öffnen sich zum Prater-Wald
Sober seminar rooms with a view to the Prater park
v

Jedes Einzelbüro verfügt über eine großzügige Fensteröffnung
Each single office has a generous window aperture
v >

STATEMENTS

MAN KANN HIER LEBEN, NICHT NUR LERNEN
STUDIEREN AM WU CAMPUS

ROBERT TEMEL

Die Rezensionen sind hymnisch, die professionellen Stichwortgeber sind euphorisch – in der Fachwelt, vor allem aber in der architekturinteressierten Öffentlichkeit kommt der neue Campus der Wiener Wirtschaftsuniversität gut an. Wie erfolgreich ist die neue Wiener Architekturikone aber im Praxistest? Immerhin war eines der zentralen Argumente für den Umzug in den Wiener Prater, dass die alte WU am Alsergrund zwar erst vor 30 Jahren bezogen worden war, aber für nur 9.000 Studierende ausgelegt wurde. Derzeit besitzt die WU jedoch 24.000 Studierende – und der Campus kann noch mehr aufnehmen. Wie sehen nun also die Studierenden ihre neuen Universitätsgebäude?

HERE YOU CAN LIVE, NOT JUST LEARN
STUDENTS ON THE WU CAMPUS

The reviews are ecstatic, the professional opinion-makers are euphoric – in the specialist world but above all among a public with an interest in architecture, the new campus of Vienna University of Economics and Business is very well received. But how successful is the new Viennese architectural icon in practice? After all, one of the main arguments for the move to the location in the Prater park was that the old WU in the 9th district, even though it was only in use for 30 years, was designed for just 9,000 students. Presently, there are 24,000 students enrolled at the WU – and the campus can accommodate even more. What are the students' opinions of their new university buildings?

STUDIERENDE / STUDENTS — STATEMENTS

FREIRAUMQUALITÄT UND RAUMSCHIFF-FEELING
OPEN SPACE QUALITY AND A SPACESHIP FEELING

HANG
Student

Zunächst bitte ich Hang, der Betriebswirtschaftslehre studiert, um Auskunft. Er kannte schon die alte WU über mehrere Jahre, außerdem arbeitet er im neuen Infopoint am Campus, der Erstanlaufstelle für alle Wissbegierigen, er kennt sich somit aus. Er findet den neuen Campus motivierend – alles sei neu und modern. Zwar hatte auch die alte WU ihre guten Seiten, aber sie sei viel weitläufiger gewesen, man hätte lange Wege zurücklegen müssen. Demgegenüber sei der neue Campus praktisch, alles liege in kurzer Gehdistanz. Die neue Anlage sei strukturierter und kleinteiliger, so gebe es jetzt neben dem großen Bibliothekszentrum auch drei kleinere Bibliotheken an anderen Orten. Der eindrucksvollste Vorteil sei jedoch die Nähe zum Prater, wo man im Grünen spazieren gehen könne. Und auch direkt am Campus bieten die großzügig gestalteten Freiräume viel Gelegenheit zum ungezwungenen Sitzen und Pause-Machen. Dem gegenüber sei die Pausen-Nutzbarkeit der grandiosen Innenräume in Hadids Learning Center ein wenig zu kurz gekommen.

Doch es sei nicht nur so, dass die neue WU von ihrem Umfeld profitiere, sondern vielmehr hätte dieser Neubau neues Interesse und neue Chancen für den Stadtteil mit sich gebracht. Derzeit werde der Campus nicht nur von Studierenden und Lehrenden, sondern auch von einer Vielzahl Interessierter besucht, die sich die neue Architektur ansehen, die moduliert geformten Freiflächen zum Skateboarden nützen und die vielen Cafés und Lokale am Campus frequentieren. Die neue WU sei ja auch „superpraktisch" mit der U-Bahn erreichbar. Dass der neue Campus aus so vielfältiger Architektur bestehe, sei ein Vorteil, die Anlage sei nicht langweilig. Jedes Mal, wenn man in ein anderes

To start with, I ask Hang, who is studying business management, for information. He was already familiar with the old WU for several years. Moreover, he works at the info point on campus, the first place to go for all those eager to know more, so he knows what he is talking about. He finds the new campus inspiring – everything is new and modern. The old WU did have its good sides, but it was much vaster and one had to overcome long distances. In contrast, the new campus is practical; everything is just around the corner. He says that the new complex is better structured and smaller scaled: for example, now there is the main library and three other libraries in other places. The most impressive advantage is the proximity to Prater, where you can go for a walk in the park. And directly on campus generously designed open spaces offer numerous opportunities to casually sit around and take a break. Having said that, the extravagant interiors in Hadid's Learning Center lack a bit in this respect.

But not only the new WU profits from its surroundings; the new buildings, in turn, stimulate new interest and new chances for the district. At the moment, the campus is not only used by its students and teachers; it is also visited by numerous enthusiasts who come to see the new architecture, use the modulated forms of the public spaces for skateboarding, or frequent the many cafés and bars on campus. After all, the new WU can be reached "super easily" with the subway. The fact that the campus consists of such multifaceted architecture is an advantage; the complex is anything but boring. Each time you go into another building, it is again totally different. Some visitors are a

STUDIERENDE / STUDENTS — STATEMENTS

Gebäude gehe, sei wieder alles anders. Manche Besucher seien etwas verwundert, dass eine Wirtschaftsuniversität so aussehe – aber er möge Überraschungen, es sei gut, wenn nicht alles traditionell bleibe, sonst gebe es keine Kreativität mehr!

Von den neuen Gebäuden findet er jedes wichtig – aber das wichtigste ist wohl das Library and Learning Center im Zentrum des Campus, in dem er auch arbeitet: Das sei sehr modern, schön und dynamisch. Er würde es mögen, hier in Ruhe in der Bibliothek zu lernen. Wenn man dieses Gebäude das erste Mal betrete, könne man kaum fassen, dass es sich um eine Universität handelt, es wirke eher wie ein Raumschiff. Viele fragen sich: Warum ist das alles so schief? Obwohl es dazu manchmal auch negative Meinungen gebe, sei das meiste Feedback positiv – viele Ältere meinten, das Gebäude würde auch ihnen „Lust zum Lernen" machen. Für seine Tätigkeit im Infopoint sei es aber manchmal nicht so leicht, in dem dynamisch konfigurierten Gebäude die richtige Richtung anzugeben: Was genau könnte hier mit „immer geradeaus" wohl gemeint sein?

Anfangs etwas gewöhnungsbedürftig sei für ihn das Teaching Center mit seiner rostigen Fassade gewesen. Vor allem am Abend finde er es aber mittlerweile sehr schön. Auch zu diesem Gebäude würde es sowohl positive als auch negative Sichtweisen von Besuchern geben. Und schließlich gebe es noch ein drittes einzigartiges Gebäude am Campus, und zwar das Administrationsgebäude mit der farbenfrohen Fassade und den Holztafeln vor den Fenstern, das von manchen Studierenden „IKEA-Kindergarten" genannt werde. Er persönlich verstehe zwar nicht, welche Funktion diese Tafeln hätten – aber sie seien praktisch zum Unterstellen, wenn es regnet.

> Wenn man dieses Gebäude das erste Mal betritt, kann man kaum fassen, dass es sich um eine Universität handelt, es wirkt eher wie ein Raumschiff.

> When you enter the building for the first time, it is hard to believe that it is a university – it seems more like a spaceship.

bit surprised that a university of economics can look like this – but he likes surprises, it is good thing when everything doesn't stick to traditions, otherwise there wouldn't be any room for creativity!

He finds each of the new buildings important – but the most outstanding one is definitely the Library and Learning Center at the heart of the campus where he also works: It is very modern, attractive, and dynamic. He likes to study in the library in peace. When you enter the building for the first time, it is hard to believe that it is a university – it seems more like a spaceship. Many people wonder: Why is everything so slanted? Although there are sometimes negative opinions on the topic, most of the feedback is positive. Many older people say that the building also makes them "thirsty to learn". In his job at the info point, however, it is often not so easy to give proper directions in the dynamically configured building: What exactly do you mean, "keep going straight ahead"?

The Teaching Center with its rusty façade took a bit of getting used to in the beginning for him. In the meanwhile, he finds it very beautiful, especially in the evening. Also this building is perceived both positively and negatively by visitors. And there is still a third unusual building on campus, namely the Department and Administration Building with its colorful façade and wood slats in front of the windows – which some students refer to as the "IKEA Kindergarten". He personally doesn't understand the function that these wood slats should have – but they are useful to hide under when it rains.

WIE IN EINEM THRILLER
LIKE IN A THRILLER

Meine zweite Gesprächspartnerin ist Karine, die Betriebswirtschaftslehre studiert und gerade nach einem Sommeraufenthalt am Campus der UCLA nach Wien zurückgekehrt ist. Im September 2013 herrschte an der neuen WU noch der „Wahnsinn", es sei laut gewesen und alle waren gestresst. Im Oktober war plötzlich alles fertig, und es kehrte etwas Ruhe ein. Während der amerikanische Campus alt und klassisch gewesen sei, „wie in Italien", hätte man hier das Gefühl, in einen aufregenden Film geraten zu sein. Vor der alten WU, die sie nur wenig kenne, hätte sie Angst gehabt: Dort sei alles tief und dunkel gewesen, hier sei es hell und freundlich. Sie hätte schon von einigen Leuten gehört,

My second discussion partner is Karine, who studies business management and has just returned to Vienna following a summer semester on the campus of the UCLA. In September 2013 "chaos" still reigned free at the new WU; it was loud and everyone was stressed out. In October suddenly everything was finished and then a bit of silence set it. While the American campus was old and classical – "like in Italy" – here it was as if you had fallen into an exciting film. She was afraid of the old WU, which she only knew a little: It was so dark and abyssal there; here everything is bright and friendly. She has also heard of a few people who would consider switching to the WU just to be able

STUDIERENDE / STUDENTS — STATEMENTS

KARINE
Studentin Student

> Die Lage ist großartig, man kann draußen liegen, essen, Sonne tanken. Am schönsten ist es mittags vor dem Learning Center in der Sonne, sogar im Winter.

> The location is perfect: You can lie outdoors, eat, soak up some sun. The best thing is to be in front of the Learning Center around midday in the sun, even in winter.

die überlegen würden, zum Studium an die WU zu wechseln, nur um in diesem neuen, coolen Campus lernen zu können. Sie finde es toll, dass die Gebäude verteilt sind und man sich deshalb hier mehr bewegen müsse. Die Lage sei großartig, man könne draußen liegen, essen, Sonne tanken. Am schönsten sei es mittags vor dem Learning Center in der Sonne, sogar im Winter. Es gebe genügend Sitzgelegenheiten im Freien, und auch drinnen, im Teaching Center, gebe es viel Platz zum Sitzen, auch außerhalb der Mensa. Wenn sie hierher komme zum Lernen, dann nicht nur für bloß zwei Stunden, wie das davor der Fall war, sondern sie bleibe von früh bis spät, den ganzen Tag. Was draußen fehlt, seien aber Fahrradabstellplätze.

Ihr Favorit am Campus sei das Teaching Center, einfach optimal für Studierende: Wenn man hineingehe, sehe man Leute sitzen, es gebe ein Café, die Farben seien hell und bunt, das Ganze wirke nicht wie ein Büro- oder Universitätsgebäude. Hier finde das Leben statt – es gebe Austausch, die Studierenden würden hier lernen, essen, diskutieren, es gebe großzügige Lernflächen, es sei nicht laut, und im Unterschied zur Bibliothek müsse man nichts vorher abgeben, um sich hier aufhalten zu können. Von außen wirke das Teaching Center zwar modern, aber andererseits auch so, als stehe es schon viele Jahre und sei langsam verrostet. Wenn im Sommer die Gitterbleche vor den Fenstern aufgeklappt würden, dann wirke das, als habe das Gebäude Landeklappen wie ein Flugzeug und würde gerade zur Landung ansetzen. Und: Die Aussicht im fünften Stock über ganz Wien sei phänomenal! Von außen sei das Learning Center ihr Liebling, es sei einfach großartig. Allerdings sei es, abgesehen

to study on this new, cool campus. She finds it nice that the buildings are spread across the campus so you have to move around more. The location is perfect: You can lie outdoors, eat, soak up some sun. The best thing is to be in front of the Learning Center around midday in the sun, even in winter. There are more than enough sitting places out in the open, and also in the Teaching Center are lots of places to sit, and not only in the cafeteria. When she comes here to study, then not just for a couple of hours as was previously the case – no, she stays from early till late, the entire day. However, what is lacking outside are bike parking areas.

Her favorite building on campus is the Teaching Center, simply ideal for students: When you go in you see people sitting; there is a café; the colors are bright and friendly; the overall impression is not of an office or university building. There is life going on: It is a place to socialize; students are here to learn, eat, discuss; there are generous study spaces; it is not loud. And in contrast to the library, you do not need to drop off things upon entry in order to stay here. The outer appearance of the Teaching Center is modern, but on the other hand, it also seems as if it has been standing here for many years slowly rusting away. When the steel lattices in front of the windows are flipped open in the summer, it looks as if the building had landing flaps like an airplane and just hit the runway. And: The view over Vienna from the fifth storey is phenomenal! From the outside, the Learning Center is her favorite; it is simply fantastic. Mind you, it is rather imprac-

vom Lernen in der Bibliothek, für Studierende eher unpraktisch, so gebe es drei verschiedene vierte Stöcke, die nicht miteinander verbunden seien. Da müsse man sich erst einmal zurecht finden.

Schließlich erzählt sie einen russischen Witz, um das Wechselspiel zwischen dem neuen Campus und dem dort stattfindenden Wirtschaftsstudium zu erläutern: Ein Mann kommt in den Himmel und sieht, wie hinter einer Mauer eine fette Party gefeiert wird mit lauter Musik und vielen schönen Frauen und Männern – das ist die Hölle! Er verlangt von Gott, dorthin zu dürfen, was ihm schließlich auch gewährt wird, jedoch landet er in der Hölle sofort am Spieß, statt mitfeiern zu können. Er fragt Gott: Warum bin ich nicht bei der Party? Das war nur die Werbung für die Hölle, sagt der. So ähnlich sei es hier: Der Campus sei schön und fröhlich, aber das Studium sei schwer.

tical for students – apart from studying in the library – for instance, there are three different fourth floors, which are not connected to one another. That takes a bit of getting used to.

In the end, she tells a Russian joke in order to explain the interplay between the new campus and the business studies that take place there: A man arrives in Heaven, and then he sees a fat party going on behind a wall with loud music and lots of beautiful men and women – that must be Hell! He asks God if he can go there, and the wish is also granted, but in Hell he immediately lands on a spit instead of joining the party. He asks God: Why am I not at the party? That's just the advertisement for the party, he replies. And that is how it is here: The WU Campus is beautiful and cheerful, but the studies are as hard as Hell.

WIRTSCHAFT UND CAMPUS MÜSSEN MODERN SEIN
ECONOMY AND THE CAMPUS MUST BE MODERN

TATJANA, SARAH
Studentinnen Students

Schließlich bitte ich zwei Studierende des Wirtschaftsrechts, Tatjana und Sarah, um ihre Meinung. Tatjana kannte die alte WU bereits, Sarah jedoch nicht. Beim ersten Gang durch den neuen Campus fanden sie ihn „unbeschreiblich", fantastisch und unglaublich schön: Inzwischen hätten sie sich daran gewöhnt, aber: „Da kompensiert die Uni wohl, was sie uns antut!" Beide finden es bemerkenswert, wie sehr die neue Anlage auf Studierende eingestellt sei. Hier habe man offensichtlich nicht bei den Studierenden gespart. Der Campus sei sehr modern, es gebe viel Holz und Natur, ökologisches Denken sei sichtbar integriert. Der neue Campus sei sehr kommunikativ, man könne sich immer auf einer Ebene bewegen, statt ständig auf und ab wechseln zu müssen. Alles sei miteinander verbunden, man müsse keine Straßen überqueren – hier gebe es ein gemeinsames Campusgefühl, die Anlage sei nicht so verzweigt. Und: Der Campus sei überaus gemütlich, es gebe viele Begegnungszonen und Cafés, man fühle sich wohl von früh bis spät. Die beiden würden schon auf den Sommer warten, wenn man die Grünlandschaft und die vielen Sitzecken besser nützen könne und die Lokale Gastgärten aufbauten. Im Vergleich dazu sei die alte WU sehr karg gewesen. Hier am neuen Campus könne man leben, nicht nur lernen, man könne

Finally, I ask two business law students, Tatjana and Sarah, for their opinions. Tatjana knew the old WU, but Sarah not. On their first walk around the campus they found it "indescribable", fantastic and unbelievably beautiful. In the meanwhile, they have gotten used to it, but: "That's where the university apparently compensates for what they lay on us!" Both find it remarkable how much the new complex is oriented toward the students. They obviously didn't make any shortcuts when it came to the students. The campus is very modern, there are wood and nature in abundance, ecological thinking is visibly integrated. The new campus is very communicative; you can continuously move on one level instead of having to constantly go up and down. Everything is connected, you don't have to cross any streets – there is a communal campus feeling, the facilities are not so scattered. And: The campus has an extremely pleasant atmosphere, there are many meeting areas and cafés, you feel good from morning till late. The two look forward to the summer when the green landscape and the various seating areas can be better used and the local pub gardens are set up. The old WU was quite austere in comparison. Here you can live, not just learn; you can meet with others for lunch, spend your leisure time, there's even

STUDIERENDE / STUDENTS — STATEMENTS

> Hier hat man offensichtlich nicht bei den Studierenden gespart. Der Campus ist sehr modern, es gibt viel Holz und Natur, ökologisches Denken ist sichtbar integriert.

> They obviously didn't make any shortcuts when it came to the students. The campus is very modern, there are wood and nature in abundance, ecological thinking is visibly integrated.

sich mit anderen zum Essen treffen, seine Freizeit verbringen, es gebe sogar einen Supermarkt. Die neue WU habe einfach einen hohen „Lässigkeitsfaktor". Eine Freundin sei extra hierhergekommen, um den Campus zu fotografieren. Immer wieder würden während den Vorlesungen im Audimax einfach Leute hereinkommen und Fotos machen.

Das Administrationsgebäude würde wie ein buntes Objekt aus dem Nichts auftauchen, aber ein wenig seltsam fänden sie es schon. Das Learning Center würde ein etwas beklemmendes Gefühl bewirken, weil es so schräg sei – man denke zuerst an ein Kreuzfahrtschiff, beim dem man vom Kapitän an Bord begrüßt würde. Die Bibliothek darin sei aber sehr gut, dort gehe man auf Teppichen wie auf Wolken und es gebe eine Vielzahl verschieden großer Projekträume zu mieten. Wichtig ist, offensichtlich, das Teaching Center, auch wenn seine Fassade durchaus unterschiedlich aufgenommen wird.

Ein wenig unsicher sind die beiden bezüglich der Frage, ob sie die Verschiedenheit der Gebäude gut fänden. Sie fänden zwar jedes einzelne schön und es sei auch praktisch, wenn man die Gebäude klar unterscheiden könne (beispielsweise das Schwarze, das Bunte, das Rostige), aber mehr Einheitlichkeit wäre eigentlich auch gut. Schlussendlich sei das aber nicht so wichtig, die Vielfalt hätte anfangs seltsam gewirkt, aber jetzt sei das OK. Grundsätzlich passe der Campus zu einer Wirtschaftsuniversität, finden die beiden, schließlich müsse Wirtschaft modern sein, und das sei der Campus auch.

a supermarket. The new WU is simply very "laid-back". A friend came here just to photograph the campus. During lectures in the Audimax, time and again people simply enter and make photos.

The Administration Building is a colorful house that seems to pop up out of nowhere, but they do find it a bit strange. The Learning Center can give you a bit of an unsettling feeling because it is so slanted – one first thinks of a cruise ship and expects the captain to come and say, "Welcome aboard!" But inside the library is very good: You walk on soft carpets that seem like clouds, and there are a number of different sized project spaces that you can rent. And the Teaching Center is naturally quite important as well, even when opinions about its façade are divided.

The two are a bit uncertain regarding the question whether the diversity of the buildings is a good thing. They find each individual building nice, and it is quite practical when you can clearly differentiate between them (for example, the black one, the colorful one, the spaceship, the rusty one), but more uniformity would perhaps not be a bad thing. But in the end, that's not so important – the diversity seemed strange at first, but now that's OK. In general, they both find that the campus is well-suited for a university of economics – in the end, economy must be modern, and the campus is just that.

D3 AD

CRAB STUDIO: DEPARTMENTS 3 / ADMINISTRATION

DEPARTMENTS 3 / ADMINISTRATION

HEITERKEIT ALS PROGRAMM
DAS DEPARTMENT- UND ADMINISTRATIONS-GEBÄUDE VON CRAB STUDIO

JOLLY GOOD FUN
THE DEPARTMENT AND ADMINISTRATION BUILDING BY CRAB STUDIO

CORDULA RAU

Cook-Robotham (CRAB studio) gewann den Wettbewerb mit einem Gebäudeensemble im Südwesten des Campus. Es birgt das Haus der juristischen Departments und die zentrale Verwaltung der WU Wien. Zum Masterplan, der sich als „offene Bildungslandschaft" versteht, gestaltete CRAB studio – in den Worten von Laura Spinadel – „eine in sich schlüssige Oase mit Pavillons im Uni-Garten". Das Haus, von Terrassen, Passagen und Enklaven umflossen, stellt ein organisch-buntes, variantenreiches Ensemble dar.

Christoph Sommer, der als Projektmanager des WU Campus die gesamte Planung des Gebäudes managte, beschreibt die Struktur folgendermaßen: „Peter Cook hat den Masterplan umgesetzt, indem er den vorgegebenen Weg in idealer Weise in eine organische Struktur eingebunden hat. Den Architekten waren diese organischen Formen und vor allem auch die Zwischenräume wichtig, die sich an den Schnittstellen ergeben. Daraus wurden facettenreiche Räume für die Kommunikation."

„University has to be jolly good fun!"
Peter Cook realisiert in dem Department- und Administrationsgebäude seine Vorstellung von Studentenleben: „University has to be jolly good fun!" Eines der ersten Bilder im Wettbewerb zeigt eine Zeichnung mit Begegnungsraum, Tisch und Stühlen. Professoren und Studenten sitzen bunt gewürfelt zu-

Peter Cook and Gavin Robotham (CRAB studio) won the competition for a building ensemble in the southwest of the campus. The house accommodates university departments and the central administrative seat of the WU. Corresponding with the master plan, which is conceived as an "open landscape for education", CRAB studio designed – in the words of Laura Spinadel – "an inherently coherent oasis with pavilions in the university garden". Numerous terraces, passageways, and enclaves wrap around the building, forming an organic, colorful, and varied ensemble.

Christoph Sommer, who managed the entire planning of the building as the project manager of the WU Campus, describes the structure as follows: "Peter Cook implemented the master plan perfectly by integrating the predefined concept in an organic structure. These organic shapes and, above all, the in-between spaces on the interfaces were important to the architect. They resulted in multifarious spaces for communication."

"University has to be jolly good fun!"
In the Department and Administration Building Peter Cook realized his notion of student life: "University has to be jolly good fun!" One of the first images in the competition phase was a drawing of a meeting room with a table and chairs. Professors

Farbe, Licht, Bewegung: Die Idee in einer Entwurfsskizze von Peter Cook
Color, light, movement: design sketch by Peter Cook
>

Abgerundet und gestapelt: Das große Volumen ist in mehrere Baukörper aufgelöst
Rounded and stepped: The large volume is divided into several organic bodies
v

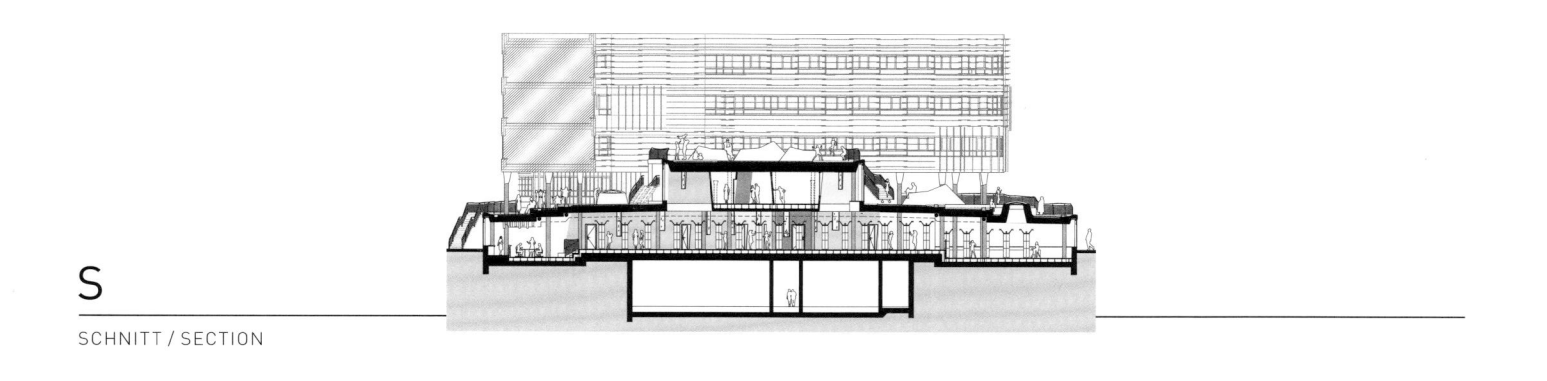

DEPARTMENTS 3 / ADMINISTRATION

S
SCHNITT / SECTION

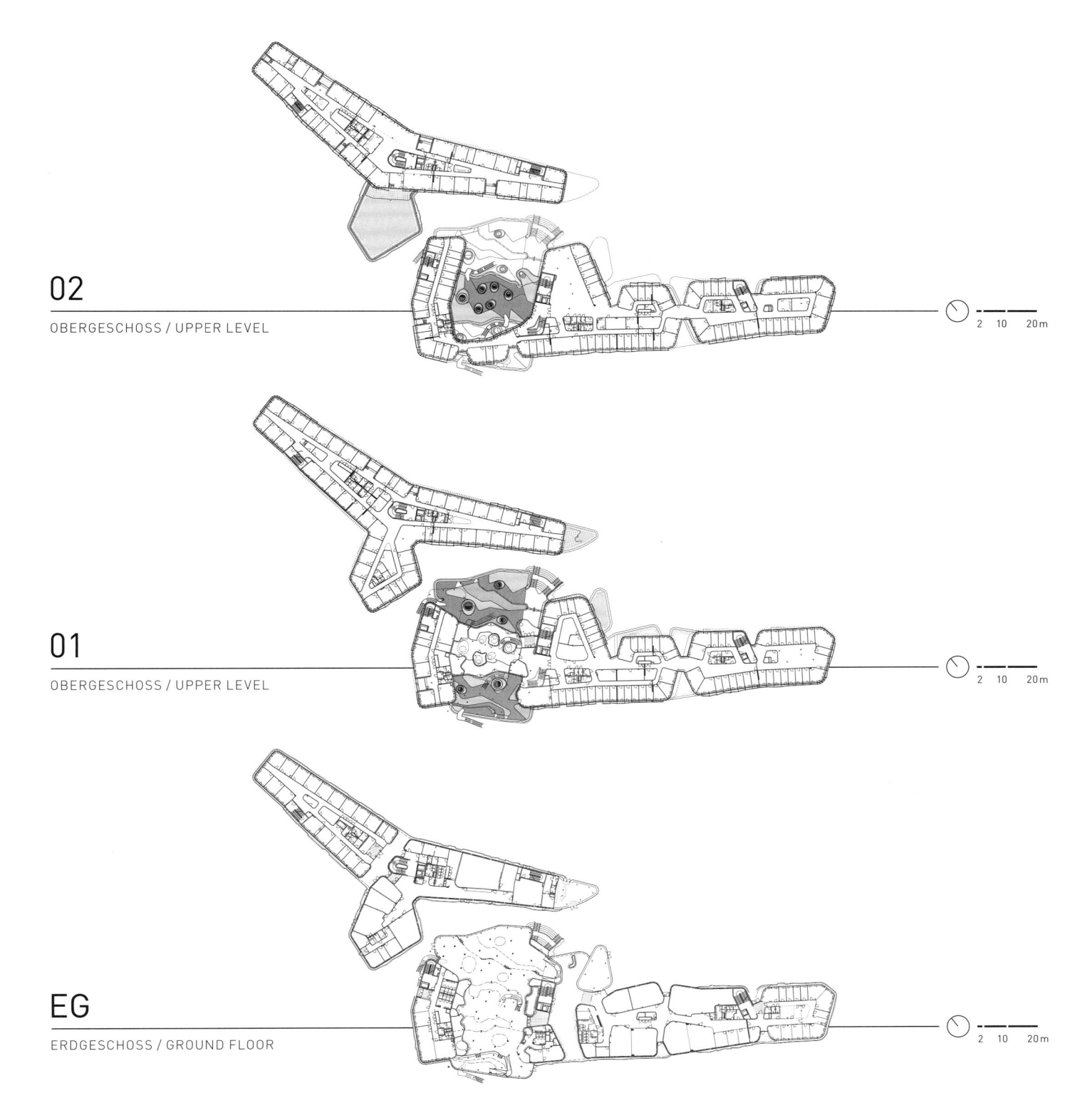

02
OBERGESCHOSS / UPPER LEVEL

01
OBERGESCHOSS / UPPER LEVEL

EG
ERDGESCHOSS / GROUND FLOOR

DEPARTMENTS 3 / ADMINISTRATION

^
Pop-Art-Ästhetik: Bunte, organische Formen mit ungewohnten Durchblicken
Pop Art aesthetics: colorful and organic forms with unexpected views

^
Bewegung im Raum: Verschlungene Wege führen durch das Gebäude
Spatial movement: Curved paths lead through the building

^
Die Holzbretter-Fassade dient der Beschattung und spielt auf den nahen Prater-Wald an
The wooden slats provide shading and allude to the adjacent Prater park

^
Begehbare Dächer: Ein Eingang führt über eine Freitreppe, die auch als Tribüne nutzbar ist
Walkable roofs: Entrance via outside steps that can also be used as a tribune

102

sammen. Unterm Tisch sieht man mehrere Weinflaschen. „Das ist Peter Cooks Bild von Universität", erläutert Christoph Sommer schmunzelnd. Mag sein, dass es Anklänge an persönliche Erfahrungen sind. Mag sein, dass es die poppig-bunten Bilder der Swinging Sixties assoziiert, die sich später in den Farben des Gebäudes niederschlagen. Es geht jedenfalls um Emotion und um ganz persönliche Bilder, an die Cook anknüpft. Und diese Bilder bleiben haften.

Britische Romantik
Cook wünschte sich sein Gebäude möglichst nah am Prater situiert. Holz für die Fassade war von Anfang als Idee vorhanden und stellt die Referenz zu dieser Grünfläche da. Dem WU Campus und der Stadt Wien, die in den Augen Cooks eher grau wirkt, schenkt er den passenden Farbklecks. Das Haus soll „urwienerisch" wirken und ist vor allem gemütlich, inspiriert von Jugendträumen. Cooks eigene Kindheitserfahrung spielt dabei eine große Rolle. Deswegen gibt es gleich zum Auftakt hinter der gerundeten Schaufensterscheibe einen Bäcker.

and students sit together in a motley group. Under the table one sees a number of wine bottles. "That's Peter Cook's image of university," explains Christoph Sommer grinning with a smile. It could be that these are echoes of personal experience. It could be that it evokes associations with the poppy technicolored images of the swinging sixties, which precipitate in the hues of the building. In any case, it is about emotion and very personal images, which motivate Cook. And these images stick.

British romance
Cook wanted his building to be situated as close as possible to the Prater. From the very beginning a timber façade was on hand as an idea to reference this green space. He would give the WU Campus and the city of Vienna – which in Cook's eyes is a shade too gray – the dab of color it needed. The house should seem "archetypically Viennese" and, above all, be cozy, inspired by boyhood dreams. Cook's own experiences growing up play an important role. That's why there is a bakery behind the rounded shop window right at the start.

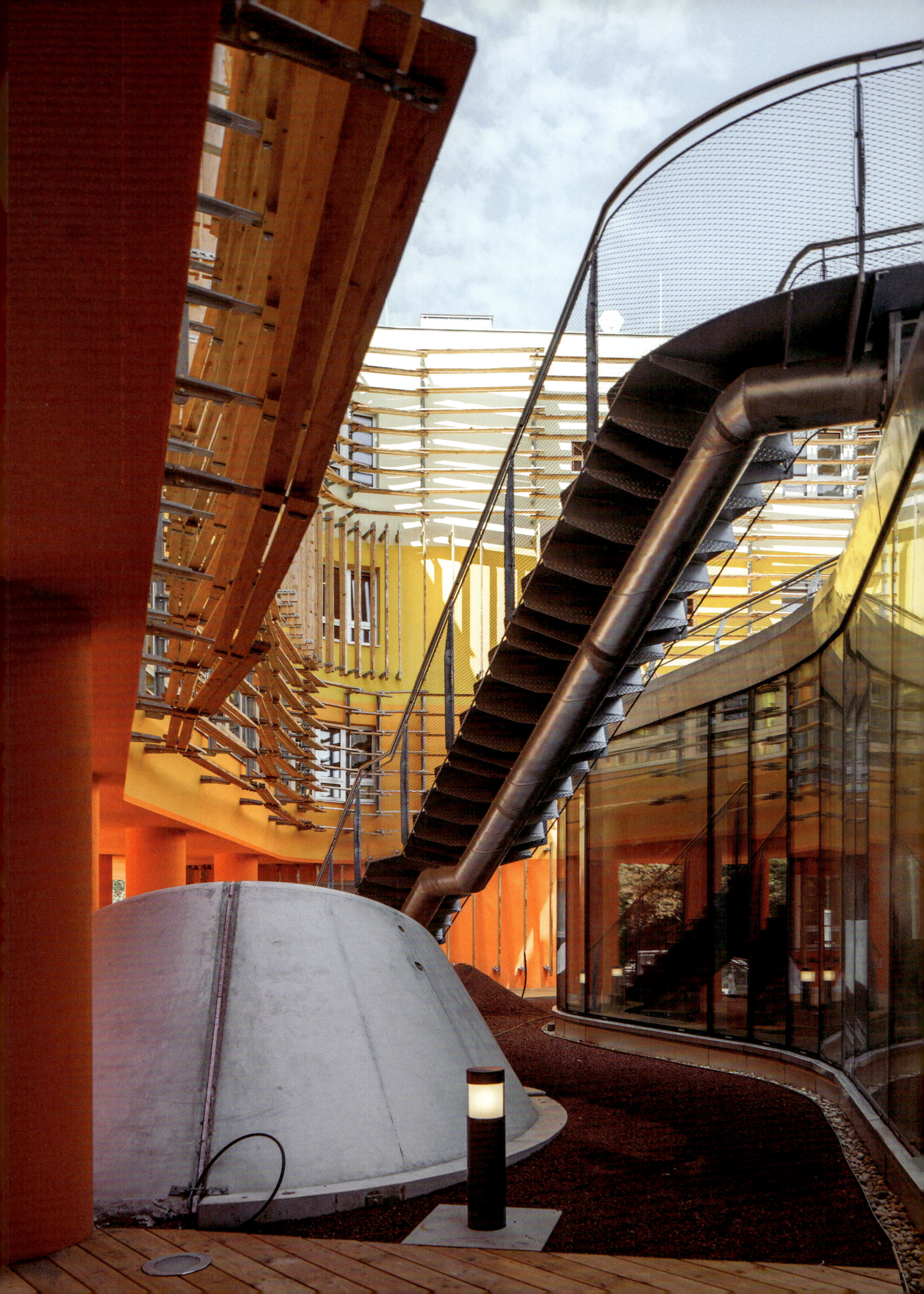

Expressive Technik: Konstruktionsdetails in voluminöser Dimensionierung
Expressive technique: structural details in bulky dimensions
◀

Gebaute Fröhlichkeit: Die Sitzbereiche sind transparent und hellfarbig
Built jollity: the seating areas are transparent and brightly colored
▶

Die als Sonnenschutz gedachten horizontalen und vertikalen Lamellen aus riesigen unbearbeiteten Brettern vermitteln gemeinsam mit den im Haus dominierenden Farben einen heiter-ironischen Bezug zur Umgebung. Die Holzfassade sollte ursprünglich dichter sein. Auf die Nutzer abgestimmt zeigt sie sich etwas aufgelockerter als geplant. Die fröhliche Farbigkeit wirkt lebendig und zieht sich von changierenden Gelb und Orange im Außenbereich zu kräftigem Blau- und Grüntönen im Innenraum. Die Akustiksegel an den Decken des Erdgeschosses sind sonnengelb, im Obergeschoss schneeweiß gestaltet. Auch der farbenfrohe Teppich ist von den Architekten selbst entworfen und zieht sich in unterschiedlichen Variationen bis in die oberen Geschosse.

Die rohen Holzbretter vor der poppigen Fassade stehen im Kontrast zu den glatteren Fassaden der Nachbarbauten. Was in der Wettbewerbsphase unbehandelte sibirische Lärche war, wurde in der Ausführung europäische Weißtanne. Auch das ist eine Geschichte für sich – und derer gibt es viele am Gebäude zu entdecken. Heute schon existiert eine Zukunftsvision der Architekten, wie sie sich das Gebäude in 20 Jahren vorstellen. Verwunschen wirkt diese Utopie, mit Efeu bewachsen, so wie das typisch englische Landhausidyll. Das Holz soll echte Patina bekommen. Mit dem Wechsel aus vertikalen und horizontalen Holzlamellen vermittelt die Fassade bereits jetzt ein abwechslungsreiches Bild, das sich vor allem im Abendlicht entfaltet. Blickt man aus dem östlich gelegenen LC auf Cooks Gebäude, lösen sich Kontur und Fassade in der Dämmerung nach und nach auf. Sobald es dunkel wird, fangen Farbe und Lichter an gemeinsam zu tanzen.

Atmosphärisches „in between"
Mittig im Ensemble liegt die von einem terrassierten Innenhof bedeckte Bibliothek. Der Department-Haupteingang im Obergeschoss ist über eine Außentreppe zugänglich. Zwischen den bepflanzten Terrassen hindurch führt der Weg nach innen. Betrachtet man die unterschiedlichen Kommunikationszonen, kommen sofort archetypische Bilder vom Spielen und Verstecken in den Sinn. „Pods und Barnacles" nennt sie Christoph Sommer. Davon gibt es viele in diesem Haus. Sie laden ein zu Kontaktgesprächen in unkonventioneller Umgebung. Die Qualität des Gebäudes entwickelt sich von innen heraus. Schnell vergisst man manch architektonisch nicht ganz akkurat gestaltetes Detail.

„Es ist eine Frage der Prioritätensetzung", erklärt Sommer die Philosophie des Gebäudes. Sieht man es streng aus Architektensicht, könnte man es leicht ablehnen. Oberflächlich betrachtet gibt es gewiss einige Detailschwächen. Jedoch auch ein

The horizontal and vertical slats of huge untreated boards were designed for sun protection, and together with the dominant colors inside the house they convey a cheerful ironic relationship to the surroundings. The timber façade was originally intended to be denser. Attuned to the users, it became a bit more diffuse than planned. The jovial colorfulness has a lively effect, fluctuating from an alternating yellow and orange on the outside to strong blue and green tones within the building. The acoustic screens on the ceilings of the ground floor are sun yellow; on the upper floor they become snow white. Also the vibrant carpet was personally designed by the architects themselves and progresses through different variations up to the top floors.

The raw wood boards in front of the poppy façade contrast the smoother facades of the neighboring buildings. What was originally intended to be untreated Siberian larch would be realized in European silver fir. And that's also a story in itself – and there are many to discover in this building. Today, there already exists a future vision in the mind of the architects about how the building will be in 20 years. This utopia seems most enchanted: grown over with ivy, like the typical English country house idyll. The timber should attain a real patina. With the interplay between vertical and horizontal wood slats the façade already communicates a varied image, which manifests the best at dusk. Viewed from the LC to the east, the contours of Cook's building gradually dissolve in the twilight. As soon as it becomes dark, color and lights begin a scintillating dance.

Atmospheric in-between
The library is situated in the middle of the ensemble and covered by a terraced inner courtyard. The main entrance to the departments on the upper floor can be accessed by an outdoor stairway. The path inside passes between garden terraces. Looking at the different communication zones, archetypical images of playing hide and seek immediately come to mind. Christoph Sommer calls them "pods and barnacles", and there are many of them in this house. They invite people to have personal talks in a casual atmosphere. The quality of the building unfolds from within. It's easy to forget one or the other not quite perfectly elaborated architectural detail.

"It is a question of setting priorities," tells Sommer about the philosophy of the building. If one looks from a strict architectural perspective, one could easily be dismissive. On the sur-

DEPARTMENTS 3 / ADMINISTRATION

^
Industrielle Rohheit: Signalanstriche und expressive Farbkontraste
Industrial rawness: signal painting and expressive color contrasts

^
Großzügige Büroräume mit Blick in die Baumkronen des Praters
Generous offices with a view of the trees of Prater park

^
Nichts wird versteckt: Abgehängte Schalldämmung und Installationen
Nothing to hide: exposed acoustic panels and ducts

^
Auch in der Bibliothek wird Farbe als raum- und strukturbildendes Element verwendet
Also in the library color is used as a means to shape and structure space

Mensch ist nicht perfekt. Die Zielgruppe, an die sich das Gebäude adressiert, ist breit gefächert. Es ist nicht nur der Architekt gemeint, sondern vor allem der Mensch, zu dem das Haus spricht. Es zeigt kaum satt glänzende Architektur im Sonntagsstaat, gemacht für das Auge des Fotografen. Nein – das Haus sträubt sich listig wie ein freches Kind gegen die Architekturkonvention. Komplementär betrachtet ist es das (un)perfekte Pendant zum stylischen (Over)flow der Nachbargebäude und auch eine Allegorie zum Prater. Das Haus wächst scheinbar über sich hinaus wie auch der „Wurstelprater" nebenan. Dazu bedarf es des gereiften Architektenblicks.

Cooks Ansatz, ein atmosphärisches Gebäude zu schaffen, ist geglückt. Es wirkt weder kühl noch unnahbar, ist warm und rund, leicht verspielt und vor allem kommunikativ. Das Haus lebt von seiner menschlich anmutenden Qualität. Es ist und bleibt ein Gebäude für den zweiten Blick. Wie man von schönen Frauen weiß, ist diese Attraktivität oft die nachhaltigere. Jedoch auch das bleibt eine Frage des Geschmacks und darüber lässt sich bekanntermaßen trefflich streiten – ganz im Sinne des Architekten.

face there are indeed a few weak details. But also a person is not perfect. The building addresses a broad target group. It is not only about the architect but moreover the people that the house speaks to. It's not a presentation of glossy architecture at its Sunday best, built for the eye of a photographer. No, the house is guilefully reluctant, like a cheeky kid against the conventions of architecture. Complementary seen, it is the (im)perfect dependant to the stylistic (over) flow of its neighbors and also an allegory to the Prater. The house seems to grow above and beyond itself, like the Wurstelprater amusement park next door. For this, one needs the view of a seasoned architect.

Cook's approach to create an atmospheric building was a success. It is neither cool nor aloof rather warm and rotund, a bit playful and, most importantly, communicative. The building lives from its human-like quality. It is and remains a building of the second glance. As we know from beautiful women, this type of attractiveness is often more sustainable. However, this, too, is a question of taste and, as we know, a matter of argument – very much in the spirit of the architect.

DEPARTMENTS 3 / ADMINISTRATION

Seminarraum mit vielfältigen Öffnungen
Seminar room with manifold apertures

Arbeitsbereiche mit Bodenleitstreifen
Work space with guidance system

DEPARTMENTS 3 / ADMINISTRATION

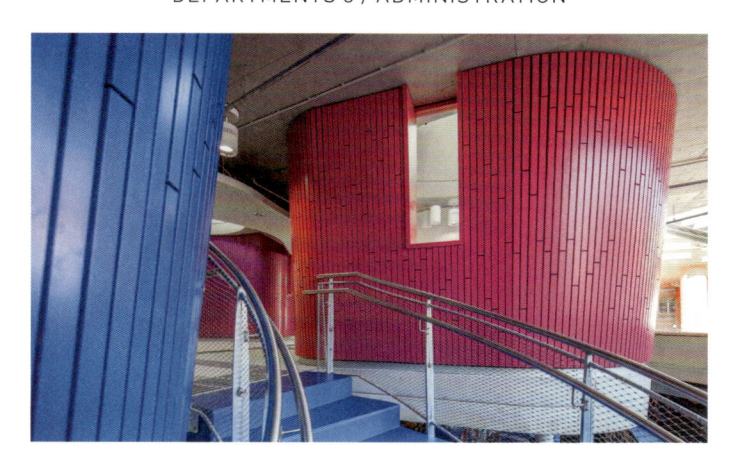

^
Organoide „Pods" als Projekträume
Organic "pods" as project rooms

ENERGY AND ECOLOGY

DER GRÜNE CAMPUS
ENERGIE-DESIGN-KONZEPTE

MALGORZATA SOMMER-NAWARA, BERNHARD SOMMER

Nicht ohne Stolz präsentierte die Bundesimmobiliengesellschaft (BIG) den WU Campus als großen Erfolg: Der gesamte Campus wird auf Basis eines „Green Building"-Konzepts errichtet. Dieses Konzept wurde gemeinsam mit internationalen Fachleuten auf Basis internationaler Zertifizierungssysteme (…) erarbeitet.[1] Letztlich sollte folgender Zertifizierungsstatus erreicht werden: ÖGNI Silber für jedes einzelne Gebäude, ÖGNI Gold für das D1 Departmentgebäude. Dieser Erfolg war wohl nur möglich, weil sich der Bauherr von Beginn an das Ziel eines „grünen" Campus gesetzt hatte, verwirklicht mit den neuesten und innovativsten technologischen Möglichkeiten. Das erfordert mehr als bloßes Optimieren haustechnischer Anlagen: Es erfordert die Entwicklung und Fortschreibung eines Energie-Designs als integralen Bestandteil aller anderen architektonischen Konzepte.

THE GREEN CAMPUS
ENERGY DESIGN CONCEPTS

The Bundesimmobiliengesellschaft (BIG – Austrian Federal Real Estate Company) were proud to announce the success of the WU Campus: "The complete campus was built on the basis of a Green Building concept. This concept was elaborated together with international specialists in accordance with international certification systems."[1] In the end the following certification statuses from the Austrian Society for Sustainable Real Estate Management (ÖGNI) were to be achieved: ÖGNI Silver for each individual building and ÖGNI Gold for the D1 Department Building. This success was probably only possible because the client focused on the goal of a "green" campus from the very beginning and implemented this ambition with cutting-edge, innovative technological solutions. This implies more than just optimizing the building systems: It requires the development and advancement of an energy design as a central component of all other architectural concepts.

ENERGY AND ECOLOGY

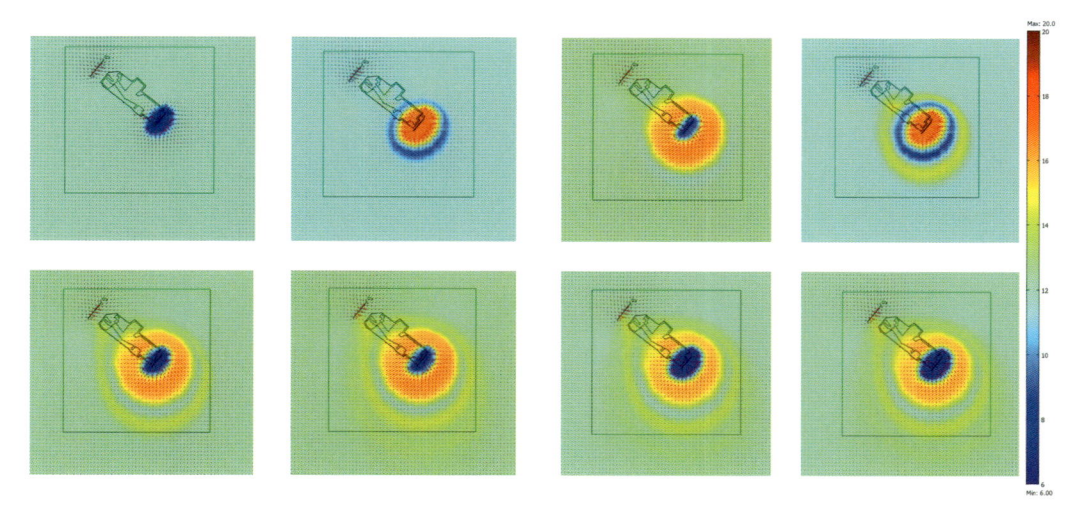

Dietmar Adam: Ermittlung der Temperaturfront durch Simulationsberechnung
Determining the temperature front through simulation calculations

Planer und Planungskultur

To design with energy in mind – so beschreibt Brian Cody, Professor am Institut für Gebäude und Energie der Technischen Universität Graz sowie Gastprofessor an der Universität für Angewandte Kunst Wien, die Intention von Energie Design. Die architektonische Gestaltung bleibt im Vordergrund. Das Energiekonzept ist aber von den ersten Entwurfsschritten an Teil des kreativen Prozesses. Ganz in diesem Sinne stand am Beginn des Prozesses ein von Brian Cody entworfenes Energiekonzept, das bereits wesentliche Merkmale des schließlich realisierten Projekts zeigte.[2] So wurde bereits zu diesem Zeitpunkt die thermische Nutzung des Grundwassers vorgeschlagen. Mit der Wettbewerbsentscheidung für die Ausarbeitung des Masterplans stand auch der Generalplaner fest, die Arbeitsgemeinschaft BUSarchitektur und Vasko+Partner. Im Zuge der Ausarbeitung des Masterplans und der Vorbereitung für den Wettbewerb zu den einzelnen Gebäuden wurde, unter der Federführung von Vasko+Partner, auch der energetische Masterplan für den Campus erstellt, der ebenfalls die Grundwassernutzung in den Mittelpunkt des thermischen Konzepts stellte. Die Gebäudetechnikplanung für den gesamten Campus wurde unter der Leitung von Günther Sammer, Vasko+Partner, durchgeführt. Das Wassermanagement wurde von Ernst Nöbl, Ingenieurbüro für Kultur- und Umwelttechnik projektiert. Und die mit der Projektsteuerung beauftragte Arbeitsgemeinschaft Drees & Sommer und DELTA wurde bereits im Rahmen des Wettbewerbs mit dem Green Building Management betraut, um sicher zu stellen, dass die angestrebten Gebäude-Zertifizierungen auch tatsächlich erreicht werden konnten.

Wie man beginnt

Ohne explizit auf die Grundwassernutzung Bezug zu nehmen, beschreibt Santiago Sánchez Guzmán von BUSarchitektur das Fließen als eines der Hauptthemen, die BUSarchitektur für den Masterplan analysiert hat.[3] Dynamische Eigenschaften finden sich in Verkehrsströmen, in Stoffströmen, im Wechsel von Licht und Schatten und eben auch in Luft-, Wärme-, Wind- und Wasserströmen. All diese Aspekte wurden Bestandteil des Integralen Masterplans[4] und können nicht losgelöst von den jeweiligen gestalterischen Lösungen betrachtet werden.

Planning and Planning Culture

To design with energy in mind. This is how Brian Cody, professor at the Institute for Buildings and Design at Graz University of Technology and guest professor at the University of Applied Arts Vienna, describes the intention behind Energy Design. Architectural design remains at the fore, but the energy concept is a part of the creative process already in the first design steps. True to this spirit, an energy concept formulated by Brian Cody was involved in the beginning of the process, which already reflected the important cornerstones of realized project.[2] For example, the thermal use of the groundwater was already proposed at this point in time. The competition decision for the elaboration of the master plan also designated the general planner: the collaborative team of BUSarchitektur and Vasko+Partner. In the development process of the master plan and the preparation phase of the second competition for the individual buildings, the energy master plan for the campus was also formulated under the guidance of Vasko+Partner, which likewise placed the use of groundwater at the heart of the thermal concept. Günther Sammer from Vasko+Partner led the building systems planning for the entire campus. Ernst Nöbl, from the engineering office Ingenieurbüro für Kultur- und Umwelttechnik, was responsible for the water management projections. And the working group commissioned with the project management, Drees & Sommer and DELTA, was already entrusted with the Green Building Management in the framework of the competition in order to ensure that the envisioned building certifications could actually be attained.

Departure Points

Without making explicit reference to the use of groundwater, Santiago Sánchez Guzmán from BUSarchitektur names flows as one of the basic principles of the master plan.[3] Dynamic properties are inherent in traffic flows, in material flows, in the interplay of light and shadow, and also in air, heat, wind, and water flows as well. All of these aspects became elements of the Integral Master Plan[4] and thus cannot be divorced from the respective design solutions.

Versucht man, diesen Integralen Masterplan aus dem Blickwinkel von Energieeffizienz und Ökologie zu betrachten, so lassen sich die wichtigsten Maßnahmen wie folgt zusammenfassen:

- Weitestgehende Nutzung lokaler und regenerativer Energiequellen
- Simulation vorhandener natürlicher Phänomene (Winde, Sonne, Grundwasserströmungen) als Planungsgrundlage
- Bedarfsanalyse durch Simulationen, Wirtschaftlichkeitsanalyse und Lebenszyklusanalyse
- Geothermie als leistungsfähiges Rückgrat der grundsätzlichen Versorgung mit Wärme und Kälte
- Fernwärme zur wirtschaftlichen und „sanften" Abdeckung der Spitzenlasten
- Vorkehrungen zur Nachrüstung für die Nutzung von Solarenergie
- Erstellung und Umsetzung eines innovativen Wasserkonzeptes, Nutzwassernutzung Versickerung der gesamten Niederschlagswässer am Grundstück, begrünte Dächer
- Aerodynamische Optimierung zur Vermeidung von Konfliktsituationen
- Tageslicht zur Orientierung und Gestaltung im öffentlichen Raum
- Tageslichtnutzung in möglichst allen Bereichen, bis in die Tiefgarage
- Präsenz- und helligkeitsabhängige Beleuchtung und strahlungsabhängiger Sonnenschutz
- Hohe Flexibilität der einzelnen Gebäude durch Hohlraum-/Doppelböden und Reversibilitätspläne
- Speichermasse und Bauteilaktivierung
- Optimierte Gebäudehülle mit Empfehlungen für U-Wert und Glasanteil
- Saisonale Konzepte zur Nutzung des Freiraums

Looking at this Integral Master Plan from the perspective of energy efficiency and ecology, the most important measures can be summarized as follows:

- Maximum use of local and regenerative energy sources
- Simulation of on-site natural phenomena (wind, sun, groundwater flows) forms the planning basis
- Requirements analysis through simulations, cost/benefit analysis, and life cycle analysis
- Geothermal energy as an efficient backbone for the basic provision of heat and cooling
- District heating for an economic and "soft" coverage of peak loads
- Retrofitting measures for the use of solar energy
- Preparation and implementation of an innovative water concept. Use of process water, seepage of all rain water into the site, green roofs
- Optimized aerodynamics to avoid conflict situations
- Daylight as an orientation and design factor in the open space
- Use of daylight in as many areas as possible, even in the underground garage
- Motion and brightness-dependent lighting and radiation-dependent sun protection
- High level of flexibility in the individual buildings through cavity and double floors and reversibility plans
- (Thermal) storage mass and building component activation
- Optimized building shell with recommendations for the U-value and glass ratio
- Seasonal concepts for the use of the open space

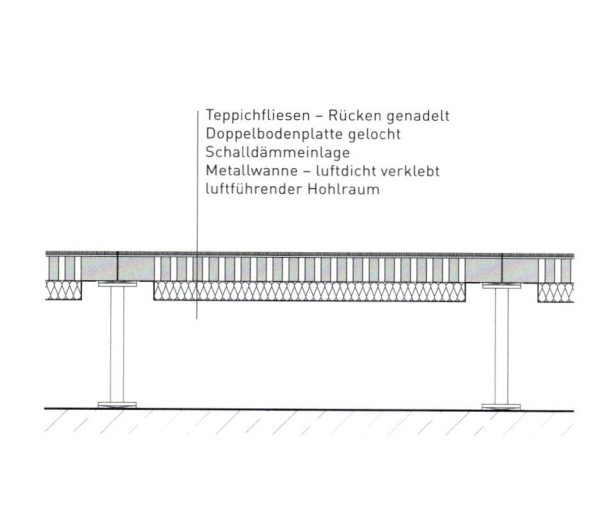

Vasko+Partner: Akustisch wirksamer Doppelboden
Acoustically effective double floors

Goga S. Nawara: Diagramm des Heiz- und Kühlsystems des Campus
Diagram of the campus' heating and cooling system

An Besonderheiten sind darüber hinaus noch das Brandschutzkonzept und die Schallschutzmaßnahmen zu nennen. Die meisten der oben angeführten Punkte waren im Wesentlichen bereits Grundlage für den zweiten Architekturwettbewerb, sicher ein Grund für das auch aus ökologischer Sicht erfolgreiche Zusammenspiel der verschiedenen Entwurfsansätze. Kritisch anzumerken bleibt, dass es mittlerweile üblich geworden ist, bei Wettbewerben nicht nur Ziele für die Gebäudehülle festzusetzen, sondern explizit U-Werte oder Glasanteil vorzuschreiben. Zum Glück blieb es bei einer Empfehlung und so konnte im Fall des Library and Learning Centers von Zaha Hadid Architects gezeigt werden, dass auch ein größerer Glasanteil nicht automatisch zu Problemen mit Überhitzung oder Behaglichkeit führen muss.[5]

Die einzelnen Gebäude sind grundsätzlich autark. Durch die zwischen den Gebäuden liegende Tiefgarage läuft die gesamte Infrastruktur der Versorgung. Ein herausragendes und energetisch sicherlich das mächtigste Element des Campus ist die thermische Grundwassernutzung.

Solide Grundlagen

Die Versorgung des Campus mit Wärme und Kälte erfolgt über die derzeit größte nicht-industrielle Grundwassernutzung Österreichs. Die bereitgestellte Kälte- bzw. Wärmeleistung beträgt rund drei Megawatt. Günther Sammer von Vasko+Partner berichtet, dass ca. zwei Drittel des Energiebedarfs für Kälte bzw. Wärme auf diese Weise gedeckt werden können. Ein Drittel wird durch Fernwärme bzw. über Kältemaschinen gedeckt.

Das Konzept der Geothermienutzung wurde von Dietmar Adam, Professor am Institut für Geotechnik der Technischen Universität Wien, und seinem Büro Geotechnik Adam ZT GmbH, gestützt auf Simulationsberechnungen, entwickelt. Es ist ein offenes System, das im saisonalen Betrieb bewirtschaftet wird. Beim offenen System wird das Grundwasser zur Nutzung direkt entnommen und, anschließend erwärmt oder abgekühlt, dem Grundwasserträger wieder zugeführt. Im saisonalen Betrieb wird die thermische Trägheit des Bodens als Energiespeicher genutzt. Die Anlage besteht aus einem Entnahmebrunnen (Horizontalfilterbrunnen) und einer Versickerungsanlage. Mithilfe von hydraulischen und thermischen Simulationen konnte gezeigt werden, dass Entnahmebrunnen und Versickerungsanlage so positioniert wurden, dass die thermische Reichweite (Thermalfront) ca. ein halbes Jahr beträgt. Durch die Entnahme kommt es zu einer Absenkung des Grundwasserspiegels. Der dadurch entstehende Grundwasserstrom läuft fast entgegengesetzt zum natürlichen Strom und benötigt für diese Strecke ein halbes Jahr. Die „versickerte Wärme" des Sommers erreicht so im Winter den Entnahmebrunnen und umgekehrt. Das führt zu einer Temperaturschwankung des Grundwassers von ±4 K. Aufgrund der halbjährlichen Verzögerung heißt das: 14° C im Winter und 10° C im Sommer! Ohne diesen Effekt wäre an diesem Ort konstant mit ca. 12° C zu rechnen. Der gewählte Aufbau verbessert den Wirkungsgrad der Anlage also erheblich.

Der Geist in der Maschine

Neben der Geothermie wird die Abwärme insbesondere der IT-Anlagen über hocheffiziente Wärmerückgewinnung genutzt. Den Ressourcen Geothermie und Abwärme steht ein Bedarf an niedrigen und hohen Temperaturen gegenüber. Das Niedrigtemperaturnetz (NT-W) der Wärmeversorgung kann weitestgehend durch die Grundwasseranlage direkt und im Heizfall mit Unterstützung der Wärmepumpe versorgt werden. Spitzenlasten der Heizung und das Hochtemperaturnetz (HT-W) werden über

Furthermore, the fire protection concept and sound proofing measures can be added to this list of special features. The majority of the abovementioned points already formed a basis in the second architectural competition – surely one of the reasons behind the successful interplay of the different design approaches, also from an ecological point of view. Nonetheless, it must be noted that today it is standard practice in competitions to not only state aims for the building shell but also explicitly prescribe U-values and glass ratios. Luckily, it remained only a recommendation and, in the case of the Library and Learning Center by Zaha Hadid Architects, it could be demonstrated that buildings with a higher glass ratio do not automatically have problems with overheating or thermal comfort.[5]

Principally, the individual buildings are autonomous. The entire infrastructure for energy provisions runs through the underground parking garage between the buildings. An exemplary and, without question, strongest element in terms of energy efficiency is the thermal use of groundwater.

Solid Foundations

The heating and cooling supply on campus is provided through the currently largest non-industrial groundwater management system in Austria. The available cooling and heating volume amounts to approximately three megawatts. Günther Sammer of Vasko+Partner reports that roughly two-thirds of the energy requirements for heating and cooling can be covered in this way. The other third is covered by district heating and with cooling machines.

The concept for the use of geothermal energy was developed by Dietmar Adam, professor at the Institute of Geotechnics of Vienna University of Technology, and his office Geotechnik Adam ZT GmbH by means of simulation calculations. It is an open system with seasonal operations. In an open system the groundwater for usage is directly obtained, warmed or cooled, and then reintroduced into the groundwater resource. In seasonal operations the thermal inertia of the earth is employed as an energy reservoir. The installation consists of an extraction well (horizontal filter well) and a seepage system. In hydraulic and thermal simulations it could be demonstrated that the extraction well and the seepage system can be positioned in such a way that the thermal range (thermal front) amounts to approximately a half year. The extraction process results in a lowered groundwater table. The subsequent groundwater flow runs almost in the opposite direction to the natural flow and needs a half-year for this distance. Hence, the "seeping warmth" of summer reaches the extraction well in winter and vice versa. This leads to a ± 4 K temperature fluctuation in the groundwater. Given the half year delay, this means: 14°C in winter and 10°C in summer! Without this effect we could estimate a constant temperature of 12°C at this location. Thus, the chosen setup considerably improves the efficiency of the system.

The Ghost in the Machine

In addition to geothermal energy also the waste heat – from the IT facilities in particular – is exploited with a highly efficient heat recovery system. The resources geothermal energy and waste heat stand opposite a need for low and high temperatures. The low temperature network can be largely supplied by the groundwater system directly and – when used for heating – with the help of the heat pump. Peak loads for heating and the high temperature network are covered by the district heating system. The peak loads for the cooling supply are covered by

Fernwärme abgedeckt. Die Spitzenlasten der Kälteversorgung werden durch die Wärmepumpe (Heiz-/Kältemaschine) des Niedertemperaturnetzes abgedeckt. Wesentlicher Verbraucher im Hochtemperaturnetz sind die bei Gebäuden hoher Besucherfrequenz erforderlichen Torluftschleier. Mit dem Niedrigtemperaturnetz sind Heizkörper (HZK) und Bodenkonvektoren, sowie die Nachheizregister (NHR) verbunden. Heizkörper und Bodenkonvektoren sind nur in sensiblen Bereichen vorgesehen. Die wesentlichen Lasten werden von der Bauteilaktivierung getragen. Mit dieser sind alle Gebäude des Campus ausgestattet und in diesen wiederum fast alle Räume. Akustikmaßnahmen sind daher in den meisten Bereichen auf Wände und Böden beschränkt. Das führt dazu, dass auch Leuchten akustisch eingesetzt werden (etwa in der Executive Academy und in den Seminarräumen). Einzig im Hörsaalzentrum (Teaching Center) und Teilbereichen des Library and Learning Centers kommen leistungsfähigere Kühldecken zum Einsatz, um Akustikmaßnahmen an der Decke zu ermöglichen. Es zeigt sich hier wieder die enge Verschränkung von architektonischer Gestaltung und Energiesystem. Die Bauteilaktivierung (BT) wird nicht vom Niedrigtemperaturnetz versorgt, sondern gemeinsam mit den Vorheizregistern (VHR) bzw. Vorkühlregistern (VKR) als Change-Over-System (CO) betrieben. Von Change-Over spricht man, wenn ein und dasselbe System zum Heizen wie zum Kühlen verwendet wird. Einzig das Warmwasser in den Sanitärräumen wird unabhängig vom Grundwassersystem durch elektrisch betriebene Untertisch-Durchlauferhitzer bereitgestellt.

Was hat das mit mir zu tun?
Alle Gebäude sind mit physikalischen Datenpunkten für die Mess-, Steuer- und Regeltechnik (MSR) ausgestattet. Inklusive Bus-System der Brandschutz- und Brandrauchsteuerklappen sind das über 11.000 Stellen. Jeweils etwa 100 m² große Zonen wurden mit Referenztemperaturfühlern ausgestattet. Die Zonengröße dient einerseits der Beschränkung von Druckverlusten im Leitungssystem der Bauteilaktivierung. Sie ermöglicht aber auch eine relativ scharfe (nutzernahe) Regelung des Innenraumklimas. Die Zonen sind nach Geschoss, Himmelsrichtung und Nutzungsart zusammengefasst. Im Kühlfall beträgt der Vorlauf ca. 16° C, der Rücklauf ca. 19° C, im Heizfall beträgt das Verhältnis 30/27° C. Die Heizkörper des Niedrigtemperaturnetzes werden über Thermostatventile geregelt. Die Schalttemperatur von Heizkörpern und Bauteilaktivierung ist unterschiedlich. Letztere bleibt länger im Kühlmodus.

Um größtmögliche Flexibilität zu erreichen, sind die meisten Räume mit einem Doppelboden (bei Teppichbelägen) oder einem Hohlraumboden (bei Parkettboden) ausgestattet. Die Zuluft kommt in all diesen Räumen durch den Boden. Um die akustische Wirksamkeit des Bodens zu erhöhen, sind in der Executive Academy die Bodenplatten gelocht.

In Seminarräumen und Hörsälen sind außer Temperaturfühlern auch CO_2-Fühler montiert. In Kombination mit variablen Volumenstromreglern (VVS) wird so im Bedarfsfall die Luftmenge automatisch erhöht. Diese Maßnahme dient sowohl der Behaglichkeit (und Konzentrationsfähigkeit!) als auch der Energieeffizienz.

Und vieles andere mehr ...
Aufgrund der sehr unterschiedlichen Räumlichkeiten und Anforderungen gestaltete sich das Brandschutzkonzept komplex. Die von der Firma Hoyer geplanten Sprinkleranlagen weisen in einigen Bereichen Besonderheiten auf. In den meisten Gebäuden

the heat pump (heating/cooling machines) of the low temperature network. Significant users of the high temperature network are the air curtain door heaters in buildings with a high frequency of visitors. Radiators, floor convectors, and the reheaters are connected to the low temperature network. Radiators and floor convectors are only provided for in sensitive areas. The majority of the load is carried by building component activation. All buildings on campus – and nearly every room – are equipped with such systems. Acoustic measures are therefore limited to the walls and the floors in most areas. This also led to the use of lights as sound proofing elements (for example, in the Executive Academy and in the seminar rooms). Only in the Auditorium Center of the Teaching Center and select areas of the Library and Learning Center are high-performance cooling ceilings employed to also facilitate acoustic measures. This is another illustration of the close interrelation between architectural design and energy systems. The building component activation is not supplied by the low temperature network rather it is operated together with the preheaters and the precooling coils as a change-over system. One speaks of "change-over" when one and the same system is used for heating and cooling. Only the warm water in the sanitary rooms is supplied independently from the groundwater system via continuous flow water heaters under the sinks.

What does this have to do with me?
All buildings are equipped with physical data points for measurement and control systems. Including the BUS system for the fire protection and smoke control dampers this amounts to over 11,000 points. Approximately 100-square-meter zones are each equipped with a reference temperature sensor. The zone size serves, on the one hand, to limit pressure loss in the thermal activation distribution system; but it also facilitates a relatively precise (user-specific) regulation of the indoor climate. The zones are subsumed according to storey, compass direction, and type of function. When used for cooling the flow temperature is approximately 16°C, the return temperature 19°C; when used for heating the relationship is 30/27°C. The radiators of the low temperature network are controlled with thermostatic valves. The switch temperature is different for the radiators and the building component activation. The latter remains longer in the cooling mode.

In order to achieve the highest level of flexibility most rooms are equipped with raised double floors (when carpets) or with cavity floors (when parquet floors). In all rooms the supply air comes from the floor. In the Executive Academy the floor slabs are perforated in order to increase the acoustic efficiency of the floors.

In addition to the temperature sensors in seminar rooms and auditoriums, CO_2 sensors have also been mounted. In combination with variable volumetric flow controllers the air volume can be automatically increased when needed. This measure serves for room comfort (and concentration when studying!) as well as energy efficiency.

And much more...
The design of the fire protection concept is quite complex given the very different spaces and their requirements. The sprinkler systems by the company Hoyer have special designs in some areas. Most buildings are equipped with wet systems. Given the room height and the size of the fire compartment in the towering atrium of the Library and Learning Center, a deluge sprin-

ENERGY AND ECOLOGY

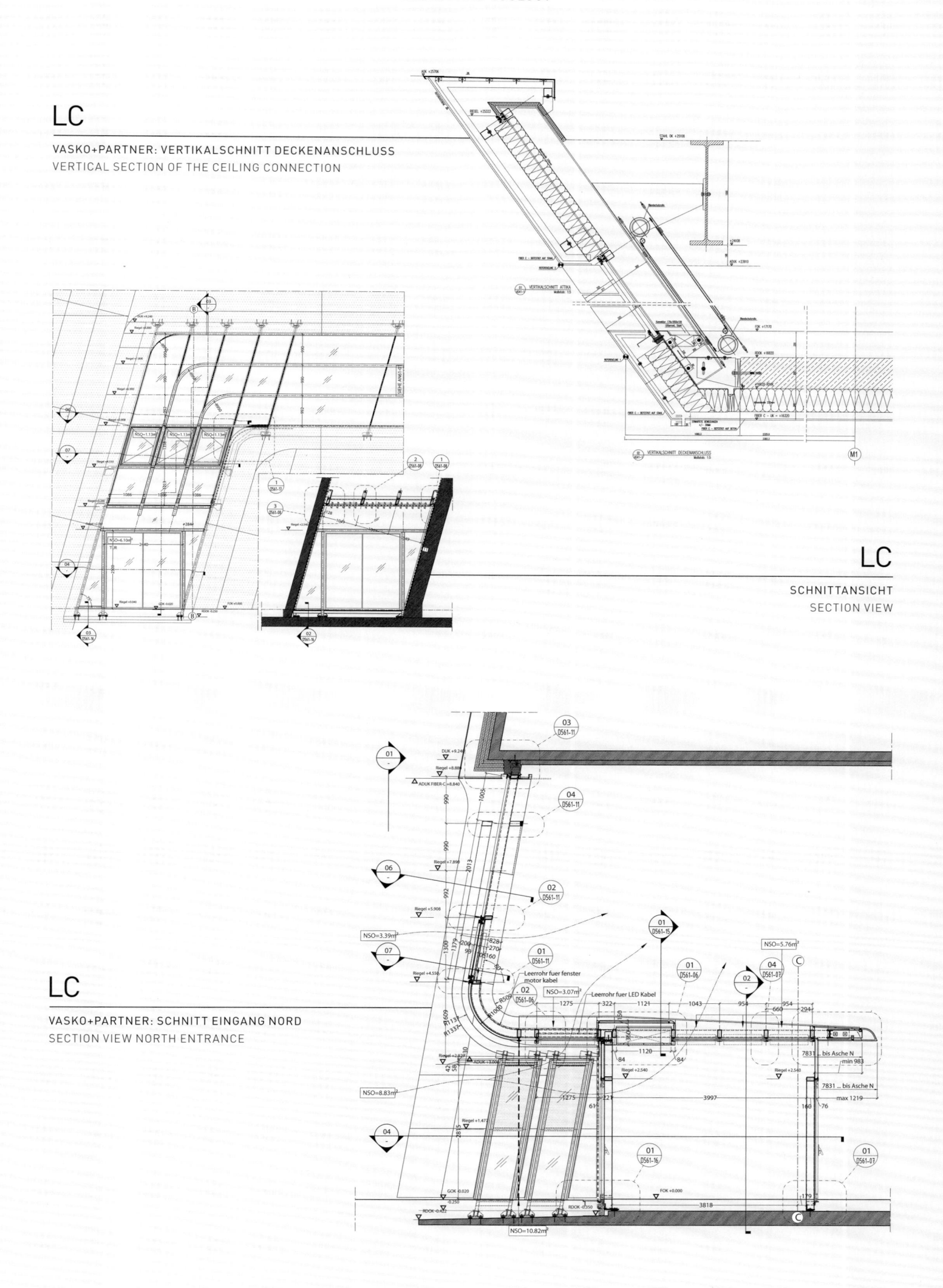

LC

VASKO+PARTNER: VERTIKALSCHNITT DECKENANSCHLUSS
VERTICAL SECTION OF THE CEILING CONNECTION

LC

SCHNITTANSICHT
SECTION VIEW

LC

VASKO+PARTNER: SCHNITT EINGANG NORD
SECTION VIEW NORTH ENTRANCE

Taktiles Leitsystem im Gebäudeinneren
Tactile guidance system inside the building

befinden sich Nass-Systeme. Im Atrium des Library and Learning Centers wurde aufgrund der Raumhöhe und der Größe des Brandabschnittes eine Sprühflutanlage vorgesehen, da normale Sprinklerköpfe zu spät oder gar nicht (abgekühlte Rauchgase) auslösen würden. In Bereichen, die mit Akustikbaffeln ausgestattet sind, wurden Steuersprinkler verwendet. In der Bibliothek und in den Archiven sind die Sprinklerleitungen mit Druckluft gefüllt, die Anlage ist von einem Zweimelder-System abhängig. Das heißt, dass sowohl mindestens ein Sprinklerkopf, als auch die Brandmeldeanlage auslösen müssen, um den Wasseraustritt herbeizuführen.

Das Wassermanagement sieht die vollständige Versickerung des Regenwassers am Campus vor. Für die Bewässerung und für die WC-Spülung wird Grundwasser eingesetzt. Urinale wurden wasserlos ausgeführt.

Für das Erlangen der ÖGNI-Zertifikate sind aber nicht nur Ökologie, Ökonomie und Energieeffizienz, sondern auch soziokulturelle Faktoren wie Barrierefreiheit, Sicherheit und Gesundheit entscheidend. Die Transparenzschaffung von Nachhaltigkeitsanforderungen in einer sehr frühen Projektphase spiegeln sich in einer außergewöhnlichen hohen Prozessqualität wieder.

So wurde bereits im Vorentwurf die Zusammenarbeit mit diversen Fachverbänden gesucht und der Campus mit einem taktilen Leitsystem, induktiven Höranlagen, Notrufsäulen und einer

kler system was used as normal sprinkler heads would be triggered too late or not at all (cooled fumes). Control sprinklers are used in areas equipped with sound absorbing baffles. In the library and the archives the sprinkler pipes are filled with compressed air, and the system is dependent on dual detectors. That means that at least one sprinkler head and the fire alarm system must both be triggered for the release of water.

The water management plan provides for the complete seepage of rainwater on campus. Groundwater is used for flushing toilets. Urinals use a waterless system.

In order to receive the ÖGNI certificates, not only ecology, economy, and energy efficiency are central, also sociocultural factors such as accessibility, safety, and health play a decisive role. The transparency of the sustainability requirements compiled in a very early stage is reflected in the extraordinarily high processual quality.

For example, collaborations with diverse associations were sought in the pre-design phase in order to equip the campus with a tactile guidance system, an assistive listening system, emergency call pillars, and a security center for the complete campus. Markus Moucka from Drees & Sommer: "We received a lot of input from the associations and the standards committees, which enabled us to reach a level far above the normative directives."

Sicherheitszentrale für den gesamten Campus ausgestattet. Markus Moucka von Drees & Sommer: „Wir bekamen viele Inputs aus den Fachverbänden und den Normenausschüssen und konnten so ein Niveau erreichen, das weit über normative Grundlagen hinausgegangen ist."

Einen Schritt weiter
Günther Sammer von Vasko+Partner berichtet, dass der energetische Masterplan weitestgehend ohne Modifizierungen realisiert werden konnte.[6] Durch den speziellen Planungsablauf habe die Integration der einzelnen Gebäude in das Gesamt-Energiekonzept sehr gut funktioniert.

Ein wichtiger gestalterischer Erfolg des Campus liegt zweifellos in seiner Differenziertheit. Das beste Gegenbeispiel ist die alte WU selbst. Während dort von einem einzigen Planungsbüro ein einziges homogenes, aber ambivalentes Großobjekt entworfen wurde, wird der neue Campus der urbanen Dimension des Projekts gerecht und liefert städtische Vielfalt. Gleichzeitig konnten ein vielschichtiger Masterplan und ein hochqualifiziertes Team die Grundlage eines intelligenten Zusammenspiels dieser Vielfalt gewährleisten. Die Chance, die Synergien eines größeren Systems zu nützen, wurde ergriffen und ohne Monotonie umgesetzt. Der WU Campus kann mit Recht als Best Practice-Beispiel bezeichnet werden.

1 http://www.big.at/projekte/campus-wu/
2 Günther Sammer von Vasko+Partner hält dazu fest, dass Prof. Cody zwar kurz seitens BUSarchitektur als Berater zugezogen wurde, das endgültige Energiekonzept jedoch von Vasko+Partner und BUSarchitektur erstellt wurde.
3 boa Büro für offensive Aleatorik [Hrsg.], Campus WU – A Holistic History, Wien, 2013, S. 92.
4 Von BUSarchitektur und boa Büro für offensive Aleatorik wurden neue Instrumente entwickelt, die über die üblichen Funktionen eines Masterplans hinausgehen, dazu gehören der Integrale Masterplan und der Konfigurator.
5 Dass es keinen zwingenden Zusammenhang zwischen Glasanteil und Überhitzungsstunden geben muss, wurde u. a. von Stefan Plesser und Johannes Lang gezeigt: Jürgen Pöschk [Hrsg.], Energieeffizienz in Gebäuden – Jahrbuch 2008, S. 87–96: Stefan Plesser und Johannes Lang, Gebäude optimieren – im laufendend Betrieb, VME-Verlag, Berlin 2008.
6 Die Autoren danken ihren Interviewpartnern Markus Moucka von Drees & Sommer und Günther Sammer von Vasko+Partner für ihre Zeit und bereitwilligen Auskünfte.

A Step Further
Günther Sammer from Vasko+Partner reports that the energy master plan was realized largely without modifications.[6] Thanks to the special planning procedure the individual buildings have been very well integrated into the overall energy concept.

An important achievement in the design of the campus is without doubt its differentiation. The best counter example is the old WU itself. Whereas a single homogenous yet ambivalent mega-building was designed there by one office, the new campus does justice to the urban scale of the project and contributes to the diversity of the cityscape. At the same time a multifaceted master plan and a highly-qualified team ensured the basis for an intelligent interplay within this diversity. The chance to use the synergies of a larger system was seized and realized without monotony. The WU Campus can rightly be called a best practice example.

1 http://www.big.at/projekte/campus-wu/
2 Günther Sammer from Vasko+Partner notes that Prof. Cody was briefly engaged by BUSarchitektur as a consultant, however the final energy concept was developed by Vasko+Partner and BUSarchitektur.
3 boa Büro für offensive Aleatorik (ed.), Campus WU – A Holistic History (Vienna: boa, 2013), 92.
4 BUSarchitektur and boa Büro für offensive Aleatorik have developed new tools that go far beyond the conventional functions of a master plan, among others the Integral Master Plan and the Configurator.
5 Stefan Plesser and Johannes Lang, among others, show that there doesn't have to be a conclusive link between the glass ratio and the overheating hours: Stefan Plesser and Johannes Lang, "Gebäude optimieren – im laufendend Betrieb," in Energieeffizienz in Gebäuden – Jahrbuch 2008, ed. Jürgen Pöschk (Berlin: VME-Verlag, 2008), 87–96.
6 The authors thank their interview partners Markus Moucka from Drees & Sommer and Günther Sammer from Vasko+Partner for their time and willingness to provide information.

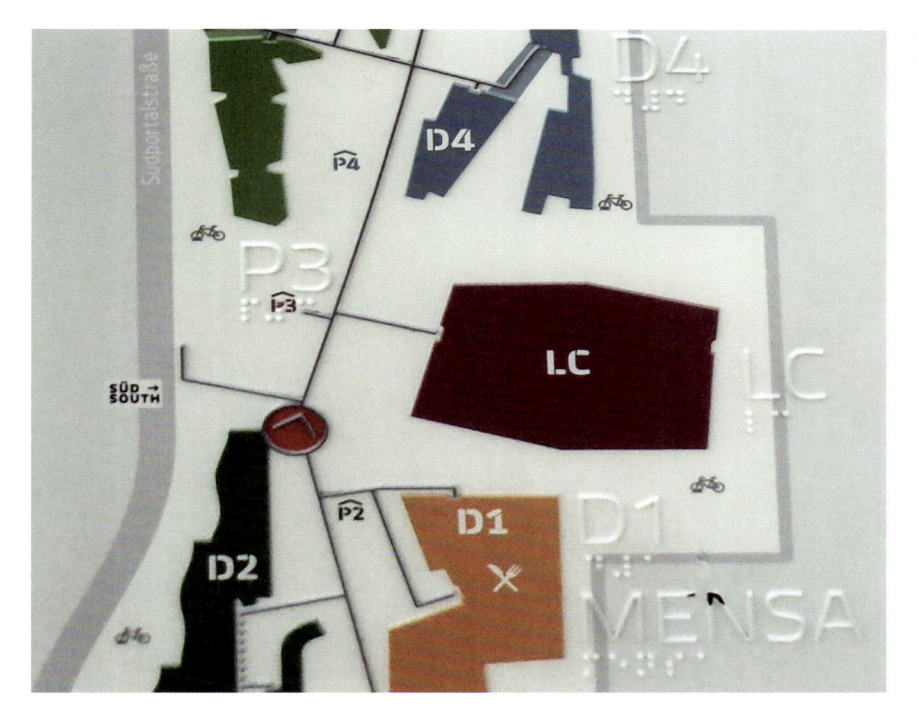

Orientierungstafel, Blindenschrift
Orientation plate, Braille

D4

ESTUDIO CARME PINÓS: DEPARTMENTS 4

DEPARTMENTS 4

EIN SPIEL MIT PARALLELOGRAMMEN
DEPARTMENTGEBÄUDE D4 VON ESTUDIO CARME PINÓS

AN INTERPLAY OF PARALLELOGRAMS
DEPARTMENT BUILDING D4 BY ESTUDIO CARME PINÓS

ULRICH TRAGATSCHNIG

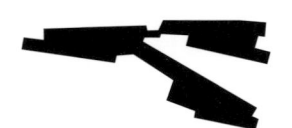

Angesichts seiner schrägen Fluchten und Schnitte, Vor- und Rücksprünge wirkt das vom spanischen Architekturbüro Estudio Carme Pinós entworfene Departmentgebäude D4 zunächst klar „dekonstruktivistisch", leicht in die vom Architekturhistoriker Heinrich Klotz beschriebene „Zweite Moderne" einzuordnen. Die nähere Betrachtung relativiert diesen Kurzschluss. Hier droht nichts auseinander zu fallen. Am Ende wirkt auch die „Tetrisfassade" wie die raffinierte Neuauflage des postmodernen Ornaments und das Ganze wie eine gefahrlose, aber tiefsinnige Spielerei.

Zusammenhalt trotz Zersplitterung
Um die Jahrtausendwende war es für Heinrich Klotz recht klar, in welcher Form sich das Neue ankündigt und wohin es sich entwickeln wird. Aus der genauen Kenntnis und Interpretation des Baugeschehens schöpfte er eine Narration, die wohltuend präzise Wertmaßstäbe verkörperte. Die Architektur seiner Zeit hatte für ihn die historisierend-ornamentalen Aspekte der sogenannten Postmoderne großteils überwunden und setzte, gleichwohl revisionistisch, das Projekt der Klassischen Moderne fort. Dieser „Zweiten Moderne" ging es, laut Klotz, zum einen wieder um die Pflege eines selbstgenügsam reinen Vokabulars. Zum anderen aber auch um dessen Überhöhung durch „erzählerisch fiktionale Sinnerweiterung".[1]

Das Departmentgebäude D4 ist auf ersten Blick ein prototypischer Vertreter dieser Tendenzen. Es setzt sich aus reinen Formen zusammen, nicht aber um damit einfach nur einem lapidaren

With its skewed alignments and slanted sections, projections and deep recesses, Department Building D4 by the Spanish architecture office Estudio Carme Pinós initially appears to be clearly "deconstructivist", easy to classify in the "second modernism" described by architectural historian Heinrich Klotz. But a closer look quickly relativizes this hasty conclusion. Here nothing threatens to fall apart. In the end, also the "Tetris façade" has the appeal of a sophisticated interpretation of postmodern ornament, and the whole seems to be a harmless yet profound game.

Coherence despite Fragmentation
Around the millennium the advent of a new architecture was quite apparent to Heinrich Klotz, and he knew the direction it would take. From a detailed knowledge and interpretation of built history, he formulated a narration that offered refreshingly precise standards. In his eyes, the architecture of his time had largely overcome the historicizing ornamental aspects of the so-called postmodern and pursued – albeit with revisions – the project of classic modernism. According to Klotz, this "second modernism" was, on the one hand, once again about cultivating a self-contained, pure vocabulary. But on the other hand, it was also about its exaggeration by adding a "narrative, fictional dimension".[1]

At first glance Department Building D4 is a prototypical representative of these tendencies. It is composed of pure forms, but not in order to simply meet the requirements of a terse functional

Einer der vielen unerwarteten Platzbildungen am Campus ergibt sich aus der Y-Geometrie des Hauses
One of the many unexpected urban squares pops up through the Y geometry of the building

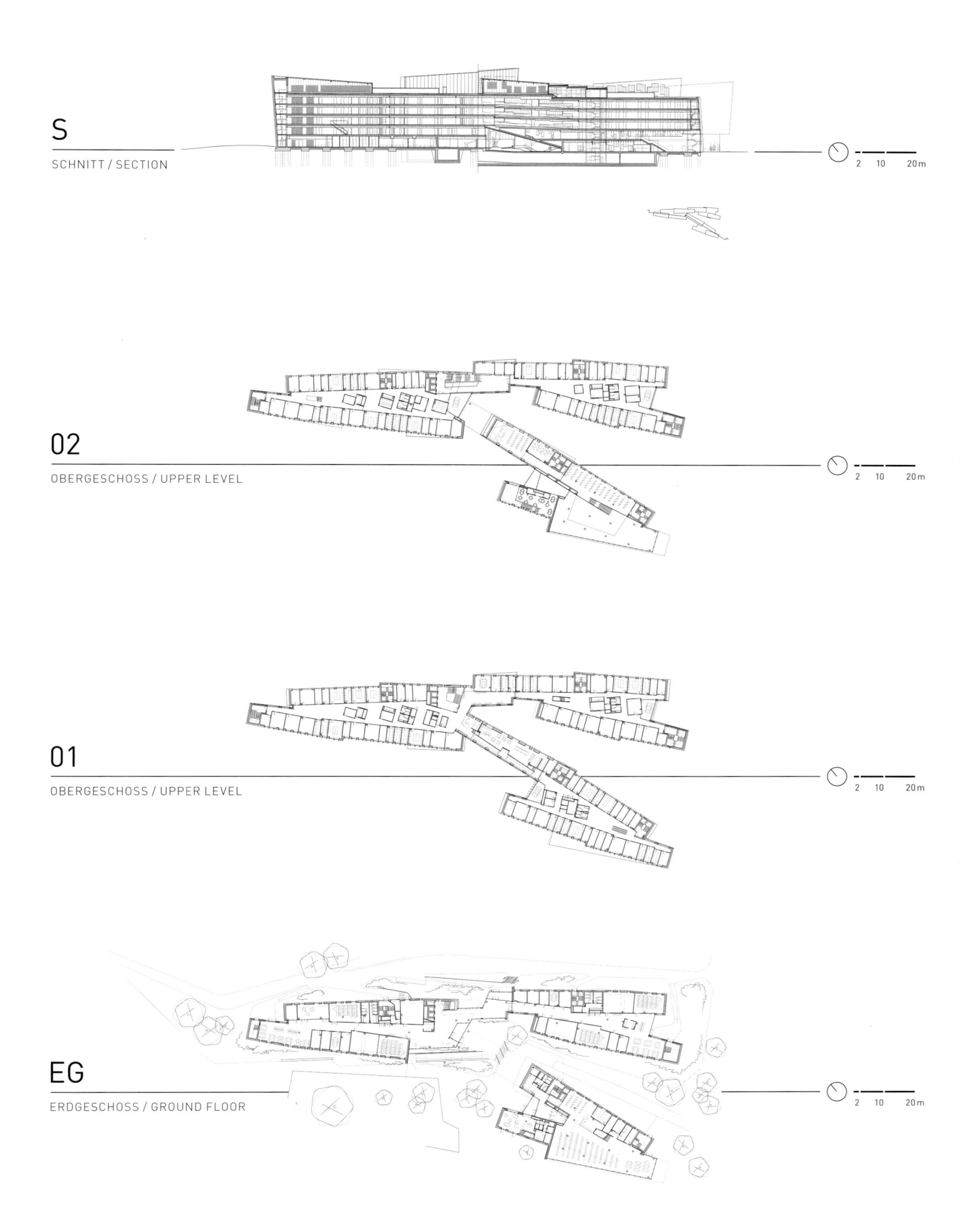

DEPARTMENTS 4

S
SCHNITT / SECTION

02
OBERGESCHOSS / UPPER LEVEL

01
OBERGESCHOSS / UPPER LEVEL

EG
ERDGESCHOSS / GROUND FLOOR

DEPARTMENTS 4

Der Haupteingang liegt im Schnittpunkt der drei Gebäudetrakte unter einer Schräge
The main entrance is at the intersection of the three wings of the building

Die zwei Schenkel des Y öffnen sich in Richtung Library and Learning Center
Two volumes of the Y plan open up toward the Library and Learning Center

Überlagerung zweier Systeme: Parallelogramm-Baukörper und Zick-Zack-Öffnungen
Two systems overlap: parallelogram volumes and zig-zag openings

Die Expo-Zone vor dem Departmentgebäude ist Teil der Freiraumplanung von BUSarchitektur
Expo zone in front of the building, designed by BUSarchitektur

Zweckrationalismus zu genügen. Gemessen am verbauten Volumen bringt es enorm viele Büros, Aufenthalts- und Nebenräume, Lehrsäle und eine Bibliothek unter Dach und Fach, bleibt dabei jedoch einer Verspieltheit verpflichtet, die ihm ein eigenes, unverwechselbares Erscheinungsbild verleiht und „Sinn" generiert.

Dabei relativiert das Haus aber auch Klotz' Architekturgeschichte, die den ins Spiel gebrachten Inhalt hauptsächlich als dekonstruktivistischen gelesen hat. Den fiktiven Charakter sah Klotz primär in „Zersplitterung", in einer „Auflösung bis an den Rand des scheinbaren Zerfalls". Bauten wie die von Günter Behnisch, Coop Himmelb(l)au, Rem Koolhaas oder Daniel Libeskind stellten für ihn die Kategorien von „Ganzheit" oder „Perfektion" durchaus theatralisch in Frage: „Wenn am Ende doch alles zusammenhält, so ist mit der entstandenen Verwunderung zugleich ein Interesse am Zustandekommen des Bauwerks verbunden."[2]

Wege und Plätze
Solche Verwunderung wird man vor dem Departmentgebäude D4 schwerlich empfinden. Gewiss, es ist keine einfache Ganzheit, die dem Betrachter hier vor Augen steht. Schon der Grund-

rationality. In terms of the built volume, it accommodates a great number of offices, lounges and common rooms, classrooms, and a library under one roof; however, it remains committed to a playfulness that lends it an own unmistakable appearance and generates "content".

But the building also relativizes Klotz's architectural history, which mainly reads the invoked content as deconstructivist. Klotz saw the fictitious nature primarily in "fragmentation", in a "dissolution to the point of apparent collapse". Buildings such as those by Günter Behnisch, Coop Himmelb(l)au, Rem Koolhaas, or Daniel Libeskind question the categories of "totality" or "perfection" in an indeed theatrical manner: "But when everything holds together in the end, then the aroused astonishment at the same time triggers an interest in the realization of the building."[2]

Paths and Places
It is hard to have such a sense of astonishment in front Department Building D4. Sure enough, the observer is not presented with a mere totality. Already the floor plan is quite complex. The

Die zweigeschossige Bibliothek ist großzügig verglast, der Ausblick ist mit einem Schleier-Vorhang vernebelt
The two-level library is generously glazed, the view outside is blurred by a hazy drop

riss ist durchaus komplex. Das Gebäude setzt sich grob aus drei zu einem Y miteinander verbundenen Teilen zusammen, die sich wiederum leicht V-förmig aufspreizen. Die nördlichen beiden bilden einen geknickten Riegel, der den Campus zur Messe hin abschließt. Durch eine schräg gestellte Scheibe ist mit ihm ein zweiter, etwas tiefer gelegter Körper am Campus verbunden. „Durch die Anhebung eines Volumens entsteht im Erdgeschoss die geforderte Fußgängerverbindung, die zum Library and Learning Center führt"[3], erläutern die Architekten.

Der Eingangsbereich des Departmentgebäudes liegt im Schnittpunkt des Ypsilons. Er ist auch der Verkehrsknotenpunkt des Gebäudes. Den Besucher empfängt ein lichtes, weil großflächig verglastes Foyer, das unkompliziert zu Lift und Treppe führt. Das Erdgeschoss reiht in zwei Achsen Seminar- und Projekträume bzw. Studierenden-Lounges aneinander. Die Obergeschosse sind durch Glaswände und Teppichböden weit privater gestaltet. Von den Front-Office-Bereichen strahlen die Gänge der jeweils über zwei Stockwerke verteilten Departments für Finance and Statistics, Sozioökonomie und Volkswirtschaft aus und erschließen recht sparsam dimensionierte Büros und Konferenzräume. Rampen vermitteln zu einer dritten Achse im tiefer gelegten Baukörper und begleiten dabei weit großzügigere Lounges, die informellen Treffen Raum bieten und als Cafeterias genutzt werden können.

Dass sich die Fluchten der langgestreckten Mittelgänge nicht geradlinig entwickeln, sondern sich in sanften Knicken aufweiten oder verengen, erhöht in den Obergeschossen die Privatheit des Ambientes. In den am stärksten aufgeweiteten Bereichen stehen Kopierräume, kleine Küchen, Archive und interne Treppen schräg im Raum, mindern die Übersicht und mildern die Gestrecktheit der Flügel. Im Erdgeschoss münden die Gänge in offene Aufenthaltsbereiche, die als Selbststudienzonen nutzbar sind.

Ein extravagantes Kleid
Die Fassaden zeigen, dass es dem Gebäude dezidiert um Rhetorik und Erzählung geht. Während die das Y zusammenbindenden Teile in dunkles Metallgitter gekleidet sind und sich die

building consists of three slightly V-shaped components, which are connected to one another in the form of a Y. The two wings to the north form a buckled bar, defining the boundary between the campus and the Messe Wien exhibition grounds. A diagonal slab connects a second, somewhat lower volume toward the campus. "By elevating one volume, the required pedestrian connection is created on the ground floor, which leads to the Library and Learning Center,"[3] explain the architects.

The entrance area of the Department Building is situated at the intersection of the Y. It is also the central movement hub of the building. Visitors are welcomed by a brightly lit, generously glazed foyer that houses the elevator and stairs. The seminar and project rooms and the study areas are rowed along two axes on the ground floor. The upper floors are designed to be far more private with glass walls and carpets. Hallways branch out from the front office areas of the Departments of Finance and Statistics, Socioeconomics, and Economics, providing access to thriftily dimensioned offices and conference rooms. Ramps form a connection to the third axis in the lower volume and pass along more spacious lounges, which can be used as spaces for informal meetings and cafeterias.

The long aisles of the central hallways are not laid out as straight lines; they expand or contract with gentle kinks and heighten the private ambience on the upper floors. Copier rooms, small kitchens, archives, and internal staircases are diagonally situated at the widest points, diffusing the overview of the whole and tempering the elongated design of the wings. The hallways on the ground floor lead to open common areas, which function as self-study zones.

An Extravagant Dress
The façades reveal that this building is decidedly about rhetoric and narrative. While the components that bind the Y are clad in a dark metal trellis and the small sides of the wings are similarly withdrawn in dark gray, the remaining fronts have a far more dynamic design. Here the windows are deeply recessed into the

Die Metallgitter-Fassade verschafft den gestaffelten Korridoren kontemplative Lichteffekte
Metal trellis on the façade creates contemplative light atmospheres in the staggered corridors

>

Bewegungsmuster von Stiegen und Fensteröffnungen in Interferenz
Interfering movement patterns of windows and stairs

>>

Ein Seminarraum mit vielfach durchbrochener Längswand und nüchterner Einrichtung
A seminar room with numerous perforations in its long wall and a sober furnishing
⌄

Auch in der Cafeteria zeichnet sich das rhythmische Fassadenmuster ab und interagiert mit der Einrichtung
Interplay between the rhythmic façade pattern in the cafeteria and the furnishings
⌄

In den Büros bieten die vertikal versetzten Fensterfelder Ausblicke auf verschiedenen Ebenen
Staggered windows create views from the offices on different levels one level
⌄

Die öffentlichen, barrierefreien Bereiche des Hauses gehen fließend ineinander über
The public barrier-free spaces of the house fluidly merge into each other
›

Schmalseiten der Flügel ebenso dunkelgrau zurücknehmen, haben die übrigen Fronten eine weit lebhaftere Gestaltung erfahren. Hier sind die tief aus dem weißen Putz geschnittenen, von Faltschiebeläden aus dunklem Aluminiumlochblech begleiteten Fenster zueinander verschoben übereinander gestapelt, was nicht von ungefähr schon zur Bezeichnung „Tetris-Fassade" führte. Leicht kommt die Vermutung auf, dass diese gezackten Furchen mehr einer von außen hinzugedachten Logik als einer Belichtungsmaxime folgen. Gewiss, die Fensterstränge scheinen das Gebäude zu zerklüften, zersplittern es dabei aber nicht. Gemeinsam mit den verputzten Flächen bilden sie ein extravagant gemustertes Kleid, als hätten Ornament und Nutzbarkeit widerstreitend doch zueinander gefunden.

Liest man die schräggestellten Fluchten der Erschließungsgänge bzw. die leichten Vor- und Rücksprünge an den Fassaden als Ausweise eigenständiger Volumina, sind es insgesamt 15 Scheiben, die sich hier zu einer Einheit zusammen gefunden haben. Dabei vermitteln sie aber nicht den Eindruck einer schwierigen, labilen Gemeinschaft. Am Ende entspricht das Ganze dem, worauf die Architekten von Anfang an hinaus wollten: Einer „Spielerei aus Parallelogrammen, welche die Anordnung der Büros und der restlichen Räume auf einfache Art und Weise löst."[4]

1 Heinrich Klotz, Architektur der Zweiten Moderne. Ein Essay zur Ankündigung des Neuen, Stuttgart 1999, Zitat S. 25. Vgl. auch ders., Kunst im 20. Jahrhundert. Moderne – Postmoderne – Zweite Moderne, München 1994.
2 Klotz, 1999, S. 34.
3 Estudio Carme Pinós S. L., Baufeld W1 – Departments, online unter: http://www.architekturwettbewerb.at/data/media/med_binary/original/1229425868.pdf (Zugriffsdatum: 11. 2. 2014).
4 Ebd.

white plaster walls, stacked and shifted above and beside one another, and furnished with folding shutters made of perforated aluminum panels – not by chance, the origin of the title "Tetris façade". It is easy to suppose that these jagged furrows are derived from a logic projected from outside as opposed to an optimal lighting maxim. The window patterns appear to fissure the building, but they do not end in fragmentation. In combination with the plastered surfaces they fashion an extravagantly patterned dress, as if the conflict between ornament and function had been reconciled after all.

If one reads the kinks in the corridors or the subtle projections and recesses on the façades as evidence of independent volumes, it is a total of 15 slabs that unite here to form a whole. However, they do not convey the impression of a complicated, unstable agglomeration. In the end the whole corresponds with the intention of the architects in the very beginning: "An interplay of parallelograms that solves the layout of the offices and the rest of the spaces in a simple way."[4]

1 Translated for this publication from: Heinrich Klotz, Architektur der Zweiten Moderne. Ein Essay zur Ankündigung des Neuen (Stuttgart: DVA, 1999), 25.; cf. Heinrich Klotz, Kunst im 20. Jahrhundert. Moderne – Postmoderne – Zweite Moderne (Munich: Beck, 1994).
2 Klotz, 1999, 34.
3 Cf. Estudio Carme Pinós S. L., "Baufeld W1 –Departments", http://www.architekturwettbewerb.at/data/media/med_binary/original/1229425868.pdf, accessed February 11, 2014.
4 Ibid.

STATEMENTS

DIE MEHRZAHL DER SACHEN IST RICHTIG GEMACHT WORDEN
DER NEUE CAMPUS AUS SICHT DER LEHRENDEN

ULRICH TRAGATSCHNIG

Der neue WU Campus beherbergt insgesamt 90 Hörsäle und Seminarräume, die sich auf alle Gebäude verteilen. Dazu kommen zahlreiche Break-Out-Zones: kleine Räume, die sowohl für Gruppenarbeiten während der Lehrveranstaltungen nutzbar, als auch von den Studierenden selbst frei buchbar sind. So unterschiedlich sie in Zuschnitt, Möblierung und Farbgebung anmuten, vereint sie doch ein Umstand, der den wohl größten Unterschied zur vorherigen Situation ausmacht und von den Lehrenden unisono gelobt wird: Alle Unterrichtsräume haben Tageslicht. Vorbei sind die Zeiten, in denen die Lehre in bunkerähnlichen und lautstark klimatisierten Schachteln stattfinden musste. Auch die technische Ausstattung der Räume ist up to date. Einfach zu bedienende Beamer und Smartboards erlauben eine multimediale Vermittlung. Befragt man die Lehrenden, ergeben die Neuerungen ein durchaus sehr positives Stimmungsbild. Natürlich werden aber auch manche Problemfelder benannt.

THE MAJORITY OF THINGS WERE DONE RIGHT
THE NEW CAMPUS FROM THE VIEWPOINT OF THE TEACHERS

The new WU Campus houses a total of 90 lecture halls and seminar rooms, which are found in all of the buildings. Additionally, there are also "break-out zones": small rooms that can be used for group work during the courses and freely booked by the individual students as well. As varied as they might seem in their layout, furniture, and color schemes, there is one aspect that they share in common, which is probably the biggest change in comparison to the previous situation and is praised by the teachers unanimously: All lecture rooms have natural daylight. The days are over when teaching had to take place in bunker-like and vociferous, climatized boxes. And the technical equipment is state-of-the-art. Easy to operate beamers and smartboards facilitate multimedia communication of the content. If you ask the teachers, the improvements yield a very positive atmospheric picture. But naturally, also some problematic issues have been identified.

LEHRENDE – TEACHERS – STATEMENTS

VERENA MADNER

Leiterin des Forschungsinstituts für Urban Management und Governance
Head of the Research Institute for Urban Management and Governance

Ulrich Tragatschnig: Haben die Visionäre beim neuen WU Campus erreicht, was sie wollten?
Verena Madner: Aus meiner Sicht schon. Bereits am ersten Tag war spürbar, dass mit dieser zentralen Achse und mit dem Zusammenrücken der vielen vorher zerstreuten Standorte unheimlich viel Kommunikation begonnen hat. Selbst viele Nutzer der Tiefgarage nehmen den Weg über die Oberfläche, statt den Lift ins Institut zu nutzen. Diese Planung war sicher ein genialer Schachzug. Im alten Gebäude wählten die meisten den Aufzug direkt zu ihrem Institut. Viele Leute hat man deshalb nie gesehen.

Ergeben sich am neuen Standort Verbesserungen für Ihre Lehre?
Ganz sicher. Ein Beispiel: Ich arbeite in einigen Lehrveranstaltungen mit Kleingruppen. Dazu gibt es jetzt spezielle Arbeitsräume, die ich gleich im Herbst bei meiner ersten Lehrveranstaltung am neuen Campus intensiv nutzen konnte. Auch das Tageslicht bewirkt sehr viel. Im Teaching Center herrscht eine unglaublich angenehme Atmosphäre. Im Departmentgebäude von Cook, in dem ich arbeite, unterrichte ich auch sehr gerne. Interessanterweise sind die Studierenden diesem Gebäude gegenüber viel skeptischer als die Lehrenden. Sie fänden es schon recht verspielt, haben mir einige konkret gesagt. Insgesamt nehme ich aber wahr, dass die Studierenden von den Lernplätzen am Campus und von der Medientechnik im Hörsaal sehr begeistert sind.

Hat der neue Standort Ihre Lehre sonst irgendwie beeinflusst?
Der neue Standort ist für mich ein Ansporn, mehr mit der Umgebung zu interagieren. Wir haben zum Beispiel an der WU schon Kontakte zur Gebietsbetreuung hier im zweiten Wiener Gemeindebezirk geknüpft und sie in verschiedenen Lehrveranstaltungen auch eingebunden. Speziell im Stuwerviertel hat sich durch den neuen Campus einiges verändert. Wenn ich eine Lehrveranstaltung zu Stadtentwicklung und Partizipation veranstalte, ist es naheliegend, sie auch vor Ort zu verankern. Das hätte man zwar auch am alten Standort machen können, man war aber nicht in derselben Art und Weise motiviert dazu. Hier herrscht tatsächlich eine andere Stimmung.

> Der neue Standort ist für mich ein Ansporn, mehr mit der Umgebung zu interagieren.
>
> The new location motivates me to interact more with my surroundings.

Ulrich Tragatschnig: Did the visionaries accomplish what they intended with the WU Campus?
Verena Madner: Yes, they have, from my point of view. Already on the first day one could feel that the central axis and the now closer proximity of the previously scattered locations had triggered a great deal of communication. Even many users of the underground parking walk over the surface instead of taking the elevator to their department. This plan was certainly a stroke of genius. In the old building many went underground from the garage directly to the office with the elevator. Hence, you never saw some people at all.

Does the new location contribute to improvements in your teaching?
Definitely. One example: I work with small groups in some courses. Now there are special work rooms available for this, which I could already make use of in autumn for my first course on the new campus. Also the daylight has a big effect. There is an incredibly pleasant atmosphere in the Teaching Center. I also truly enjoy teaching in the Department and Administration Building by Cook where I work. Interestingly, the students are far more skeptical about this building than the teachers. They find it quite playful, some of them clearly told me. But in general I sense that the students are very fond of the study areas on campus and the media technology in the auditoriums.

Did the new location have any other influences on your teaching?
The new location motivates me to interact more with my surroundings. For example, we have already made contacts with the local Gebietsbetreuung (urban renewal office) here in the second district and also involved them in various courses. Especially in the Stuwer neighborhood a lot has changed because of the new campus. When I organize a course on urban development and participation, it seems only logical to also make a connection with the site on hands. Naturally, this could have been done at the former location of the WU as well, but one was somehow not as encouraged to do so. There is certainly a different vibe around here.

MONIKA KNASSMÜLLER
Public Management und Governance

> Raumklima und Lichtverhältnisse sind eindeutig besser. Fein ist auch die technische Ausstattung der Hörsäle, das Schleppen von Beamer und Laptop ist endlich Geschichte.

> The indoor climate and the light conditions are clearly better. A nice thing is also the technical equipment in the auditoriums; dragging around the beamer and laptop is finally history now.

Ulrich Tragatschnig: Eignen sich die neuen Räume besser für Ihre Lehrveranstaltungen?
Monika Knassmüller: Auf jeden Fall. Raumklima und Lichtverhältnisse sind eindeutig besser. Fein ist auch die technische Ausstattung der Hörsäle, das Schleppen von Beamer und Laptop ist endlich Geschichte. Man kann die Bestuhlung in den kleineren Unterrichtsräumen umstellen, was gut für diskursive Lehrveranstaltungsformate ist. Die Standard-Aufstellung ist allerdings immer sehr vortragsorientiert. In vielen Hörsälen ist die Aufstellung primär auf die Screens ausgerichtet, und das Pult der Vortragenden steht seitlich daneben, das heißt, es steht quasi im Off. Das lässt sich auch durch Umstellen nicht vermeiden. Das ist das einzige, was für mich gewöhnungsbedürftig ist. Die Break-Out-Zonen sind ideal für meine Veranstaltungen und bieten neue Möglichkeiten, die ich in den nächsten Semestern auf jeden Fall ausloten werde.

Einzigartig ist die Nähe des Campus zum grünen Prater. Könnten Sie sich auch Open-air-Lehrveranstaltungen vorstellen?
Das ist wie mit der Technik: Nicht alles, was geht, ist auch sinnvoll. Wenn es mir darum geht, die Leute irgendwo rauszuholen – im wörtlichen wie übertragenen Sinn – dann kann das schon was bringen. Oder für Kreativphasen. Es muss eben inhaltsorientiert sein. Bei unserem quantitativen Verhältnis von Studierenden zu Lehrenden ist die Zeit, in der man Kontakt zu den Studierenden hat und eine direkte Auseinandersetzung mit ihnen als Personen möglich ist, sehr wertvoll und muss gut geplant sein.

Ulrich Tragatschnig: Are the new rooms better suited for your courses?
Monika Knassmüller: Yes, for sure. The indoor climate and the light conditions are clearly better. A nice thing is also the technical equipment in the auditoriums; dragging around the beamer and laptop is finally history now. You can rearrange the seats in the smaller classrooms, which is useful for discursive course formats. However, the standard set-up is always very lecture-oriented. In many auditoriums the set-up is primarily oriented toward the screens with the speaker's desk positioned to their side, meaning that it stands off-stage, so to speak. Reorganizing the seats cannot change this either. This is the only thing that I find needs getting used to. The break-out zones are ideal for my courses and bear new possibilities that I will definitely explore in the next semesters.

The proximity of the campus to the green Prater park is unique. Can you also imagine open air courses?
This is the same thing like with technology: Not everything that is possible makes sense, too. When it is about getting people out of somewhere – in the literal and the virtual sense – this can indeed be helpful. Or for creative breaks. After all, it has to be content-oriented. Given our quantitative relationship between students and teachers, the time in which one has contact with the students and when direct personal interaction is possible is very precious and should be carefully planned.

LEHRENDE – TEACHERS – STATEMENTS

MARTIN SPITZER
Leiter des Bereichs Unternehmensrecht
Chair of Civil Procedure Law

Ulrich Tragatschnig: Wie fühlt sich das Unterrichten am neuen Campus für Sie an, welche Unterschiede gibt es gegenüber dem alten Standort?
Martin Spitzer: Neben dem vielen Tageslicht und der Luftigkeit sind hier auch die Bedingungen von technischer Seite ganz ausgezeichnet. Die Smartboards etwa, die Anbindung ans Internet, das ist alles State of the Art. Ich selbst habe das jedenfalls noch nirgendwo besser erlebt.

Haben die neuen Möglichkeiten Ihre Lehre beeinflusst?
Wenn wir uns ehrlich sind: Nein. Ob man etwas in der Platonischen Akademie mit dem Stock in den Sand zeichnet, ob man mit Kreide auf eine Tafel schreibt oder ein Smartboard verwendet: Davon hängt der Kern der Lehre ja nicht ab. Die Technik macht die Dinge leichter, die mathematischen Fächer profitieren davon natürlich besonders, aber die haben das ja auch früher schon gut bewältigt.

Vom technischen Equipment abgesehen: Wie würden Sie die neuen Räume beschreiben?
In vielen Bereichen kann man eine neue Großzügigkeit bemerken. Architektonisch merkt man sie wohl am stärksten beim Learning Center. Man soll dort reinkommen, im vier Stockwerke hohen Atrium stehen und denken: Na bumm! Das ist natürlich schon ein Stück Bombast-Architektur, das auch eine Funktion erfüllt. Der Überhang zum Campus ist von der Message her allerdings sehr sympathisch. Man hätte ja auch sagen können, dass dort, im prominentesten Teil des ganzen Campus, von dem aus man auch noch einen traumhaften Ausblick hat, das Rektorat hinein kommt. Dass dieser Platz den Studierenden gehört, finde ich super.

> „Na bumm! Das ist natürlich schon ein Stück Bombast-Architektur, das auch eine Funktion erfüllt.
>
> Wow! Of course, this is a bombastic work of architecture, which also fulfills a function."

Ulrich Tragatschnig: How does it feel to teach on the new campus? What is different in comparison to the old location?
Martin Spitzer: In addition to plenty of daylight and the airiness also the technical outfitting is fantastic. Take the smartboards, for example, or the Internet connectivity – everything is state-of-the-art. At least I have never seen this better implemented anywhere else.

Have the new possibilities influenced your teaching?
To be honest: No. Whether one draws something with a stick in the sand at the Platonic Academy, writes with chalk on a blackboard, or uses a smartboard, the core of the teaching doesn't depend on this. Technology makes things easier, with mathematical subjects naturally benefiting the most, but they managed well enough in the past, too.

Aside from the technical equipment: How would you describe the new spaces?
In many areas you can notice a new generosity. Architecturally speaking, this is probably the most striking in the Learning Center. One comes in, stands in the four-storey-high atrium and thinks: Wow! Of course, this is a bombastic work of architecture, which also fulfills a function. The cantilever into campus is actually quite appealing because of its message. One could have just as well decided that there – in the most prominent part of the campus where one also has a fantastic view – is the office of the Rectors. I find it great that this place belongs to the students.

LEHRENDE – TEACHERS – STATEMENTS

EDELTRAUD HANAPPI-EGGER

Leiterin des Department Managements und des Instituts für Gender und Diversität in Organisationen
Chair of the Department of Management and Professor at the Institute for Gender and Diversity in Organizations

Ulrich Tragatschnig: Wenn Sie die jetzige Situation mit früher vergleichen, welche Vor- und Nachteile fallen Ihnen auf?
Edeltraud Hanappi-Egger: Die Studierenden haben jetzt viel mehr Raum. Ich kann mich außerdem noch an Zeiten erinnern, als ich einen Trolley brauchte, um mein Equipment in den Hörsaal zu bringen. Inzwischen bin ich maximal noch mit einem Memory-Stick unterwegs. Schwierig ist die Theaterbestuhlung in den größeren Hörsälen. Die Klappstühle können ein echtes Lärmproblem werden. Und die Seminarräume für die Masterprogramme sind eher knapp bemessen. Die Atmosphäre in den Räumen hat sich aber stark verbessert. Es gibt keine bunkerartigen Hörsäle mehr. Die Akustik ist sehr gut. Gerade auch im Audimax, was mich verblüfft hat. Es wirkt im Vergleich zum alten auch kleiner, überschaubarer.

Hat sich somit auch die Kommunikation mit den Studierenden am Campus verbessert?
Das kann ich leider nicht behaupten. Früher haben sich Studierende und Lehrende öfter zufällig getroffen, weil die Bereiche durchmischter waren. Wir haben jetzt eine sehr effiziente Weise, die Lehre zu organisieren, die sich baulich ableitet. Die strikte Trennung von Lehr- und Departmentbereich ist schwer überbrückbar.

Viele behaupten das genaue Gegenteil und meinen, dass man sich durch diese Campus-Situation viel öfter trifft.
Am Weg über den Campus treffe ich wirklich viel mehr Kolleginnen und Kollegen als früher. Bei den Studierenden merke ich aber eine deutliche Zurückhaltung im Kontaktaufnehmen. Durch die Aufspaltung der Funktionsbereiche und durch die Einführung der Frontoffices kommen die Leute nicht mehr zufällig ans Institut. Das hat Vorteile, aber ich habe immer öfter das Gefühl, dass wir dadurch, dass wir die Bereiche voneinander so strikt trennen, auch eine stärkere Trennung in der Begegnung und damit in der Beziehung zwischen Studierenden und Lehrenden aufbauen.

Ulrich Tragatschnig: When you compare the current situation with the previous one, what advantages and disadvantages do you notice?
Edeltraud Hanappi-Egger: Students have much more space now. I can also remember the times when I needed a trolley to carry my equipment to the auditorium. Now I'm on my way with no more than a memory stick. The theater seating in the larger auditoriums is tricky. The fold-down chairs can pose a real noise problem. And the seminar rooms for the master programs are quite small. However, the atmosphere in the rooms has greatly improved. There are no more bunker-like auditoriums. The acoustics are good. Especially in the Audimax, which surprised me. It also seems smaller and more manageable than the old one.

Has communication with students on campus thereby improved, too?
Unfortunately, I cannot confirm that. Previously students and teachers met more often by coincidence as the areas were more mixed. Now we have a very efficient structure for the study programs, which is reflected in the architecture. The strict separation of teaching and department areas is hard to overcome.

Many people say exactly the opposite, that far more spontaneous meetings occur with the new campus situation.
On my way through the campus I do indeed meet far more colleagues than before. However, among students I notice an obvious reluctance when it comes to making contact. Due to the separation of the functional areas and the introduction of the front offices, people don't end up in the institutes by coincidence anymore. For sure, there are advantages to this, but I have the growing suspicion that by separating the areas so strictly we have also built up a stronger barrier for encounters and thus in the relationship between students and teachers as well.

> Die Akustik ist sehr gut. Gerade auch im Audimax, was mich verblüfft hat.

> The acoustics are good. Especially in the Audimax, which surprised me.

LEHRENDE – TEACHERS – STATEMENTS

RONY G. FLATSCHER
Bereich Betriebswirtschaftslehre und Wirtschaftsinformatik
Institute for Management Information Systems

Ulrich Tragatschnig: Über das Sounding-Board waren Sie von Anfang in die Planung des neuen Campus involviert. Ist das Ergebnis aus Ihrer Sicht gelungen?
Rony G. Flatscher: Dass man den Campus auf die grüne Wiese gestellt hat, brachte eine Jahrhundertgelegenheit mit sich. Organisatorisch konnte man vieles anders gestalten. Der Campus brachte eine massive Verbesserung für die WU. Nicht ausdrückbar, schwer messbar. Man merkt es an den Stimmungen. Wie wir eingezogen sind, haben die Angestellten einen neuen Bezug zu ihrer Universität hergestellt.

Mit welchen Worten würden Sie die Stimmung am Campus auf den Punkt bringen?
Aufbruch, Optimismus, Frische. Man fühlt sich hier zum ersten Mal zusammengehörig. Jeder weiß, dass der Campus ein Unikat ist. Auch die Studenten sind stolz, hier zu studieren. Das gibt einen Motivationsschub, der bisher nicht verweht ist. Die Kollegen, die von außen kommen, sind so sprachlos, wie man selbst am Anfang war.

Haben sich auch die Bedingungen für den Lehrbetrieb verbessert?
Grosso modo ja. In der Forschung und Lehre ergibt sich eine massive Verbesserung allein daraus, dass man einander täglich über den Weg laufen kann. Probleme gibt es dort, wo die Betroffenen nicht ins Boot geholt worden sind, oder dort, wo sich das neoliberale Gehabe zu stark durchsetzen konnte. Auf der alten WU gab es zum Beispiel überall an den Instituten leere Seminarräume, die nun der neoliberalen Kosten/Nutzen-Rechnung zum Opfer gefallen sind. Sie hatten aber eine wichtige Pufferfunktion, wenn man zum Beispiel einen Wissenschafter aus dem Blauen für drei Tage bekommt. Außerdem haben wir erst nach einer Krisensitzung zwei PC-Schulungsräume bekommen, die für uns Wirtschaftsinformatiker enorm wichtig sind, weil man bei komplexer Software nicht mit Laptops unterrichten kann, wie das sonst inzwischen üblich ist. Insgesamt muss man aber die Kirche im Dorf lassen. Die Mehrzahl der Sachen ist richtig gemacht worden. Das glaube ich wirklich.

Ulrich Tragatschnig: You were involved in the planning of the new campus from the beginning as a member of the Sounding Board. Do you think the result is a success?
Rony G. Flatscher: The fact that the campus was constructed on a green field brought along a once-in-a-century opportunity. It was possible to organize many things differently. The campus entailed enormous improvements for the WU – not all can be verbalized, and it's difficult to measure. One can read it from the ambience. When we moved in, the staff established a new relationship with their university.

Which words would you use to encapsulate the atmosphere on campus?
Good spirits, optimism, freshness. For the first time there is a sense of togetherness here. Everyone knows that the campus is one of a kind. Also the students are proud to study here. This generates a thrust of motivation, which has not subsided thus far. Colleagues coming from outside are as speechless as we were in the beginning.

Have teaching conditions also improved?
For the most part, yes. For research and teaching there has been a massive improvement alone due to the fact that we can run into each other on a daily basis. Problems arise where the concerned people were not involved or where a neoliberal mindset could prevail all too strongly. For example, in the old WU there were empty seminar rooms all over the institutes, which have now fallen prey to the neoliberal cost-benefit calculation. But they had an important buffer function, for example, when you get a scientist out of the blue for three days. A crisis meeting was also needed to get two PC training rooms, which are incredibly important to us information system managers as one cannot teach with laptops – the common practice now – when a complex software is involved. However, all in all, we have to see things in proportion. The majority of things were done right. I truly believe this.

> Aufbruch, Optimismus, Frische. Man fühlt sich hier zum ersten Mal zusammengehörig.

> Good spirits, optimism, freshness. For the first time there is a sense of togetherness here.

EA

NO.MAD ARQUITECTOS: EXECUTIVE ACADEMY

NICHT-KARTESIANISCHE GEOMETRIEN

EDUARDO ARROYO ÜBER DIE EXECUTIVE ACADEMY IM GESPRÄCH MIT GUDRUN HAUSEGGER

NON-CARTESIAN GEOMETRIES

EDUARDO ARROYO ON THE EXECUTIVE ACADEMY IN CONVERSATION WITH GUDRUN HAUSEGGER

Außen ein schwarzer, in sich verdrehter Baukörper, in dessen unterschiedlich transparenten Aluminium- und Glasflächen sich die Umgebung spiegelt. Innen reihen sich um einen zentralen, verspiegelten Installationskern auf vier Etagen Büroflächen der Executive Academy sowie des WU Alumni Clubs im Open Space-System. Ein hellgrüner Teppich markiert diese teilweise zweigeschossigen Arbeitsflächen.

From the outside a distorted cubic volume with aluminum and glass surfaces in different degrees of transparency that reflect the surroundings. Inside, four storeys of open-plan offices for the Executive Academy and the WU Alumni Club are arranged around a mirrored structural core. A bright green carpet defines these in part two-storey work areas.

Im Gegensatz zu den anderen Bauten am Campus und auf Initiative des Architekten Eduardo Arroyo (NO.MAD Arquitectos, Madrid) sind hier die Lehrbereiche der Studierenden mehrerer MBA-Curricula in den obersten Geschossen auf den Ebenen fünf und sechs untergebracht. Zweigeschossige Hörsäle im „Arenastil", großzügige Ruhezonen und ein bevorzugter Blick durch bewusst platzierte Fensteröffnungen werden hier geboten. Der violette Teppich spielt ironisierend auf Farben des Klerus an: „Studieren ist eine ernste Sache", meint der Architekt.

In contrast to the other buildings on campus and on the initiative of the architect Eduardo Arroyo (NO.MAD Arquitectos, Madrid), the teaching areas for the students of various MBA programs are situated on the uppermost floors – levels five and six. This zone accommodates two-storey "arena-style" lecture halls, spacious places for relaxation, and privileged views through strategically placed window openings. The violet carpet makes an ironic comment on the color of the clergy: "Studying is a serious matter," opines the architect.

Die Lage bestimmt die Geometrie: Drehungen in Richtung dominierender Beziehungen
The site defines the geometry:
twisting in dominant directions

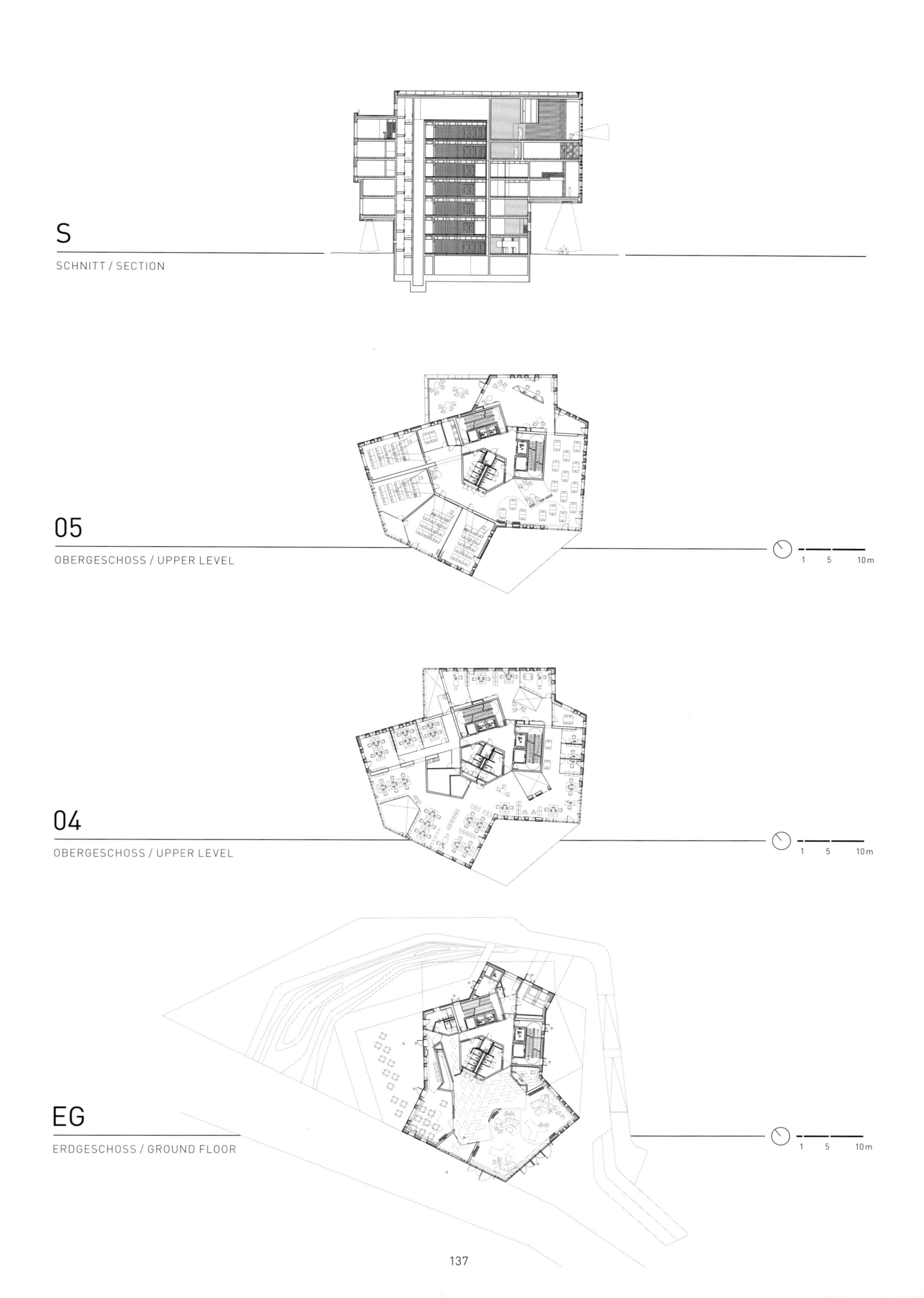

EXECUTIVE ACADEMY

S
———
SCHNITT / SECTION

05
———
OBERGESCHOSS / UPPER LEVEL

04
———
OBERGESCHOSS / UPPER LEVEL

EG
———
ERDGESCHOSS / GROUND FLOOR

**Form und Funktion: Fenster sind Teil des Fassaden-
systems und erfüllen verschiedene Funktionen**
Form and function: Windows are part of the façade
system and fulfill different functions

Wandbekleidungen und Beleuchtungskörper ziehen sich – auch aus schalltechnischen Gründen – einheitlich durch das Gebäude. Die Sichtbetonflächen zeigen die tragenden Teile des Baus – Lesbarkeit und eine verfeinerte Wahrnehmung sind grundlegende Entwurfsprinzipien der Executive Academy.

Gudrun Hausegger: Die Executive Academy hat die Form eines verdrehten Kubus mit zentralem Installationskern. Spiegelt diese Form ihren üblichen Entwurfsprozess wider, der auf geometrischen Prinzipien basiert?

Eduardo Arroyo: Die Hauptidee des Entwurfs war, kein gewöhnliches Gebäude zu bauen. So versuchten wir im Wettbewerb den Entwurf mit etwas anzureichern, das eine verfeinerte Wahrnehmung ermöglicht. Wir wollten einen gewöhnlichen Container in etwas transformieren, das zwischen den Menschen im Gebäudeinneren und der Umgebung vermittelt, wie Prater und Wiener Innenstadt: In einem Transformationsprozess öffneten wir ein gewöhnliches Gebäude gegenüber fernen oder nahen Punkten der Umgebung. Zudem versuchten wir bestimmte Bereiche wie Cafeterias oder Aufenthaltsräume aufzuwerten, in-

A uniform procession of wall panels and lighting fixtures – also for soundproofing purposes – meanders through the building. Visible concrete surfaces reveal the structural components of the house – readability and refined perception are the underlying design principles of the Executive Academy.

Gudrun Hausegger: The Executive Academy is shaped as a distorted cube with a central installation core. Does this concept reflect your preferred design process based on geometry?

Eduardo Arroyo: The main idea of the design was to avoid building a generic building. In the competition we aimed to enrich the design with something that would foster refined perception. In other words, we wanted to transform a generic container into something that mediates the users of the building with their surroundings, such as the Prater park and the old city of Vienna. We employed a transformational system to open up a generic building form toward points in the immediate environment and distant landscape. Additionally, we tried to enhance certain areas, such as the cafeterias or common rooms, by making them larger than initially planned. These spaces act as a fil-

EXECUTIVE ACADEMY

Tektonik: Die schwarzen Aluminiumtafeln der Fassade markieren tragende Bauteile
The black aluminum panels of the façade indicate load-bearing building elements

> ^

An der Fassade werden transparente und spiegelnde Glassorten verwendet
The façade employs transparent and reflective types of glass

> >

Der westliche Campus-Eingang wird von einem markanten Turm bezeichnet
The west entrance of the campus is defined by a striking tower

>

dem wir sie größer als geplant veranschlagten. Sie sind die Filter zwischen dem pragmatischen Programm und den sensiblen Teilen des Hauses. Da diese aufwertenden Faktoren Geschoss für Geschoss eingeführt wurden, ergibt das unterschiedliche Grundrisse in jedem Stockwerk. Das heißt, für die Executive Academy wurde keine a priori-Form festgelegt, sondern die Form ist das Ergebnis dieses Deformationsprozesses.

Ihre Konzepte beruhen oft auf Verhaltens- und Nutzungsmustern. Waren derartige Instrumente auch hier die Entwurfstools?
Architektur kann die Wahrnehmung gegenüber der Realität steigern: Wenn man die „Welt" mit unterschiedlichen Fensterformaten rahmt, so werden den Benutzern unterschiedliche Eindrücke der äußeren Welt geboten. Die Vielzahl der Fenster im Gebäude reagiert auf ergonomische Gegebenheiten: Einige sind niedriger, da die Studierenden sitzen, wenn sie lernen. Einige sind größer, da man so, wenn man in Gruppen beieinander sitzt, gut in die Landschaft sehen kann. Ich denke, dass diese „Laune" des Architekten ein Muster ist, das unterschiedliche Bedeutungen hat – am Ende verbindet es die Benutzer des Gebäudes mit

ter between the pragmatic program and the sensitive parts of the building. As these enhancements were introduced floor by floor, the building attained different geometries and floor plans on each storey. This means the design of the Executive Academy did not have a form a priori; rather the form is the result of this process of deformation.

Your concepts often incorporate behavior and usage patterns. Did such strategies influence the design of the Executive Academy?
Architecture can enhance your perception of reality: When you frame "the world" with different types of windows, users are offered an array of impressions of the outside world. Many of the windows in the building respond to ergonomic factors: Some of the windows are lower as the students are seated while studying. Some of the windows are larger so that when people sit together in a group they can view out to the landscape together. I think that this "caprice" of the architect is a pattern with very different meanings – and in the end it is something that connects the user and the outside world. This pattern – this system of different modes of perception – recurs throughout the building and

Öffentlicher Raum: Die Eingangshalle setzt den Walk Along Park fort und führt zu Liften und Restaurant
Public space: The lobby continues the Walk Along Park and leads to the elevators and to the restaurant

Raumplan: In der Lobby treffen niedrigere Büroräume auf die hohe Eingangshalle
The high space of the lobby adjacent to lower office rooms
‹

Gestaffelte Sitzreihen in den Arena-Hörsälen
Stepped seating rows in the arena lecture halls
‹

Der violette Teppichboden markiert die Veranstaltungsbereiche
The violet carpet defines the event areas
⌄

der Außenwelt. Dieses Muster – das System der unterschiedlichen Wahrnehmungen – wiederholt sich in einer homogenen Gestaltung im gesamten Gebäude: Von den tragenden Teilen über die Glasflächen bis hin zu den Vorhängen.

Das heißt, die Fenster wurden nicht einem bestimmten Algorithmus folgend platziert? So wird zumindest die Fassade des Baus oft interpretiert.
Das ist das Problem der Architektur heutzutage: Sie wird sehr schnell interpretiert. Normalerweise, wenn jemand einen Bau wie die Executive Academy sieht, denkt er, die Fenster sind willkürlich gesetzt. Nein, die Fassade ist eine präzise Bezugnahme auf die innere Nutzung des Baus.

Der gesamte Campus sowie alle Gebäude unterliegen dem Green-Building-Konzept. Haben diese Anforderungen Ihren Entwurf beeinflusst?
Ich möchte eine Bemerkung voranschicken: Niemand in der Architektur kann im Moment sagen, wie die bauliche Umsetzung von Nachhaltigkeit aussehen sollte. Nachhaltigkeit hat keine konkrete bauliche Umsetzung. Was in diesem Zusammenhang zählt, sind korrekte Energiekennzahlen oder nachhaltig produzierte Materialien. Nachhaltigkeit gehört in den Bereich der Ingenieure. So hat uns das Konzept eines Green Buildings viele architektonische Entscheidungen aufgezwungen. Entscheidungen, die von einem traditionellen Weg des Bauens zu einem innovativen führten. Für mich waren folgende Überlegungen die wichtigsten: Wie realisiere ich eine neue Art der Isolierung, wie eine neue Art der Struktur – und vor allem, wie löse ich eine neue Art des Schallschutzes? Am Ende ist der Bau ein Green Building geworden, obwohl die Fassade aus Aluminium ist. Diese Botschaft der Academy mag ich: Man kann ein Gebäude grün und nachhaltig bauen und trotzdem falsche Vorstellungen von Nachhaltigkeit außen vor lassen.

generates homogeneity: from the structure to the glass surfaces and even to the curtains.

That means the positions of the windows do not follow a particular algorithm? This is how the façades of the building are often interpreted.
This is the problem with architecture these days: It is interpreted very fast. Usually when someone sees a building like the Executive Academy he or she thinks that the windows were placed randomly. On the contrary, the façade is a precise reference to the inner functions of the building.

The entire WU Campus and every single building are based on a Green Building concept. To what extent did these requirements influence your design?
First, I have a remark: Nobody in architecture presently knows what the built image of sustainability should look like. Sustainability does not have a fixed image. What really counts in this context are correct low energy coefficients or the sustainable production of materials. Sustainability belongs to the domain of the engineers. So the concept of a Green Building imposed many architectural decisions, decisions that led from a traditional method of building to a more innovative one. For me, the most important deliberations were how to implement new types of insulation, new approaches to structure – and, above all, how to develop new strategies for soundproofing. In the end, the Executive Academy is a Green Building, even though its façade is made of aluminum. This message is what I like about the Academy: You can build a green and sustainable building and nevertheless avoid pretended images of sustainability.

Zweigeschossige Hörsäle im Arena-Stil
Two-storey lecture halls in arena style

Die sternförmigen Lampen in den hohen Hörsälen sind auch Akustikelemente
The star-shaped lamps in the high lecture halls also serve as acoustic elements

Aus den Veranstaltungsräumen bietet sich ein spektakulärer Blick in Richtung Innenstadt
Spectacular view from the event rooms to the city center

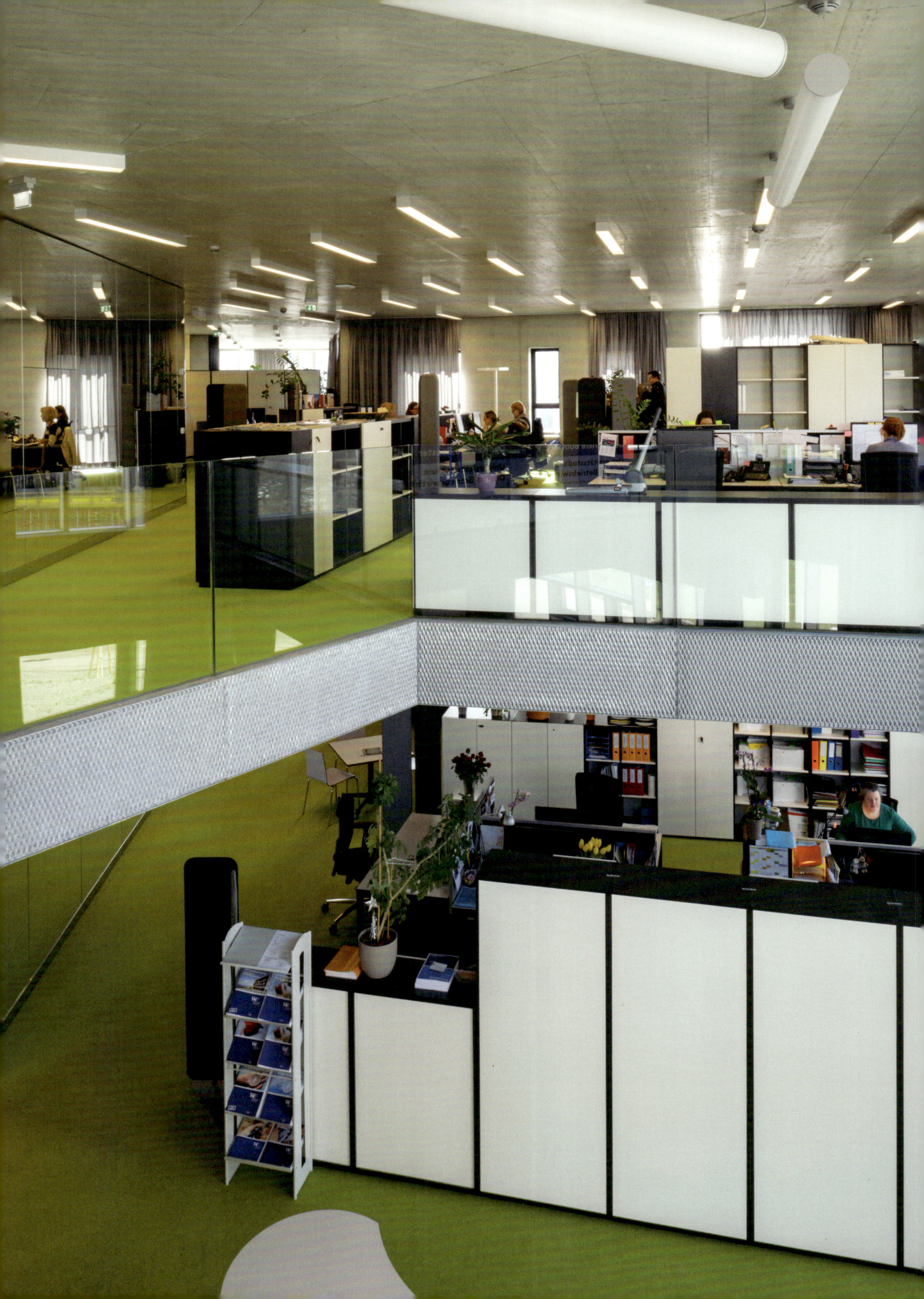

Die Schalldämmung in den Büros erfolgt über Akustikböden und Vorhänge
Soundproofing with "acoustic floors" and curtains

Innovative Raumerlebnisse: Zweigeschossige Büros
Innovative spatial experiences: two-storey offices

Wie haben Sie die Herausforderungen der Akustik gelöst?
Da wir gezwungen waren, die aktivierten Bauteile, die das Kühlwasser transportieren, in den Geschossplatten unterzubringen, konnten wir keine Akustikdecken anbringen. Gegen den Vorschlag der Ingenieure, aber zugunsten einer reinen und freundlichen Architektur, ließen wir die Schallschutz-Vorrichtungen nicht sichtbar von den Decken hängen, sondern erfanden stattdessen einen „Akustikboden", der nun unter den bunten Teppichen liegt. Da dieser Boden zwar die hohen Töne absorbieren kann, nicht aber die tiefen, erfanden wir zusätzlich das System der Vorhänge. Auch die sternförmigen Lampen sind voll mit Akustikvorrichtungen für die tiefen Töne.

Warum haben Sie sich für die Materialien Glas, Aluminium und – einen sehr glatten – Beton entschieden?
Architektur muss eine Botschaft vermitteln: Die Bedeutung dieses Gebäudes liegt für mich darin, eine bestimmte Sensibilität zu erzeugen, die im Inneren wie auch von Außen spürbar wird. Man soll die Struktur des Gebäudes nachvollziehen können und dabei erkennen, dass das Gewicht von oben nach unten verläuft. So sind die schwarzen Teile tragend, alle anderen, nicht tragenden Teile sind transparent und aus Glas. Das Schwarz ist Aluminium und überzieht die tragenden Betonteile. Der Vorschlag in Beton zu bauen, kam von den Auftraggebern. Da das Muster, das sich durch das ganze Gebäude zieht, sich auch in den Aluminium- und Glasbereichen der Fassade fortsetzen muss, kamen zwei unterschiedliche Glassorten zum Einsatz: ein transparentes und ein spiegelndes. Auch das Aluminium spiegelt ein wenig. Die Botschaft ist: Architektur ist keine Konstante, sie ändert sich je nach Wetter und mit den unterschiedlichen Tageszeiten.

Im Inneren wollte ich den Beton sichtbar lassen, im Anklang an die sichtbaren aktivierten Geschossplatten. Aber er sollte glatt sein, um eine angenehme Atmosphäre zu erzeugen. Die gläsernen Teile im Inneren, die Spiegel, erfüllen zwei Funktionen: Sie verdecken den tragenden Kern und wir konnten so mit Geometrien spielen, die nicht kartesianisch sind und die Räume aufwerten.

How did you solve the challenges with the acoustics?
We were unable to mount acoustic ceilings as we were obliged to house the activated building components that transport cooling water in the floor construction. For the better of coherent and friendly architecture – albeit against the advice of the engineers, who suggested visible soundproofing provisions hanging from the ceilings – we invented an "acoustic floor" underneath the colorful carpets. As this acoustic floor could absorb high tones but not the lower ones, we also devised a special system of curtains. Even the star-shaped lamps are acoustically equipped for bass absorption.

Why did you decide for the materials glass, aluminum, and – very smooth – concrete?
Architecture has to convey a message. For me, the ambition of this building was to create a certain sensibility from both the inside and the outside. One should be able to comprehend the structure of the building and recognize that the load travels from the top to the ground. Hence, the black parts are structural, the rest of the non-load bearing elements are transparent and made out of glass. The black is aluminum and covers the concrete structure beneath. It was the client's idea to build in concrete. As the pattern that runs through the entire building should also carry over on the aluminum and glass of the façade, we chose two different kinds of glass: a transparent one and a reflective one. Also the aluminum is a bit reflective. The message is: Architecture is not stable; it changes with weather conditions and with different times of day. On the inside I wanted the concrete to remain visible, an echo of the surfaces of the activated floor slabs. But it should be smooth and create a pleasant atmosphere. The glazed elements inside, the mirrors, fulfill two functions: On the one hand, they hide the presence of the structural core; on the other, we could play with non-Cartesian geometries and enrich the spaces.

STATEMENTS

SCHNITTSTELLEN
ARBEITS-BEZIEHUNGEN ZUR GEBAUTEN CAMPUS-UMWELT

DANIEL GRÜNKRANZ

Der Abschluss einer Bauaufgabe – die schlussendliche Präsenz des Bauwerks – ist im Lebenszyklus des Hauses nur eine Momentaufnahme. Sie lässt für den Augenblick Meinungen und Kritiken entstehen. Doch wie gestaltet sich der weitere alltägliche Umgang mit der gebauten Umwelt für jene, die sie nutzen? Angesichts eines Projekts wie dem neuen Campus der Wirtschaftsuniversität Wien, der allein schon durch seine Dimension hervorsticht, stellt sich die Frage nach Abläufen und Situationen, die sich in Interaktion mit der höchst präsenten Architektur entwickelt haben.

INTERFACES
WORK RELATIONSHIPS IN THE ARCHITECTURE OF THE CAMPUS

The completion of a building process – the presence of the architecture in the end – is but a snapshot in the life cycle of a house. In this moment it provokes opinions and criticism. But how do the future everyday encounters with the built environment evolve for those who use it? In light of a project like the new Vienna University of Economics and Business campus, which already stands out with its sheer scale, the question arises of what types of processes and situations emerge in interaction with the highly prominent architecture.

WORKING ENVIRONMENTS – STATEMENTS

> Der Architektur des Campus und ihren Elementen wird immer wieder neue Aufmerksamkeit zuteil.

> The campus architecture and its elements receive attention time and again from different directions.

Architektur spüren

Beobachtet man das rege Treiben auf dem Campus, so erscheinen manche Beziehungen zwischen den dort anwesenden Menschen und der gebauten Umwelt schon recht deutlich umrissen. Architekturtouristen spazieren aufmerksamen Blicks über den Campus, sie nehmen immer wieder ausgesuchte Stand- und Blickpunkte ein, um den Konturen der Gebäude eindringlicher folgen zu können. Während sie Eindrücke sammeln, gilt ihre Aufmerksamkeit den architektonischen und landschaftsgestalterischen Elementen, die sie umgeben. Studierende gehen wiederum telefonierend oder sich unterhaltend zielstrebig auf Eingänge zu, besetzen im Inneren der Gebäude Lern-, Projekt- und Aufenthaltsräume. Sie nehmen die Umgebung bereits als gegeben hin und haben sich eingelebt. So rückt die Architektur bald in den Hintergrund. Oft tritt sie aber wieder deutlich hervor, beispielsweise unter dem Eindruck der vielen noch unbekannten räumlichen Situationen, in denen es sich noch zurechtzufinden gilt, oder auch in der Begegnung mit Einrichtungen, die für manche Abläufe des Campuslebens noch nicht vollständig zur Routine gereift sind. Der Architektur des Campus und ihren Elementen wird so immer wieder neue Aufmerksamkeit zuteil.

Die architektonische Umsetzung des Campus bedeutet für jene, die dort arbeiten und studieren, auch Herausforderungen. Zum einen treffen die vor dem Umzug der Lern- und Forschungseinrichtungen gehegten Vorstellungen oder aktiv geäußerten Wünsche des Universitätspersonals nun auf die konkrete Beschaffenheit der neuen Arbeitsräume. Für einige hat sich zum Beispiel die gewohnte Einteilung der Büroarbeitsplätze geändert, manche Elemente der Bürointerieurs erweisen sich als wohltuend praktisch und die neuen Gebäude ermöglichen veränderte Organisationsformen für die einzelnen Abteilungen. Zum anderen gibt nicht allein der funktionelle Charakter Anlass zur Auseinandersetzung mit dem Bau. Die Häuser reflektieren auch die von ihren ArchitektInnen gehegten konzeptuellen und gestalterischen Vorstellungen. Das Herzstück des Campus, das von Zaha Hadid Architects geplante Library and Learning Center (LC), vermittelt mit seinen schrägen Flächen, Durchschlitzungen und dynamisch geschwungenen Formen außergewöhnliche räumliche Eindrücke. Wie schon bei Zaha Hadids erstem realisierten Bau, der Vitra Feuerwache in Weil am Rhein, beschäftigt auch hier eine starke und körperlich spürbare Wirkung der architektonischen Formen die Nutzer.

Sensing Architecture

If one observes the bustling activities on campus, certain relationships between the people present and the built surroundings seem to have already assumed a rather concrete shape. Architecture tourists stroll through the campus with watchful eyes, stopping time and again at select viewing points to trace the contours of the buildings from their most dramatic perspective. While collecting impressions their attention is focused on the architectural and landscape design elements that surround them. Students, on the other hand, walk directly toward entrances, on the telephone or chatting with others; they occupy the learning, project, or common areas inside the buildings. Their surroundings are matter of fact, and they have already settled in. The architecture has quickly faded into the background. But then again it comes to the fore: for example, in face of many yet unknown spatial situations, which still require finding one's way, or in encounters with facilities where certain processes of campus life have not fully matured into routine. Hence, the campus architecture and its elements receive attention time and again from different directions.

The architectural manifestation of the campus also implies challenges for those working and studying there. For one, the university staff's imaginations or expressed wishes for the study and research facilities prior to the move now concur with the physical conditions of the new working spaces. For others, the familiar layout of the workspaces has changed, for example, some elements of the office interior have turned out to be pleasantly practical, and the buildings enable new organizational forms for the individual departments. On the other hand, not only the functional aspect calls for engagement. The houses also reflect the architects' concepts and design strategies. At the heart of the campus the Library and Learning Center (LC), planned by Zaha Hadid Architects, grants exceptional spatial experiences through its slanted surfaces, slit incisions, and dynamic winding shapes. As was the case with Hadid's first realized building, the Vitra Fire Station in Weil am Rhein, the bold and physically tangible effect of the forms preoccupies the users.

CHRISTIAN CSIKOS
Abteilung für Facility Management: Komplexe Betriebsanforderungen
Facility Management Department: Complex Operational Requirements

> Mit dem Einzug in ein neues Haus werden Bedürfnisse gegenüber der Planungsphase noch einmal deutlicher konkretisiert, und das bedingt einige Adaptierungarbeiten.

> Upon moving into a new house, needs immediately become more obvious than they were in the planning phase, which leads to adaptations.

Für manche, die am Campus beschäftigt sind, geht der Umgang mit der Architektur über das allgemeine Einleben in ihre neuen Arbeitsräume hinaus. Ihre Arbeit an Schnittstellen in unterschiedlichen Abteilungen der Universität erfordert einen besonderen Blick auf die gebaute Umwelt. Christian Csikos ist stellvertretender Leiter der Abteilung für Facility Management und somit in einem Bereich tätig, der in eine anhaltende Aufmerksamkeit gegenüber den baulichen Einrichtungen übergeht. In seinen Verantwortungsbereich fallen Instandhaltungen, Umbaumaßnahmen und ausstattungsmäßige Anpassungen an den laufenden Unibetrieb. Dass die einzelnen Gebäude von unterschiedlichen Architekten geplant wurden, bedeutet für ihn eine professionelle Herausforderung, da es überall andere Problemstellungen zu bewältigen gilt. Dazu kommt eine Vielzahl an technischen Einrichtungen, welche der jeweiligen funktionellen und gestalterischen Auslegung der einzelnen Gebäude entsprechen. Jedes Bauwerk hat seinen eigenen Charakter, das verlangt nach Flexibilität. Das Gebäude der Executive Academy von NO.MAD Arquitectos etwa ist mit vielen gläsernen und spiegelnden Flächen ausgestattet. Damit steht auch die Reinigung vor besonderen Aufgaben, um den repräsentativen Eindruck des Gebäudes zu bewahren. Für Christian Csikos ist der Campus ein gut nutzbares Ensemble, wenn auch hinsichtlich des laufenden Betriebs noch Erfahrungswerte gesammelt werden. Es wird immer wieder nachgebessert. Aber darin unterscheidet sich die Situation am Campus nicht von anderen Neubauten, wie er meint. Die Architektur erfüllt noch nicht alle Wünsche der Nutzer, Departments und Institute. Darum fallen laufend Veränderungen an. Mit dem Einzug in ein neues Haus werden Bedürfnisse gegenüber der Planungsphase noch einmal deutlicher konkretisiert, und das bedingt einige Adaptierungsarbeiten. Das Campusmodell und die Umsetzung der im Konzept angestrebten Offenheit werden von Herrn Csikos jedenfalls als Erfolg bewertet. Das zeige sich schließlich auch an den vielen Besuchern und Touristen, die den Campus besichtigen!

For some people on campus, the interaction with the architecture goes beyond simply settling into their new workspaces. Their work at the interfaces of different university departments requires a special awareness of the built environment. Christian Csikos is deputy head of the Facility Management Department, and as such he is active in a field that demands constant attention toward the architectural amenities. He is responsible for maintenance, reconstruction work, and adaptations of equipment to running university operations. The designs of the individual buildings by different architects poses a professional challenge as there are always different problems to tackle. Additionally, there are numerous technical facilities that are particular to the respective design and functional concept of the individual buildings. Each building has its own character – this demands flexibility. The Executive Academy building by NO.MAD Arquitectos, for example, is outfitted with many glazed and reflective surfaces. Cleaning these surfaces poses a particular challenge in order to maintain the representative impression of the house. For Christian Csikos the campus is a user-friendly ensemble, albeit some experience still needs to be accumulated for ongoing operations. There is constant touch-up work. However, the situation at the campus is no different from any other new buildings, he finds. The architecture does not fulfill every desire of the users, departments, and institutes just yet, so there are regular changes. Upon moving into a new house, needs immediately become more obvious than they were in the planning phase, which leads to adaptations. At any rate, the campus model and the implementation of the aspired openness were a success in Csikos' eyes. The many visitors and tourists exploring the campus are the best evidence of this!

WORKING ENVIRONMENTS – STATEMENTS

BARBARA ENZINGER

Marketing und Kommunikation: Visitkarte für Weltoffenheit
Marketing and Communication: A Trademark for Open-Mindedness

> Es ist eine Weltoffenheit, es ist eine internationale Agenda, es ist kein Elfenbeinturm. Dieser Campus hat keine Zäune, jeder kann hinein- oder hinausgehen, alles durchmischt sich.

> It's open-mindedness, an international agenda, no ivory towers. The campus doesn't have fences, everyone can come in and go out, different worlds mix together.

Dass das Campusmodell gut funktioniert, und dabei besonders als Kommunikationsraum dienlich ist, in dem man am Weg von einem Gebäude zum anderen Kollegen und Mitarbeiter trifft oder sich plötzlich Studierende und Lehrende in den gleichen Cafés finden, empfindet auch Barbara Enzinger. Sie leitet den Bereich Marketing und Kommunikation der Wirtschaftsuniversität. Sie vergleicht den lang gezogenen öffentlichen Raum des Campus mit einer dörflichen Hauptstraße oder auch der Kärntner Straße, eine der belebtesten Fußgängerzonen Wiens. Ihr Büro liegt wie jenes von Christian Csikos in dem von CRAB studio gestalteten Verwaltungsgebäude AD. Von ihrem Arbeitsplatz aus kann sie auf den zentralen Platz vor dem Learning Center sehen – ein Ausblick, den sie sich zwar nicht ausgesucht hat, wie sie sagt, aber fantastisch findet. Sie hält das Haus, in dem sie arbeitet, für etwas Besonderes. Es mag zwar in seiner äußeren Erscheinung umstritten sein, gleichzeitig empfindet sie seine Innenräume im Vergleich zu den anderen Gebäuden am wohnlichsten. An dem kleinen Besprechungstisch in ihrem großzügigen

Barbara Enzinger also feels that the campus model functions well. It is particularly effective as a space of communication: On the way from one building to another one can meet colleagues and employees; students and teachers can be found in the same cafés. She is the head of Marketing and Communication at the university. She compares the long stretch of open space on campus with a small town main street or with Kärntner Straße, one of the liveliest pedestrian zones in Vienna. Like Christian Csikos, her office is located in the Department and Administration Building by CRAB studio. From her workspace she looks toward the central plaza in front of the Learning Center – a view she did not choose personally, as she says, but she finds it fantastic. Although its outer appearance may be a subject of debate, she finds the interior the most comfortable in comparison to the other buildings. On a small conference table in her spacious office she explains the special role the campus and its architecture play in the projects of her department. Namely, a part of her work involves the sponsoring of the auditoriums and li-

Büro erklärt sie die besondere Bedeutung des Campus und seiner Architektur für die Projekte ihrer Abteilung. Denn ein Teil ihrer Aktivitäten betrifft das Sponsoring von Hörsälen und Bibliotheken durch Unternehmen – ein Modell, das der Universität ermöglichen soll, Drittmittel zu lukrieren. Bei diesen Aktivitäten spielen der Campus und seine Architektur natürlich eine entscheidende Rolle, denn Marketingunternehmungen brauchen derartige interessante Objekte. Überhaupt ist der Campus für die Visualisierung der Marke „Wirtschaftsuniversität" sehr wichtig geworden. Jetzt verstehen die Leute, wie diese Uni denkt, sich darstellt und wofür sie steht, sagt Barbara Enzinger: Es ist eine Weltoffenheit, es ist eine internationale Agenda, es ist kein Elfenbeinturm. Dieser Campus hat keine Zäune, jeder kann hinein- oder hinausgehen, alles durchmischt sich. Gleichzeitig entstehen neuartige Aktivitäten wie zum Beispiel Architekturführungen, die mit dem ungestörten Unibetrieb in Einklang zu bringen sind. Oder Filmproduktionen stellen Anträge für eine Dreherlaubnis. Auch dafür liegt die Schnittstelle bei Barbara Enzinger – eine neue Agenda, die sie im Zusammenhang mit dem Campus und seiner Architektur nun beschäftigt. —

braries by businesses – a model designed to enable the university to acquire financial support from third parties. For these kinds of activities the campus and its architecture are quite decisive because marketing endeavors can play off such interesting objects. The campus was also crucial in visualizing the brand "University of Economics and Business". Now people understand how this university thinks, represents itself, and what it stands for, says Enzinger: It's open-mindedness, an international agenda, no ivory towers. The campus doesn't have fences, everyone can come in and go out, different worlds mix together. At the same time, new kinds of activities emerge: Architecture tours are organized parallel with undisturbed university operations. Or there are film productions applying for permission to shoot. And this is where the interface resides for Barbara Enzinger – a new agenda that she is now busy with in connection with the campus and its architecture. —

WOLFGANG MAYRHOFER

Interdisziplinäres Institut für Verhaltenswissenschaftlich Orientiertes Management:
Ein mögliches Studienobjekt für Übergangssituationen
Interdisciplinary Institute of Management and Organizational Behavior:
A Potential Research Object for Transitional Situations

Während die Inbesitznahme des Campus sich bei vielen Nutzern mit spürbarem Enthusiasmus verbunden hat, wirft Professor Wolfgang Mayrhofer – er ist Leiter des Interdisziplinären Instituts für Verhaltenswissenschaftlich Orientiertes Management – einen differenzierten Blick auf den Campus und seine unmittelbare Arbeitsumgebung. In der Planungsphase war er unter anderem im Sounding Board tätig und fungierte als Baubeauftragter seines Departments. In seinen Arbeitsbereich fiel somit die anspruchsvolle Pflege eines Kommunikationsscharniers zwischen Neubauteam und akademischen Bereich sowie das Handling der zukünftigen Belegung der geplanten Räumlichkeiten durch die

While the transition to the new campus was accompanied with the distinct enthusiasm of many users, professor Wolfgang Mayrhofer, head of the Interdisciplinary Institute of Management and Organizational Behavior, casts a more differentiated view on the campus and his own immediate work surroundings. In the planning phase he was a member of the Sounding Board and building representative of his department. Hence, his work involved a delicate balance of communication between the construction team and the academic unit as well as managing the future occupancy of the planned spaces by the employees. To this end, he would have a special engagement with the campus pro-

> Dass unter WissenschafterInnen, die in unterschiedlichen Bereichen tätig sind, sich aber nun Örtlichkeiten teilen oder in räumlicher Nähe wiederfinden, plötzlich Kooperationen erblühen, mag er nicht glauben. Günstig ist es jedoch für persönliche Begegnungen.

> He cannot really believe that suddenly cooperations will blossom among scientists who are working in different fields but now share certain locations or find themselves in closer proximity. However, it does encourage personal encounters.

Mitarbeiter. Auf diese Weise ergab sich für ihn bereits zu einem frühen Zeitpunkt eine besondere Auseinandersetzung mit dem Campusprojekt. Sein Arbeitsplatz befindet sich in dem vom Atelier Hitoshi Abe geplanten Gebäude D2. „Das Büro ist groß genug, dass ich mich wohl fühle", sagt Wolfgang Mayrhofer. Während am alten Standort einiges an Verkehrslärm herrschte, blickt er nun in den ruhigen grünen Prater. Die größte Veränderung betrifft für ihn aber die Situation, dass zum ersten Mal die Einheiten des Departments einigermaßen in räumlicher Nähe liegen. Ob sich dadurch ein Fortschritt ergibt, muss sich noch weisen. Aber es bedeutet insgesamt eine Umstellung, weil die Institute zuvor voneinander getrennt waren – jetzt bewegt man sich hier in öffentlichen und halböffentlichen Bereichen. Ob das auch für den wissenschaftlichen Austausch förderlich ist? Wolfgang Mayrhofer hält diesen Zugang eher für „Ideologie". Dass unter WissenschafterInnen, die in unterschiedlichen Bereichen tätig sind, sich aber nun Örtlichkeiten teilen oder in räumlicher Nähe wiederfinden, plötzlich Kooperationen erblühen, mag er nicht glauben. Günstig ist es jedoch für persönliche Begegnungen. Und wenn man einmal kooperiert, dann bringt es sicher auch Erleichterungen, weil nicht immer umständlich irgendwo Treffen organisiert werden müssen. Tatsächlich sind die Departments auf großzügige Weise mit Loungebereichen und Küchen ausgestattet, die Raum für Kommunikation und Plätze zum Verweilen schaffen. Aus organisationstheoretischer Sicht böte die Aneignung der Räumlichkeiten mit allen ihren neuen Möglichkeiten auch die Chance für ein Forschungsprojekt. Schon anlässlich des Einzugs in den neuen Campus hätte Wolfgang Mayrhofer gerne Vorher/Nachher-Transitionen unter theoretischen Perspektiven zu Struktur, Infrastruktur, Form und Verhalten untersucht. Leider wurde da die Gelegenheit nicht wahrgenommen.

ject already at an early point in time. His workspace is located in building D2, designed by Atelier Hitoshi Abe. "The office is big enough so that I feel comfortable," says Wolfgang Mayrhofer. While there was plenty of traffic noise in the old location, now he has a view into the quiet and green Prater park. In his opinion, the biggest change is that now, for the first time, the department units are located within reasonable distance of each other. Whether this implies progress remains to be seen. In any case, it results in an overall transitional situation since the departments were previously separated – now one navigates in public and semi-public areas. But does this encourage scientific exchange? Wolfgang Mayrhofer considers this approach more of an "ideology". He cannot really believe that suddenly cooperations will blossom among scientists who are working in different fields but now share certain locations or find themselves in closer proximity. However, it does encourage personal encounters. And once a cooperation is on the go, there are certainly improvements as it doesn't require great efforts to organize meetings. Sure enough, the departments are generously equipped with lounge areas and kitchens, which create space for communication and socializing. From an organizational-theoretical perspective, the appropriation of the spaces with all their new possibilities could also form the basis for a research project. When they moved into the new campus Wolfgang Mayrhofer would have liked to investigate the before/after transition from the theoretical perspectives of structure, infrastructure, form, and behavior – unfortunately, this opportunity has been missed.

SICH NICHT FÜRCHTEN
ÜBER DIE GROSSE AUFGABE, EINE UNIVERSITÄT
AUF DIE GRÜNE WIESE ZU BAUEN

MAXIMILIAN PAMMER, CHRISTOPH SOMMER

Auf die häufige Frage, was ausschlaggebend für den Erfolg eines Projekts war, fällt Projektleitenden die Antwort meist gar nicht so schwer. „Die gut überlegte Projektstruktur", „unsere motivierten Projektpartner", „eine ausgezeichnete Planung" sind klassische Antworten, die jeden Baumanagement-Theoretiker mit Stolz erfüllen. Auch auf das Bauprojekt WU Campus treffen diese Feststellungen und noch weitere Klassiker zu. Bei näherer Betrachtung findet man aber einen Faktor, der dieses Projekt wie ein roter Faden durchzieht und vielleicht ein bisschen auszeichnet: Den Mut, sich nicht zu fürchten.

TO NOT BE AFRAID
ABOUT THE CHALLENGE OF CONSTRUCTING
A UNIVERSITY FROM SCRATCH

When project managers are asked about the reasons behind a project's success, answers are usually not too hard to come by. "A well-designed project organization", "our motivated project partners", "excellent planning" are standard answers, which will make any theorist of project management proud. Of course, these statements and other classics also hold true for the WU Campus construction project. Looking more closely, however, one will find an aspect that permeates and possibly distinguishes this project: the courage to not be afraid.

> **Bei näherer Betrachtung findet man aber einen Faktor, der dieses Projekt wie ein roter Faden durchzieht und vielleicht ein bisschen auszeichnet: Den Mut, sich nicht zu fürchten.**

Looking more closely, however, one will find an aspect that permeates and possibly distinguishes this project: the courage to not be afraid.

Natürlich wurde das Projekt mit der entsprechenden Sorgfalt und der einem öffentlichen Bauprojekt angemessenen Vorsicht abgewickelt. „Due Diligence" wurde geübt, Varianten wurden untersucht, Konzepte entwickelt, geändert, verworfen, Gutachten beauftragt. Dennoch siegte in entscheidenden Momenten immer der Mut zu Großem über die Sorge, Fehler zu machen.

Bereits die Entscheidung der WU, auf eine Sanierung ihrer alten Gebäude zu verzichten und stattdessen alles auf die Karte „Neubau" zu setzen, war eine mutige. Schließlich mussten bereits vor der politischen Entscheidung wichtige Schritte gesetzt werden, um das Projekt voranzutreiben. Als in der Finanzkrise die politisch Verantwortlichen rasch Konjunkturpakete geschnürt haben wollten, konnte die WU mit einem quasi-fertigen Projekt punkten. Dazu war es jedoch nötig, planerisch und konzeptionell bereits so weit zu sein, dass einer Realisierung nichts mehr im Wege stand. Dafür lehnten sich die WU und ihre kongeniale Partnerin, die Bundesimmobiliengesellschaft (BIG), etwas weiter aus dem Fenster, als es im öffentlichen Bereich üblich ist.

Schon alleine diese Kooperation zwischen BIG und WU war eine spannende, weil vollkommen neue Sache. Die Grenze zwischen Mieterin und Vermieterin bewusst aufgelöst, entwickelten die beiden Unternehmen das Projekt gemeinsam als gleichberechtigte Partnerinnen, immer das große Ziel vor Augen, langfristig einen Mehrwert zu schaffen, der über die bloße Lieferung von Universitätsflächen hinausgeht. Dazu gehörte auch die Entscheidung, einem jungen, unbelasteten Team eine Chance zu geben. Dieses Team machte sich frohen Mutes daran, die von der WU entwickelten Ideen für eine neue Universität im Rahmen der – selbstverständlich mutigen – Entscheidung der Wettbewerbsjury in die Realität umzusetzen.

Dazu entwickelte man eine Planungsorganisation, die einerseits die architektonische Vielfalt und Qualität sicherstellen sollte, andererseits durch Zentralisierung der Generalplanung so-

Naturally, the project was handled with due diligence and the prudence fitting for a public construction project of this magnitude. However, after developing, changing, and discarding many concepts, exploring alternatives and paying heed to experts' opinions, the courage to realize visions always prevailed over the concerns about making mistakes.

To fully commit to a new construction of the university campus instead of refurbishing and renovating the old buildings was the first of many spirited decisions. A number of important steps already needed to be taken to further the project before a political agreement could be achieved. At the height of the financial crisis political leaders were searching for stimuli packages for a stagnant economy. The WU seized the chance to present a conceptually and strategically well-prepared project, ready for prompt realization. In order to get this far, the WU and her congenial partner, the Bundesimmobiliengesellschaft (BIG – Austrian Federal Real Estate Company), had to venture further ahead than usual in the public sector.

This partnership between the BIG and the WU was exciting in its own right due to its innovative form of cooperation. The two organizations dissolved the usual boundaries between landlord and tenant. They developed the campus project as equal partners, together striving for an added value that achieves goals beyond the pure provision of university infrastructure. Part of this process was the decision to put faith in a young and dynamic team. With this – naturally courageous – choice by the architectural competition jury, it became this team's challenge to realize the WU's ideas for a new and modern university.

The basis for the realization process was an organizational structure for the planning phase that guaranteed high architectural quality and variety while ensuring an effective cost control system and an integrated planning process by centralizing the technical engineering. From the architects' view this plan-

wohl die Kostenkontrolle gewährleisten als auch eine integrierte technische Planung der Gebäude ermöglichen würde. Aus Sicht der Architekturbüros bedeutete diese Planungsorganisation eine Einschränkung der Möglichkeiten, die ihnen zuerst nicht geheuer schien. Dennoch gingen alle Wettbewerbssiegerinnen und -sieger das Risiko ein, im Zweifelsfall von einer inhaltlichen Entscheidung der Auftraggeber abhängig zu sein, anstatt auch alle Technikplaner in der eigenen Hand zu haben. Als Projektverantwortliche trauten wir uns wiederum, trotz einer klassischen „Sollbruchstelle" im System und aller damit zu erwartenden Reibungsverluste, diesen Weg zu beschreiten. Ausschlaggebend für den Erfolg des Systems war sicherlich die intensive Kommunikation zwischen den Auftraggebern und den Architekturbüros, wodurch die Rahmenbedingungen für alle Beteiligten transparent und die Prozesse klar waren. Aufgrund natürlicher Interessenskonflikte entstanden auch in diesem Projekt manchmal Situationen, die unpopuläre Entscheidungen nötig machten. Die Internationalität der handelnden Personen erzeugte zusätzliche Herausforderungen – Sprachbarrieren, unterschiedliche Normen und Prozesse – die es durch großen persönlichen Einsatz aller Beteiligten zu überwinden galt.

Ähnlich neue Wege wie bei der Gestaltung der Planungsstruktur beschritt das Projekt hinsichtlich der Vergabe der Bauleistungen: Anstatt den vermeintlich sicheren Weg zu gehen, ein oder mehrere Generalunternehmerpakete auszuschreiben, suchten wir eine Methode, die uns genug Möglichkeiten zur Gestaltung und Einflussnahme geben konnte, dabei aber die Situation des österreichischen Ausschreibungsmarkts berücksichtigen und trotzdem technisch sinnvolle Unterteilungen ergeben würde. Schließlich wurden die Baumeister-Arbeiten und die großen Haustechnik-Gewerke jeweils in drei Bereichsvergaben (Ost, West, Mitte) aufgeteilt, einige Gewerke wie Sicherheitstechnik oder Brandmeldeanlage für den gesamten Campus ausgeschrieben, viele andere Leistungen aber in sehr kleinen, spezialisierten Paketen umgesetzt. So wurden am WU Campus beispielsweise zwölf verschiedene Aufträge für Schlosserarbeiten vergeben. Am Ende bedeuteten rund 110 einzelne Aufträge zwar einen sehr hohen Koordinationsaufwand und natürlich gab es auch einige Reibungsverluste, mit denen das Projektmanagement-Team fertig werden musste, dennoch spricht das Ergebnis für sich: Sowohl Kostenrahmen als auch das von Anfang an sehr enge Zeitkorsett wurden eingehalten, die Qualitätsziele wurden trotzdem erreicht.

Die eigentliche Bauphase ist wohl jene Periode eines Bauprojekts, in dem der Bedarf an mutigen Entscheidungen den geringsten Anteil haben sollte. Andererseits gab es gerade in dieser Phase auch im Projekt WU Campus genug Momente, in denen einen der Mut nicht verlassen durfte. Wie bei jedem Bauvorhaben

> **Sowohl Kostenrahmen als auch das von Anfang an sehr enge Zeitkorsett wurden eingehalten, die Qualitätsziele wurden trotzdem erreicht.**

---

the overall results speak for themselves: Both the narrow time schedule and the budget were met, and the quality objectives were achieved.

ning structure meant an unusual restriction of their flexibilities and possibilities, which initially did not evoke unwavering optimism among the designers. Nevertheless, all of the competition winners accepted the risk to be dependent on the owners' decision in case of conflicts between design objectives and technical requirements as opposed to having full control over the planning as usual. The principals and their representatives, on the other hand, were not afraid to accept a predetermined breaking point in the organizational structure and all the associated frictions to be expected. A decisive factor for the success of this system was the intensive communication between the principals and architects, which created a transparent environment with clear-cut responsibilities and processes. Naturally, conflicting interests still caused situations in this project that sometimes necessitated less-than-popular decisions. The internationality of the involved parties added more challenges – language barriers, different codes and processes – which needed to be tackled through the strong personal commitment of all project members.

Just as the organizational structure of the planning was based on an innovative concept, the tendering of the construction contracts was also conducted in an unusual way: Instead of taking the presumably safe road of one or a small number of EPC contract packages, the WU searched for a model to retain flexibility and control over the implementation while taking the size of the Austrian and regional markets into account and creating technically still feasible partitions of the scope. To achieve this the construction and main building systems works (HVAC etc.) were each separately contracted in three sector packages (East, West, Middle), whereas some trades such as security equipment or the fire safety system were commissioned in campus-wide contracts. Many other services, however, were contracted in rather small, specialized packages: For example, twelve different commissions were tendered for metal works in this project. This resulted in roughly 110 separate contracts, which, of course, implied a lot of effort for coordination and management and led to some conflicts that had to be resolved by the project management team. Nevertheless, the overall results speak for themselves: Both the narrow time schedule and the budget were met, and the quality objectives were achieved.

The actual construction phase should theoretically be the stage of such an endeavor during which courageous decisions should play the smallest role. However, also in the case of the

> **Wenn hier immer wieder von Mut gesprochen wird, so darf nicht vergessen werden, dass dieser eine Eigenschaft der beteiligten Personen ist. Die handelnden Menschen sind somit das eigentlich Spezielle an einem Projekt wie dem Campus WU.**

When speaking of courage time and again, one should not forget that it is an attribute of the involved individuals. Thus, it is the people actively involved who make a project like WU Campus a truly special one.

gab es größere und kleinere Verzögerungen, Fehler sind passiert, obwohl die knappen Kalkulationen des Budgets und des Zeitplans eigentlich keinen Platz für Abweichungen ließen. Und in Wirklichkeit war es meist doch etwas komplexer, als man sich das zu Projektbeginn vorgestellt hat. Letztendlich wurden wie oft gegen Projektende sowohl für die Ausführenden als auch für die Auftraggeber die Zeit und dadurch das Geld knapp: Wenige Wochen vor der offiziellen Eröffnung am 4. Oktober 2013 hätte die Besiedlung des Campus durch die Mitarbeiterinnen und Mitarbeiter der Wirtschaftsuniversität eigentlich die komplette Fertigstellung anzeigen sollen. Tatsächlich zogen die neuen „Bewohnerinnen" in Gebäude, in denen noch an vielen Ecken gearbeitet wurde. Nachdem damit bis zur Übernahme und Eröffnung Anfang Oktober die Restleistungen bei laufendem Betrieb erbracht werden mussten, bedeutete das eine zusätzliche Belastung der bereits ausgereizten Reserven. In einer derartigen Situation ist ein bisschen Panik durchaus vertretbar, auch wenn diese selten einen positiven Effekt hat. Dass zum Schluss doch noch alles gut und fertig geworden ist, liegt daran, dass die entscheidenden Projektpartner sich ganz und gar nicht davor gefürchtet haben, alles zu tun, was nötig war – auch wenn es vielleicht nicht immer zu ihrer unmittelbaren Aufgabe gehörte.

Wenn hier immer wieder von Mut gesprochen wird, so darf nicht vergessen werden, dass dieser eine Eigenschaft der beteiligten Personen ist. Die handelnden Menschen sind somit das eigentlich Spezielle an einem Projekt wie dem WU Campus. Hunderte von ihnen haben das Projekt in der Planung und im Management begleitet, über tausend waren gleichzeitig als Arbeitende auf der Baustelle tätig. Egal, ob für wenige Wochen oder über die gesamten sieben Jahre, sie alle haben ihre Spuren an der neuen Heimat der Wirtschaftsuniversität hinterlassen. Sie haben ein Stück dieser großen Aufgabe WU Campus mitgestaltet, weil sie begeistert mitgearbeitet haben, anstatt sich zu fürchten.

WU Campus, precisely in this phase there were enough moments when one was not to lose the before-found courage in the wake of adversity. As always in construction projects, shorter and longer delays occurred and mistakes happened, even though the time schedules and the tight budget calculations did not allow many aberrations. Furthermore, the realization was often much more complex than imagined during the planning phases. Toward the finalization point, as usual, time and therefore money were at a premium for both contractors and principals alike: The relocation of the employees of the University of Economics and Business a few weeks before the grand opening on October 4, 2013 should have signalized the completion of construction works at the new campus. In reality, the new "residents" moved into buildings, which were still being finished at that time. To reach the formal hand-over and official opening in early October, the final works therefore had to be done while the campus was in full use. This caused additional stress on already depleted resources. In a situation like this, a bit of panic is understandable, even though it is rarely helpful. The fact that everything was completed and turned out well in the end has to be attributed to the main project partner's resolve and courage to go beyond their immediate tasks and do everything necessary to finish the project just-in-time.

When speaking of courage time and again, one should not forget that it is an attribute of the involved individuals. Thus, it is the people actively involved who make a project like WU Campus a truly special one. Hundreds of them participated in the planning and in management; more than a thousand workers were on site during the main construction phases. No matter if for a few weeks or for the whole seven years, each and every one of them took part in shaping the new home of the University of Economics and Business. They left their mark on the WU Campus because they joined in enthusiastically, instead of being afraid.

ZAHLEN · DATEN · FAKTEN
FACTS AND FIGURES

**WIRTSCHAFTS-
UNIVERSITÄT WIEN (WU)**
VIENNA UNIVERSITY
OF ECONOMICS
AND BUSINESS (WU)

Gegründet Founded
1898
Studierende Students (2013)
ca. 24.000
MitarbeiterInnen Employees (2013)
ca. 1.500
Rektor Rector
Christoph Badelt

**NEUER WU CAMPUS IN
WIEN-LEOPOLDSTADT,
WELTHANDELSPLATZ 1**
NEW WU CAMPUS, VIENNA,
WELTHANDELSPLATZ 1

Bauherr Owner and developer
Projektgesellschaft Wirtschafts-
universität NEU GmbH (BIG
Bundesimmobiliengesellschaft
mbH, Wirtschaftsuniversität Wien),
2014: Campus WU GmbH
gegründet founded
2007
Geschäftsführung Management
Maximilian Pammer,
Christoph Sommer
Standortwahl Choice of site
Oktober October 2007
**Auslobung eines offenen,
einstufigen Realisierungswett-
bewerbs für die Generalplanung**
Open one-phase competition
for the general planning
Dezember 2007 (24 Einreichungen)
December 2007 (24 submissions)
**Auslobung eines zweistufigen,
nicht-offenen Verfahrens mit
vorgeschalteter, offener Präquali-
fikationsstufe für die Planung von
Einzelbauten**
Two-phase competition with prior
pre-qualification for the design of
the individual buildings:
Juli 2008 (133 Einreichungen)
July 2008 (133 submissions)
Beauftragung der Planer
Commissioning of planners
Frühjahr Spring 2009
Bauzeit Construction
2009–2013
Eröffnung Opening
4. Oktober October 4, 2013
**Projektsteuerung,
begleitende Kontrolle**
Project management,
controlling:
ARGE PS WU Neubau;
Drees & Sommer Wien GmbH /
Delta Baumangement GmbH; FCP
Fritsch, Chiari & Partner ZT

Generalplaner General planning
ARGE Campus WU; BUSarchitektur /
Vasko+Partner Ingenieure
Örtliche Bauaufsicht
Site management
ARGE ÖBA Campus WU; InGenos.
Gobiet.ZT GmbH; iC consulenten

Grundstücksfläche Site area
90.000 m² (560 m × 150–210 m)
Bebaute Fläche Built-up area
35.000 m²
Netto-Nutzfläche Net usable area
100.000 m²
Öffentlich zugängliche Freifläche
Publicly accessible open space
55.000 m²
Räume Rooms
ca. 4.000, davon 1.000 Büros
thereof 1,000 offices
Hörsäle und Seminarräume
Lecture halls and seminar rooms
90
**Kapazität Hörsäle
und Seminarräume**
Capacity lecture halls
and seminar rooms
5.000
Arbeitsplätze für Studierende
Working places for students
3.000
Fahrradabstellplätze
Bicycle parking places
1.000
Neugepflanzte Bäume
Trees planted
230
Beton Concrete
150.000 m³
Einrichtungen Facilities
Kindergarten, Buchhandlungen,
8 Gastronomiebetriebe, Sport-
zentrum, Lebensmittelmarkt,
2 U-Bahn-Anschlüsse
Kindergarten, book shops, 8 cafés,
gym, grocery store, 2 subway
stations
Gesamtbudget netto
Total net budget
492 Mio EUR

**MASTERPLAN UND
FREIRAUMPLANUNG**
MASTER PLAN AND
OPEN SPACE PLANNING

Planung Design
BUSarchitektur & boa Büro für
offensive Aleatorik & Landschafts-
Architektur, Wien Vienna
Projektleitung Project management
Laura P. Spinadel, Bernd Pflüger,
Jean Pierre Bolivar, Hubert Marz
Statik Structural consultant
kppk ZT GmbH
Grundstücksfläche Freiraum
Open space area
63.820 m²

**LC, LIBRARY AND LEARNING
CENTER (BAUFELD PLOT LLC)**

Planung Design
Zaha Hadid Architects, Hamburg
Projektleitung Project management
Cornelius Schlotthauer
Technische Konsulenten
Engineer
Vasko+Partner Ingenieure
Fassadenplanung Facade engineers
Arup Deutschland
Nutzfläche Usable area
ca. 28.000 m²
Heizwärmebedarf
Heating energy demand
16,00 kWh/m²/a
PE gesamt aus Ökobilanz
Total PE from ecobalance
260,00 kWh

**D1 TC, DEPARTMENTS 1 –
TEACHING CENTER
(BAUFELD PLOT 01)**

Planung Design
BUSarchitektur, Wien Vienna
Projektleitung Project management
Laura P. Spinadel, Bernd Pflüger,
Jean Pierre Bolivar
Statik Structural consultant
kppk ZT GmbH
Technische Konsulenten
Engineer
Vasko+Partner Ingenieure
Kapazität
Capacity Auditorium Maximum
650 Personen people
Nutzfläche Usable area
28.349 m²
Heizwärmebedarf
Heating energy demand
15,68 kWh/m²/a
PE gesamt aus Ökobilanz
Total PE from ecobalance
211,45 kWh

**D2 SC, DEPARTMENTS 2 –
STUDENT CENTER
(BAUFELD PLOT 02)**

Planung Design
Atelier Hitoshi Abe, Sendai/
Los Angeles
Projektleitung Project management
Pierre de Angelis, Christian
Schwarz
Technische Konsulenten
Engineer
Vasko+Partner Ingenieure
Nutzfläche Usable area
20.903 m²
Heizwärmebedarf
Heating energy demand
26,91 kWh/m²/a
PE gesamt aus Ökobilanz
Total PE from ecobalance
235,00 kWh

**D3 AD, DEPARTMENTS 3
ADMINISTRATION
(BAUFELD PLOT W2)**

Planung Design
CRAB studio, London
Primary team
Peter Cook, Gavin Robotham, Mark
Bagguley, Stefan Lengen, Theresa
Heinen
Technische Konsulenten
Engineer
Vasko+Partner Ingenieure
Nutzfläche Usable area
ca. 20.000 m²
Heizwärmebedarf
Heating energy demand
16,57 kWh/m²/a
PE gesamt aus Ökobilanz
Total PE from ecobalance
230,60 kWh

**D4, DEPARTMENTS 4
(BAUFELD / PLOT W1D)**

Planung Design
Estudio Carme Pinós, Barcelona
Projektleitung Project management
Carme Pinós
Technische Konsulenten
Engineer
Vasko+Partner Ingenieure
Nutzfläche Usable area
8.806 m²
Heizwärmebedarf
Heating energy demand
20,98 kWh/m²/a
PE gesamt aus Ökobilanz
Total PE from ecobalance
256,80 kWh

**EA, EXECUTIVE ACADEMY
(BAUFELD / PLOT W1E)**

Planung Design
NO.MAD Arquitectos, Madrid
Projektleitung Project management
Eduardo Arroyo
Technische Konsulenten
Engineer
Vasko+Partner Ingenieure
Nutzfläche Usable area
4.727 m²
Heizwärmebedarf
Heating energy demand
18,99 kWh/m²/a
PE gesamt aus Ökobilanz
Total PE from ecobalance
287,00 kWh

KURZBIOGRAFIEN
SHORT BIOGRAPHIES

ARCHITEKTEN UND INGENIEURE
ARCHITECTS AND ENGINEERS

HITOSHI ABE, geboren 1962 in Sendai/Japan. Nach Studien am Southern California Institute of Architecture und der Universität Tōhoku gründete er 1992 ATELIER HITOSHI ABE (AHA) mit Sitzen in Los Angeles und Sendai. Neben zahlreichen Wohnhäusern in Japan entwarf er standardisierte Doppelhäuser für Katastrophenopfer in den USA sowie das Kanno Museum in Shiogama. Hitoshi Abe lehrt an der School of the Arts and Architecture der University of California in Los Angeles.

▬▬▬▬▬▬ Born 1962 in Sendai, Japan. Following studies at Southern California Institute of Architecture and Tōhoku University, in 1992 he founded ATELIER HITOSHI ABE (AHA) with offices in Los Angeles and Sendai. In addition to numerous residences in Japan he designed standardized duplexes for disaster victims in the USA as well as the Kanno Museum in Shiogama. Hitoshi Abe teaches at the School of the Arts and Architecture at the University of California in Los Angeles.

EDUARDO ARROYO, geboren 1964 in Bilbao, Studium an der ETSAM in Madrid, gründete 1989 sein Büro NO.MAD in Amsterdam, zog nach Paris und Bilbao, seit 1996 in Madrid. Lehrte an zahlreichen Universitäten. Wichtige Bauten: Lasesarre Football Stadium in Bilbao, Haus Levene in Madrid, Kindergarten in Sondika, Desierto Square in Barakaldo, Arquia Bank in Bilbao und Haus Zafra-Uceda in Aranjuez.

▬▬▬▬▬▬ Born 1964 in Bilbao, studied at the ETSAM in Madrid, founded his office NO.MAD in Amsterdam in 1989, moved to Paris and Bilbao, based in Madrid since 1996. He has taught at numerous universities. Important buildings: Lasesarre Football Stadium in Bilbao, Levene House in Madrid, kindergarten in Sondika, Desierto Square in Barakaldo, Arquia Bank in Bilbao, and Zafra-Uceda House in Aranjuez.

PETER COOK, geboren 1936 in Southend-on Sea (UK), gehörte 1963 nach Studium am Bournemouth College of Art und der Architectural Association, London, zu den Gründern der Gruppe Archigram. Seit 2004 CRAB studio, gemeinsam mit Gavin Robotham. Cook war Direktor des Institute for Contemporary Art in London sowie der Bartlett School of Architecture, London. Bautätigkeit unter anderem in Osaka, Nagoya, Berlin, Frankfurt, Madrid und Graz (Kunsthaus). 2002 wurde Cook mit der RIBA Gold Medal (für Archigram) geehrt, er ist Knight of the British Empire.

▬▬▬▬▬▬ Born 1936 in Southend-on-Sea, UK. Following studies at Bournemouth College of Art and the Architectural Association, London, one of the founders of the group Archigram. Since 2004 he has run CRAB studio together with Gavin Robotham. Cook was the director of the Institute for Contemporary Art in London and of the Bartlett School of Architecture, London. Built works in Osaka, Nagoya, Berlin, Frankfurt, Madrid, and Graz (Kunsthaus), among other places. In 2002 Cook was awarded the RIBA Gold Medal (for Archigram); he is also a Knight of the British Empire.

DIETMAR EBERLE, geboren 1952 in Hittisau/Vorarlberg, Architekturstudium an der TU Wien, 1979–82 gemeinsam mit Markus Koch, Norbert Mittersteiner und Wolfgang Juen Gründer der „Vorarlberger Baukünstler", 1985 Gründung von be (Baumschlager & Eberle), Lehrtätigkeit in Hannover, Wien, Linz, New York und Darmstadt, seit 1999 an der ETH Zürich. be-Bürostandorte in Lustenau, Vaduz, Wien, St. Gallen, Zürich und Hongkong, zahlreiche Wohn-, Büro-, Industrie- und Kulturbauten in zehn europäischen Ländern, USA, Vietnam und China.

▬▬▬▬▬▬ Born 1952 in Hittisau in Vorarlberg, Austria. Architectural education at Vienna University of Technology. 1979–82 co-founder of "Vorarlberger Baukünstler" together with Markus Koch, Norbert Mittersteiner, and Wolfgang Juen. 1985 founded be (Baumschlager & Eberle). Teacher in Hannover, Vienna, Linz, New York, and Darmstadt, since 1999 at the ETH Zurich. be offices in Lustenau, Vaduz, Vienna, St. Gallen, Zurich, and Hong Kong. Numerous residential, office, industrial, and cultural buildings in ten European countries, USA, Vietnam, and China.

ZAHA HADID, geboren 1950 in Bagdad, studierte an der Architectural Association School in London. Internationale Lehrtätigkeit, unter anderem in New York, Chicago, London, Hamburg und Wien. Zu ihren wichtigsten Bauten zählen die Vitra Feuerwache in Weil am Rhein, die Bergisel-Sprungschanze und die Nordkettenbahn in Innsbruck, das Opernhaus in Ghuangzhou und das Lois & Richard Rosenthal Center for Contemporary Art in Cincinnati. Zaha Hadid ist Dame Commander of the Order of the British Empire und Trägerin des Pritzker Architecture Prize.

▬▬▬▬▬▬ Born 1950 in Baghdad, studied at the Architectural Association in London. International teaching activities in, among other places, New York, Chicago, London, Hamburg, and Vienna. Some of her most important buildings are the Vitra Fire Station in Weil am Rhein, the Bergisel Ski Jump and the Nordpark Railway Stations in Innsbruck, the Guangzhou Opera House, and the Lois & Richard Rosenthal Center for Contemporary Art in Cincinnati. Zaha Hadid is Dame Commander of the Order of the British Empire and recipient of the Pritzker Architecture Prize.

CARME PINÓS, geboren 1954 in Barcelona, Diplom 1979 an der Escuela Técnica Superior de Arquitectura in Barcelona, 1982–91 Büro mit Enric Miralles, lehrte an der University of Illinois, an der Kunstakademie Düsseldorf, Columbia University, ETH Lausanne, ETSAB Barcelona, Harvard University und an der Accademia di Archittetura di Mendrisio. Wichtige Bauten: Fußgängerbrücke in Petrer/Alicante, Ufergestaltung in Torrevieja/Alicante, Mittelschule in Mollerussa, Parks und Platzgestaltungen in Palma de Mallorca, Cube Tower in Guadalajara und Grundschule in Castelldefels. In Arbeit sind mehrere Wohn-, Regierungs- und Schulbauten in Katalonien.

▬▬▬▬▬▬ Born 1954 in Barcelona, diploma from Escuela Técnica Superior de Arquitectura in Barcelona in 1979, 1982–91 office with Enric Miralles. He taught at the University of Illinois, Düsseldorf Arts Academy, Columbia University, ETH Lausanne, ETSAB Barcelona, Harvard University, and at the Accademia di Archittetura di Mendrisio. Important built works: Petrer/Alicante Pedestrian Bridge, waterfront design in Torrevieja/Alicante, Mollerussa Secondary School, parks and squares in Palma de Mallorca, Cube Tower in Guadalajara, and Castelldefels Primary School. Numerous residential, governmental, and school building projects are underway in Catalonia.

KURZBIOGRAFIEN / SHORT BIOGRAPHIES

ARCHITEKTEN UND INGENIEURE
ARCHITECTS AND ENGINEERS

WOLF D. PRIX, geboren 1942 in Wien, Architekturstudium an der TU Wien, gründete 1968 mit Helmut Swiczinsky und Michael Holzer die Architektengruppe Coop Himmelb(l)au, deren Design Principal und CEO er ist. Lehrte an der Architectural Association in London, an der Harvard University, Columbia University, an der UCLA und am SCI-ARC in Los Angeles sowie an der Universität für angewandte Kunst in Wien. Wichtige Bauten: UFA Kino Dresden, Gasometer Wien, Akron Art Museum, BMW Welt München, High School # 9 Los Angeles, Dalian Conference Center in China, Busan Cinema Center in Südkorea, EZB Frankfurt, Musée des Confluences Lyon.
▬▬▬ Born 1942 in Vienna. Architectural education at Vienna University of Technology. In 1968 co-founded the architecture group Coop Himmelb(l)au with Helmut Swiczinsky and Michael Holzer, where he is the design principal and CEO. He taught at the Architectural Association in London, Harvard University, Columbia University, UCLA, SCI-ARC in Los Angeles, and at the University of Applied Arts Vienna. Important built works: UFA Cinema Center in Dresden, Gasometer Vienna, Akron Art Museum, BMW World Munich, High School #9 Los Angeles, Dalian Conference Center in China, Busan Cinema Center in South Korea, EZB Frankfurt, and Musée des Confluences Lyon.

LAURA P. SPINADEL, geboren 1958 in Buenos Aires, studierte an der Universidad de Buenos Aires und gründete 1986 gemeinsam mit Claudio J. Blazica BUSarchitektur in Buenos Aires. Nach einem Studium an der Universität für angewandte Kunst in Wien gründete sie 1992 ein weiteres Büro in Wien. Zahlreiche Städtebaustudien sowie Wohn- und Bildungsbauten, u. a. Kindergarten in Wien-Favoriten und Compact City in Wien-Floridsdorf.
▬▬▬ Born 1958 in Buenos Aires, studied at the University of Buenos Aires and founded BUSarchitektur there together with Claudio J. Blazica in 1986. Following studies at the University of Applied Arts Vienna she founded another office in Vienna in 1992. Numerous urban planning studies and residential and educational buildings, among others, a kindergarten in Vienna-Favoriten and Compact City in Vienna-Floridsdorf.

VASKO+PARTNER wurde 1976 in Eisenstadt und Wien von Wolfgang Vasko gegründet, geboren 1943, Studium an der TU Wien, ausgebildeter Mediator, ehemaliger Präsident des Verbandes der Ziviltechnikerbetriebe Österreichs, Aufsichtsratsvorsitzender der Arch+Ing-Akademie und Projektausschussvorsitzender der Arge-AKH. Im Management von Vasko+Partner sind Christian Marintschnig, Wolfgang Poppe, Heinz Peter Rausch, Günther Sammer, Arnold Vielgut und Thomas Wetzstein tätig.
▬▬▬ Was founded in Eisenstadt and Vienna in 1976 by Wolfgang Vasko, born 1943, studied at Vienna University of Technology, trained mediator, former president of the Austrian Association of Civil Engineers, chairman of the Arch+Ing Academy supervisory board, and Arge-AKH project committee chairman. Christian Marintschnig, Wolfgang Poppe, Heinz Peter Rausch, Günther Sammer, Arnold Vielgut, and Thomas Wetzstein are active in the management of Vasko+Partner.

AUTOREN
AUTHORS

CHRISTOPH BADELT, geboren 1951, Studium der Volkswirtschaftslehre an der Wirtschaftsuniversität Wien, Promotion 1976, Leiter des Instituts für Sozialpolitik, seit 2002 Rektor der Wirtschaftsuniversität Wien.
▬▬▬ Born 1951, studies in economics at Vienna University of Economics and Business (WU), doctorate 1976, head of the Institute for Social Policy, since 2002 rector of the WU.

MATTHIAS BOECKL, geboren 1962, Studium der Kunstgeschichte in Salzburg und Wien, Autor und Kurator zahlreicher Bücher und Ausstellungen zu Kunst und Architektur der klassischen Moderne und Gegenwart, Chefredakteur der zweisprachigen Zeitschrift architektur.aktuell und Herausgeber des Kunstmagazins Parnass. Lehrt an der Universität für angewandte Kunst in Wien.
▬▬▬ Born 1962, studies in art history in Salzburg and Vienna, author and curator of numerous books and exhibitions on classical modern and contemporary art and architecture, editor-in-chief of the bilingual magazine architektur.aktuell and publisher of the art magazine Parnass. Teaches at the University of Applied Arts Vienna.

ANDREI GHEORGHE, geboren 1980, Architekturstudium an der Akademie der bildenden Künste in Wien und an der Harvard University, lehrte an der SCI-ARC in Los Angeles, Harvard University und Portland State University, Mitarbeit bei Jakob + MacFarlane in Paris und FOA in London, Fachkolumnist bei architektur.aktuell, lehrt an der Universität für angewandte Kunst in Wien, Schwerpunkt interface of design & technology in architecture, structures and digital media.
▬▬▬ Born 1980, studies in architecture at the Academy of Fine Arts Vienna and Harvard University. He has taught at SCI-ARC in Los Angeles, Harvard University, and Portland State University; worked as an architect for Jakob + MacFarlane in Paris and Foreign Office Architects London; trade columnist for the magazine architektur.aktuell; teaches at the University of Applied Arts Vienna with a focus on the interface between design and technology in architecture, structures, and digital media.

DANIEL GRÜNKRANZ, geboren 1978, Architekturstudium an der Aarhus School of Architecture und der Universität für angewandte Kunst Wien, Diplom 2005, Promotion 2011. Monografie „Architektur und Bewegung. Mensch-Architektur-Beziehungen im Wirkungsfeld architektonischer Systeme", 2013. Seit 2012 Partner von FORM SOCIETY – architecture, design, theory, consulting. Tätig in den Bereichen Architekturproduktion, Theorie und Journalismus.
▬▬▬ Born 1978, studies in architecture at Aarhus School of Architecture and the University of Applied Arts Vienna, diploma degree in 2005, doctorate in 2011. Monograph Architektur und Bewegung. Mensch-Architektur-Beziehungen im Wirkungsfeld architektonischer Systeme, 2013. Since 2012 partner at FORM SOCIETY – architecture, design, theory, consulting. Active in the fields of architectural production, theory, and journalism.

GUDRUN HAUSEGGER, studierte Kunstgeschichte in Wien und an der University of California in Los Angeles, 1996–98 Kommunikationsmanagement bei Coop Himmelb(l)au, 1998–2000 Assistentin an der Universität für angewandte Kunst in Wien. Seit 1998 Projektleitungen im Architekturzentrum Wien. Mitarbeit bei den Fachzeitschriften Architektur & Bauforum und Zuschnitt, Internet-Redaktion von proHolz Austria, Autorin und Onlineredaktion bei architektur.aktuell.
▬▬▬ Studied art history in Vienna and at the University of California in Los Angeles, 1996–98 communication management at Coop Himmelb(l)au, 1998–2000 assistant at the University of Applied Arts Vienna. Since 1998 project director at the Architekturzentrum Wien. Contributor to the trade journals Architektur & Bauforum and Zuschnitt, online editor of proHolz Austria, author and online editor of architektur.aktuell.

MARKUS KRISTAN, studierte Kunstgeschichte an der Universität Wien, Kurator der Architektursammlung der Albertina, zahlreiche Veröffentlichungen zur österreichischen Architektur der Moderne und Gegenwart, u. a. über Martin Kohlbauer, Carl König, Oskar Marmorek, Gustav Peichl, Joseph Urban und Ernst Epstein sowie Bauten österreichischer Architekten in Europa.

KURZBIOGRAFIEN / SHORT BIOGRAPHIES

AUTOREN
AUTHORS

Studied art history at the University of Vienna, curator of the Albertina's Architectural Collection, numerous publications on modern and contemporary architecture in Austria, among others, about Martin Kohlbauer, Carl König, Oskar Marmorek, Gustav Peichl, Joseph Urban, and Ernst Epstein, and on buildings by Austrian architects in Europe.

FRANZISKA LEEB, geboren 1968, Studium der Kunstgeschichte in Wien und Innsbruck, Architekturpublizistin und -vermittlerin in Wien. Regelmäßig Beiträge in Fachmedien, freie Mitarbeiterin bei architektur.aktuell, 1996–2003 Mitarbeiterin der Tageszeitung Der Standard, seit 2006 Architekturkritikerin für das Spectrum der Tageszeitung Die Presse.
Born 1968, studies in art history in Vienna and Innsbruck, architectural publicist and mediator in Vienna. Regular contributions in the trade press, freelancer for architektur.aktuell, 1996–2003 worked for the daily newspaper Der Standard, since 2006 architecture critic for Spectrum, the weekend supplement of the daily newspaper Die Presse.

ISABELLA MARBOE, geboren 1970, Architekturstudium an der TU Wien, Architekturjournalistin. Zahlreiche Publikationen in Die Presse, Der Standard, Die Furche, architektur.aktuell, dbz, oris und in Büchern. 2012–14 in der Chefredaktion der deutschen Ausgabe von DOMUS, seit März 2014 Redakteurin bei architektur.aktuell.
Born 1970, studies in architecture at Vienna University of Technology, architectural journalist. Numerous publications in Die Presse, Der Standard, Die Furche, architektur.aktuell, dbz, oris, and in books. 2012–14 chief editorial staff member of the German edition of DOMUS, since March 2014 editor at architektur.aktuell.

GERLINDE MAUTNER, Professorin und Institutsvorstand am Institut für Englische Wirtschaftskommunikation der Wirtschaftsuniversität Wien (WU). Ihre Forschungsinteressen im Bereich der angewandten Wirtschaftslinguistik führen sie regelmäßig auch an britische Universitäten. An der WU war sie Mitglied des Sounding Board, eines den Neubau-Planungsprozess begleitenden Beratungsgremiums.
Professor at Vienna University of Economics and Business (WU) and head of the Institute for English Business Communication. Her research interests, pursued both at the WU and at British universities, are located at the interface of language, society, and business. She was a member of the Campus Sounding Board, a consultative committee accompanying the building process.

MAXIMILIAN PAMMER, geboren 1974, Studium des Bauingenieurwesens an der TU Wien, seit 2007 Mitarbeiter Bundesimmobiliengesellschaft m.b.H., seit 2007 Projektleiter für das Projekt WU Campus und seit 2008 Geschäftsführer der Projektgesellschaft Wirtschaftsuniversität Wien Neu GmbH, seit April 2014 Leiter des Unternehmensbereichs Universitäten der BIG.
Maximilian Pammer, born 1974, studies in engineering at Vienna University of Technology, since 2007 employee of the Austrian Federal Real Estate Company (BIG), since 2007 project manager for the project WU Campus and since 2008 managing director of the project company Wirtschaftsuniversität Wien Neu GmbH, since April 2014 head of the BIG universities division.

CORDULA RAU, geboren 1961, Studium der Architektur, Autorin, Kuratorin und Journalistin in München. Planungs- und Projektleitungstätigkeit u. a. bei Stephan Braunfels Architekten und der BMW AG. 2004 Gründung des Netzwerkes für Architektur, Kunst und Design „Die Walverwandtschaften". Publikationen, Marketing und Moderation, Vorträge, Veranstaltungen und Ausstellungen. 2008 Buch „Why Do Architects Wear Black?", 2010 Generalkommissariat Deutscher Pavillon, Architekturbiennale Venedig. 2010 Publikation der Bücher „SEHNSUCHT" und „What Architects Desire".
Born 1961, bachelor of architecture, lives and works as a writer, curator, and journalist in Munich. Planning and project management activities with, among others, Stephan Braunfels architects and BMW AG. 2004 foundation of the network for architecture, art, and design "Die Walverwandtschaften" (The affinities of the whale). Publications, marketing and moderation, lectures, events, and exhibitions. 2008 publication of the book "Why Do Architects Wear Black?" 2010 curator of the German Pavilion, Venice Architecture Biennale. 2010 publication of the books "SEHNSUCHT" and "What Architects Desire".

EDITH SCHLOCKER, Kunsthistorikerin, Kulturpublizistin im Bereich bildende Kunst, Architektur und Kulturpolitik. Regelmäßige Mitarbeiterin unter anderem bei der Tiroler Tageszeitung, Parnass, architektur.aktuell, lebt in Innsbruck.
Art historian, cultural publicist in the fields of fine art, architecture, and cultural policy. Regular contributor to, among others, the daily newspaper Tiroler Tageszeitung, Parnass, and architektur.aktuell. She lives in Innsbruck.

BERNHARD SOMMER, geboren 1969, Studium an der TU Wien, Arch+ Preis 2000, Schindlerstipendium (Los Angeles) 2002, Preis für Experimentelle Tendenzen in der Architektur 2006. Forscher und Projektmanager 2007–08 bei Kas Oosterhuis an der TU Delft, 2002–06 Assistent an der TU Wien bei Prof. Richter. Lehrt Energie Design an der Universität für Angewandte Kunst und an der Universität Innsbruck, Seminare an der TU Graz und der University of Cagliari. Mitbegründer und Miteigentümer des Architekturbüros EXIKON arc &dev und EXIKON skins.
Born 1969, studied at Vienna University of Technology. Arch+ award 2000, Max Schindler Scholarship (Los Angeles) 2002, Outstanding Artist Award – Experimental Tendencies in Architecture 2006. 2007–08 researcher and project manager with Kas Oosterhuis at the TU Delft. 2002–06 assistant at Vienna University of Technology with Prof. Richter. Teaches Energy Design at the University of Applied Arts Vienna and the University of Innsbruck, seminars at Graz University of Technology and the University of Cagliari. Co-founder and owner of the architecture offices EXIKON arc&dev and EXIKON skins.

CHRISTOPH SOMMER, geboren 1977, Studium an der Wirtschaftsuniversität Wien, seit Anfang 2007 Gesamtprojektleiter WU-Neubau an der Wirtschaftsuniversität Wien, seit Ende 2007 Geschäftsführer der Projektgesellschaft Wirtschaftsuniversität Wien Neu GmbH.
Born 1977, studied at Vienna University of Economics and Business (WU), since 2007 the general project manager of the new WU Campus, since end of 2007 managing director of the project company Wirtschaftsuniversität Wien Neu GmbH.

MALGORZATA SOMMER-NAWARA, geboren 1972, Studium an der TU Wien, 2004–11 Assistentin am Institut für Interdisziplinäre Bauprozessplanung an der TU Wien, Leiterin und Miteigentümerin von EXIKON architektur & entwicklung, spezialisiert auf Anwendung neuester Planungstechnologien mit dem Ziel der frühzeitigen Integration wissenschaftlicher Erkenntnisse in den Entwurfsprozess.
Born 1972, studied at Vienna University of Technology, 2004–2011 assistant at the Institute of Interdisciplinary Construction Process Management at Vienna University of Technology, head and co-owner of EXIKON arc&dev, specialized in the application of innovative planning technologies with the aim of integrating scientific knowledge into the design process at an early stage.

ROBERT TEMEL, Studium der Architektur an der Universität für angewandte Kunst Wien und Soziologie am IHS Wien. Architektur- und Stadtforscher in Wien sowie Sprecher der Plattform Baukultur, Kolumnist bei der Zeitschrift architektur.aktuell. Publikationen u. a.: Baugemeinschaften in der Wiener Seestadt Aspern, Studie für die Wiener Wohnbauforschung, 2012; Evaluierung der kooperativen Verfahren, Studie im Auftrag der Stadt Wien, 2014.
Studies in architecture at the University of Applied Arts Vienna and in sociology at the Institute for Advanced Studies Vienna. Architecture and urban researcher in Vienna and speaker of the platform "Baukultur". Columnist for the magazine architektur.aktuell. Publications, among others: "Building Cooperatives in Seestadt Aspern, Vienna", a study for Vienna Housing Research, 2012; "Evaluierung der kooperativen Verfahren", a study commissioned by the City of Vienna, 2014.

ULRICH TRAGATSCHNIG, geboren 1972, Studium der Kunstgeschichte in Graz, Kunst- und Architekturkritiker sowie Lektor am Institut für Architekturtheorie, Kunst- und Kulturwissenschaften der TU Graz und am Institut für Kunstgeschichte der Karl-Franzens-Universität Graz.
Born 1972, studies in art history in Graz, art and architecture critic and lecturer at the Institute of Architectural Theory, Art History and Cultural Studies at Graz University of Technology and at the Institute of Art History at the University of Graz.

IMPRESSUM
IMPRINT

Herausgeber Editor
Matthias Boeckl

Mit Beiträgen von
With contributions by
Christoph Badelt
Andrei Gheorghe
Daniel Grünkranz
Gudrun Hausegger
Markus Kristan
Franziska Leeb
Isabella Marboe
Gerlinde Mautner
Maximilian Pammer
Cordula Rau
Edith Schlocker
Bernhard Sommer
Christoph Sommer
Malgorzata Sommer-Nawara
Robert Temel
Ulrich Tragatschnig

Das Werk ist urheberrechtlich geschützt.
Die dadurch begründeten Rechte, insbesondere die der Übersetzung, des Nachdruckes, der Entnahme von Abbildungen, der Funksendung, der Wiedergabe auf photomechanischem oder ähnlichem Wege und der Speicherung in Datenverarbeitungsanlagen, bleiben, auch bei nur auszugsweiser Verwertung, vorbehalten.
This work is subject to copyright.
All rights are reserved, whether the whole or part of the material is concerned, specifically those of translation, reprinting, re-use of illustrations, broadcasting, reproduction by photocopying machines or similar means, and storage in data banks.

© 2014 AMBRA | V
AMBRA | V is part of Medecco Holding GmbH, Vienna
Printed in Austria

Die Wiedergabe von Gebrauchsnamen, Handelsnamen, Warenbezeichnungen usw. in diesem Buch berechtigt auch ohne besondere Kennzeichnung nicht zu der Annahme, dass solche Namen im Sinne der Warenzeichen- und Markenschutz-Gesetzgebung als frei zu betrachten wären und daher von jedermann benutzt werden dürfen.
Product Liability: The publisher can give no guarantee for the information contained in this book. The use of registered names, trademarks, etc. in this publication does not imply, even in the absence of a specific statement, that such names are exempt from the relevant protective laws and regulations and are therefore free for general use.

Layout, Cover Design
Martin Gaal, Wien Vienna
Bildbearbeitung Lithography
Manfred Kostal, Wien Vienna, pixelstorm.at
Übersetzung Translation
Peter Blakeney & Christine Schöffler, www.whysociety.org
Druck Printing
Holzhausen Druck GmbH, Wolkersdorf

Bildnachweis Illustration credits
Dietmar Adam 111, Atelier Hitoshi Abe 19, 84 o, 85, Iwan Baan 2, 42, 47 u, 50 r o, 51 u, Berger + Parkkinen 15 l, Anna Blau 102 l o, 102 r u, 106 l u, 120, 122 l o, 123, 126 u, BOAnet 17, 28, 30, 46, 47 o, 48, 49 r u, 50 l o, 50 u, 54 u, 55 o, 55 u, 62, 66, 68/69 u, 70, 71, 72 u, 80, 81, 87 l, 98, 100 u, 102 l u, 104, 106 l o, 107, 108/109 u, 109 o, 118, 122 r o, 122 l u, 124, 125, 127, 138, 140, 141 o, 143, BUSarchitektur 14, 65, Matthias Boeckl 10 l, 10 u, 11 r u, 12 o, 49 l u, CRAB studio 21 l, 100 o, 101, Estudio Carme Pinós 20 o, 121, Flatz-Zeytinoglu 15 r, Guillermo Vázquez Consuegra 21 r, Roland Halbe 49 o, 52 u, 54 o, 134, 136, 139, 141 m, 141 u, 142 r, 145, Hans Hollein & Partner 18 l, Pez Hejduk 29, 30, 34, 35, 36, 37, 52/53 o, 53 u, 64, 67, 68 o, 72 o, 73, 91, 103 o, 106 r u, 108 o, 126 l o, 126 r o, 142 l, 144, Markus Kristan 11 l, 11 r o, Duccio Malagamba 82, 84 o, 86, 87 r, 88, 89, 90, Morphosis Architects 18 r, Goga S. Nawara/Vasko+Partner 112 r, 116, NO.MAD 20 u, 137, Privat/AMBRA | V 22, 25, 57, 59, 60, 93, 95, 96, 129, 130, 131, 132, 133, 148, 149, 150, Vasko+Partner 75, 76, 77, 78, 79, 112 l, 115, 117, Wien Museum 8, Wikimedia Commons 10 o, Wirtschaftsuniversität Wien 12 u, Zaha Hadid Architects 18 o, 44, 45
Die Zahlen sind Seitenangaben Figures indicate page numbers
l = links left, m = Mitte center, o = oben top, r = rechts right, u = unten bottom

Cover
© fibreC by Rieder. Fotograf Photographer: Rasmus Norlander

Gedruckt auf säurefreiem, chlorfrei gebleichtem Papier – TCF
Printed on acid-free and chlorine-free bleached paper

Mit 184 farbigen Abbildungen
With 184 colored illustrations

Bibliografische Informationen der Deutschen Nationalbibliothek
Die Deutsche Nationalbibliothek verzeichnet diese Publikation in der Deutschen Nationalbibliografie; detaillierte bibliografische Daten sind im Internet über http://dnb.d-nb.de abrufbar.

ISBN 978-3-99043-645-5 AMBRA | V